ELECTIONS

Seeking public office

Meeting the candidate, Harlem, October 29, 2010

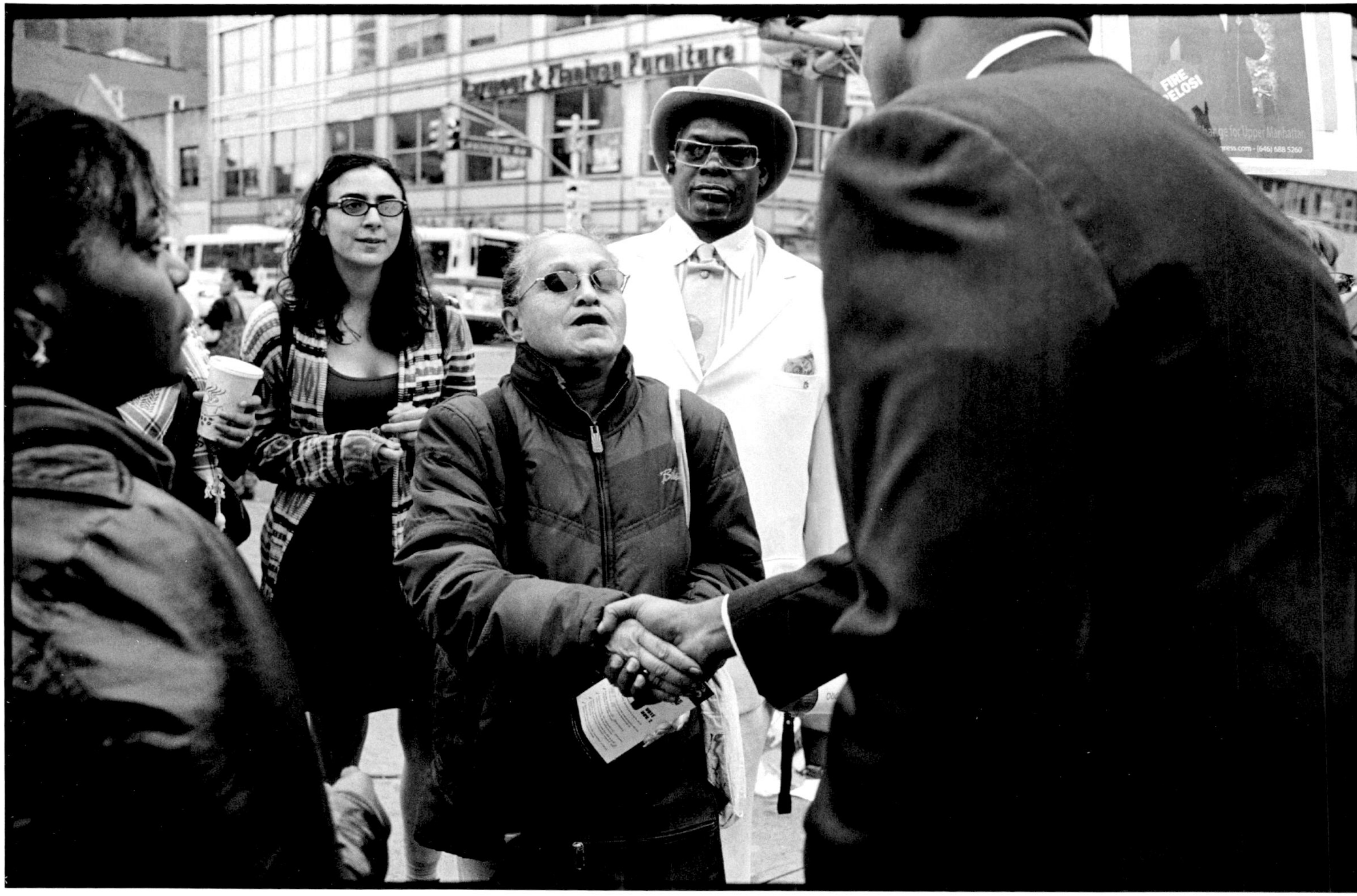
Furniture
FIRE

Listening to the candidate, Rego Park, Queens, August 25, 2011

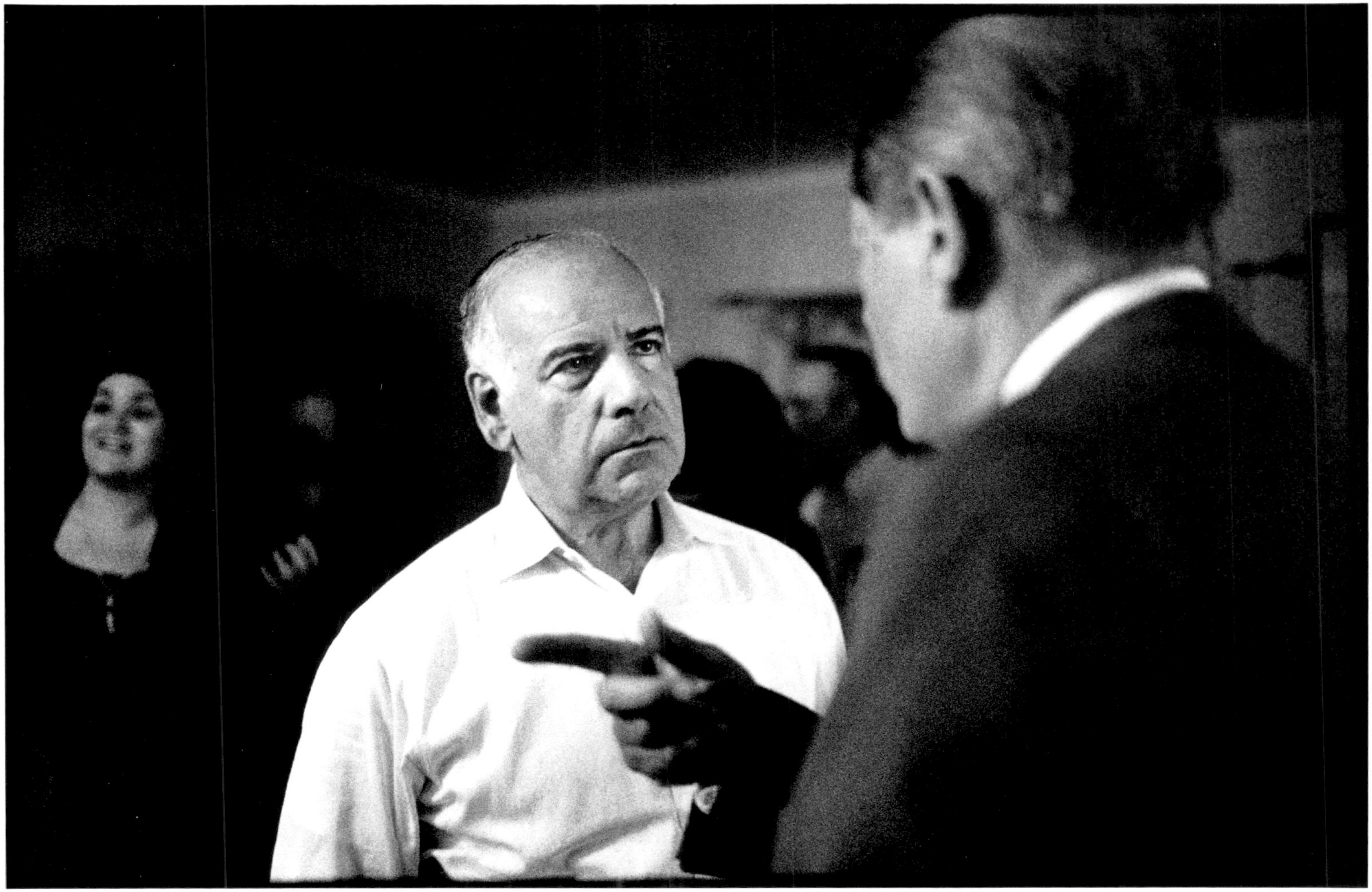

American Majority Candidates Workshop, Baruch College, Kips Bay, December 4, 2011

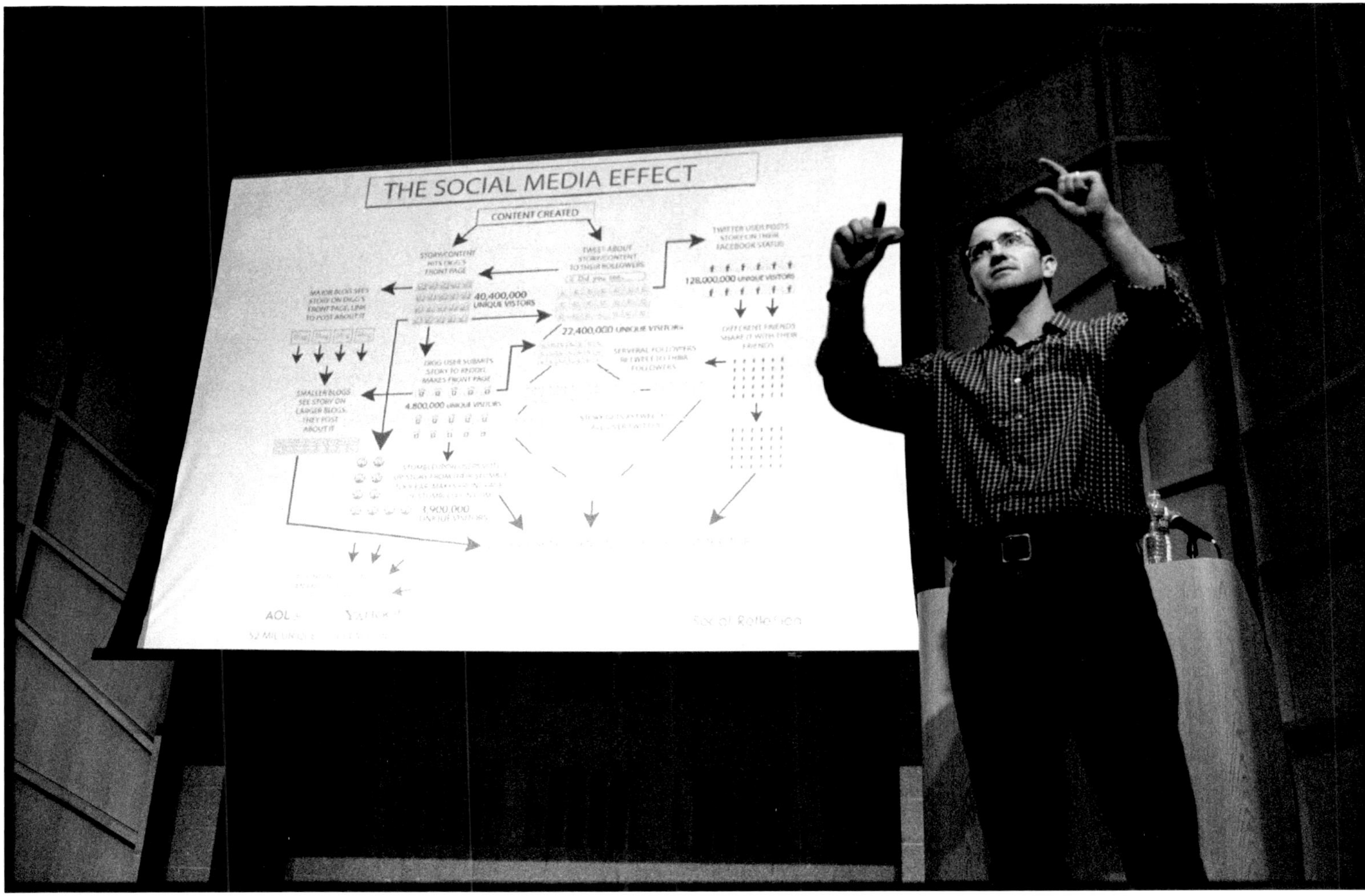
THE SOCIAL MEDIA EFFECT
CONTENT CREATED
40,400,000 UNIQUE VISTORS
22,400,000 UNIQUE VISITORS

Leafleting, Upper East Side, October 19, 2010

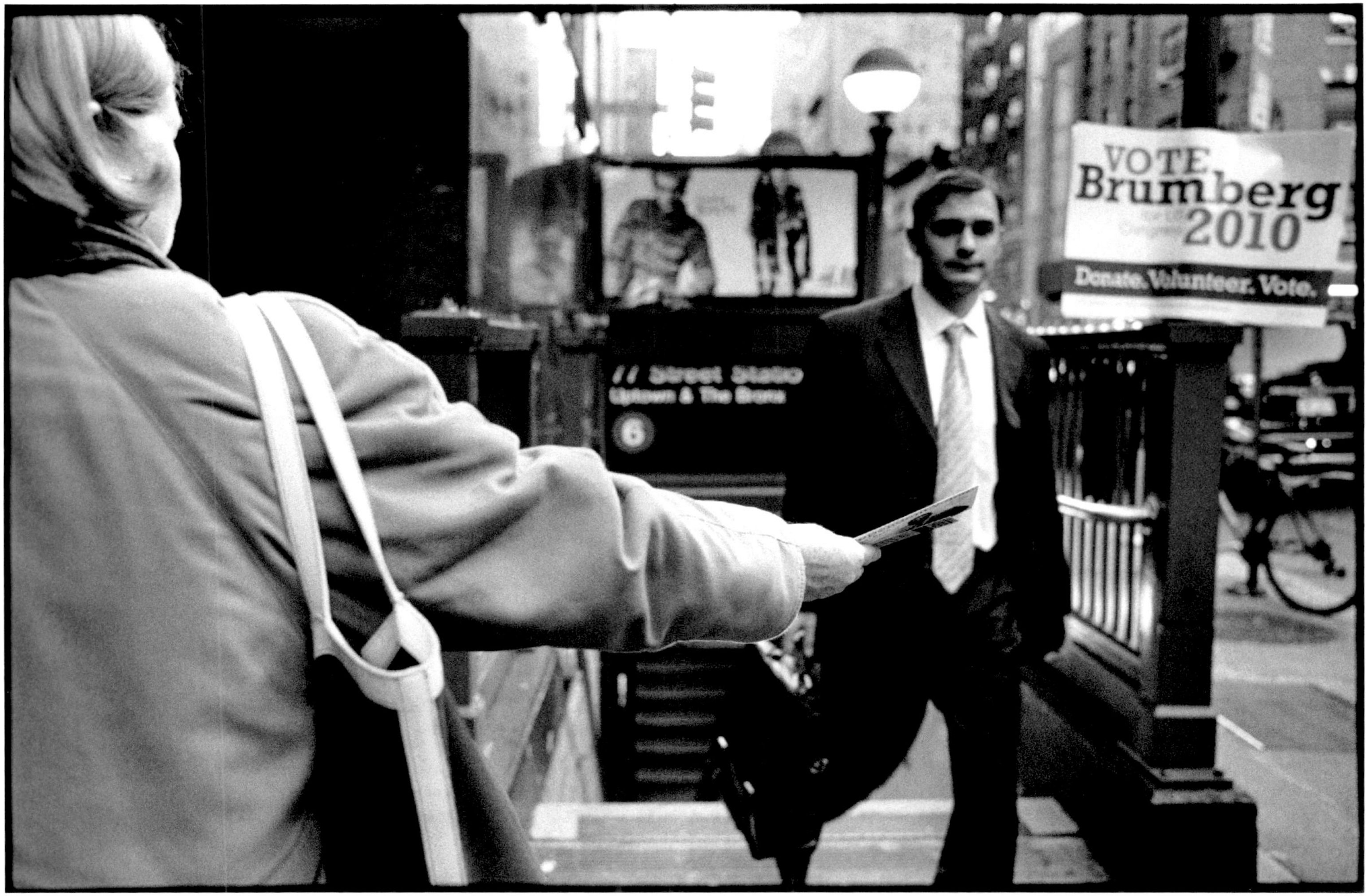
Uptown & The Bronx
6
VOTE
Brumberg
2010
Donate. Volunteer. Vote.

Candidate working the phone, Midtown, September 28, 2010

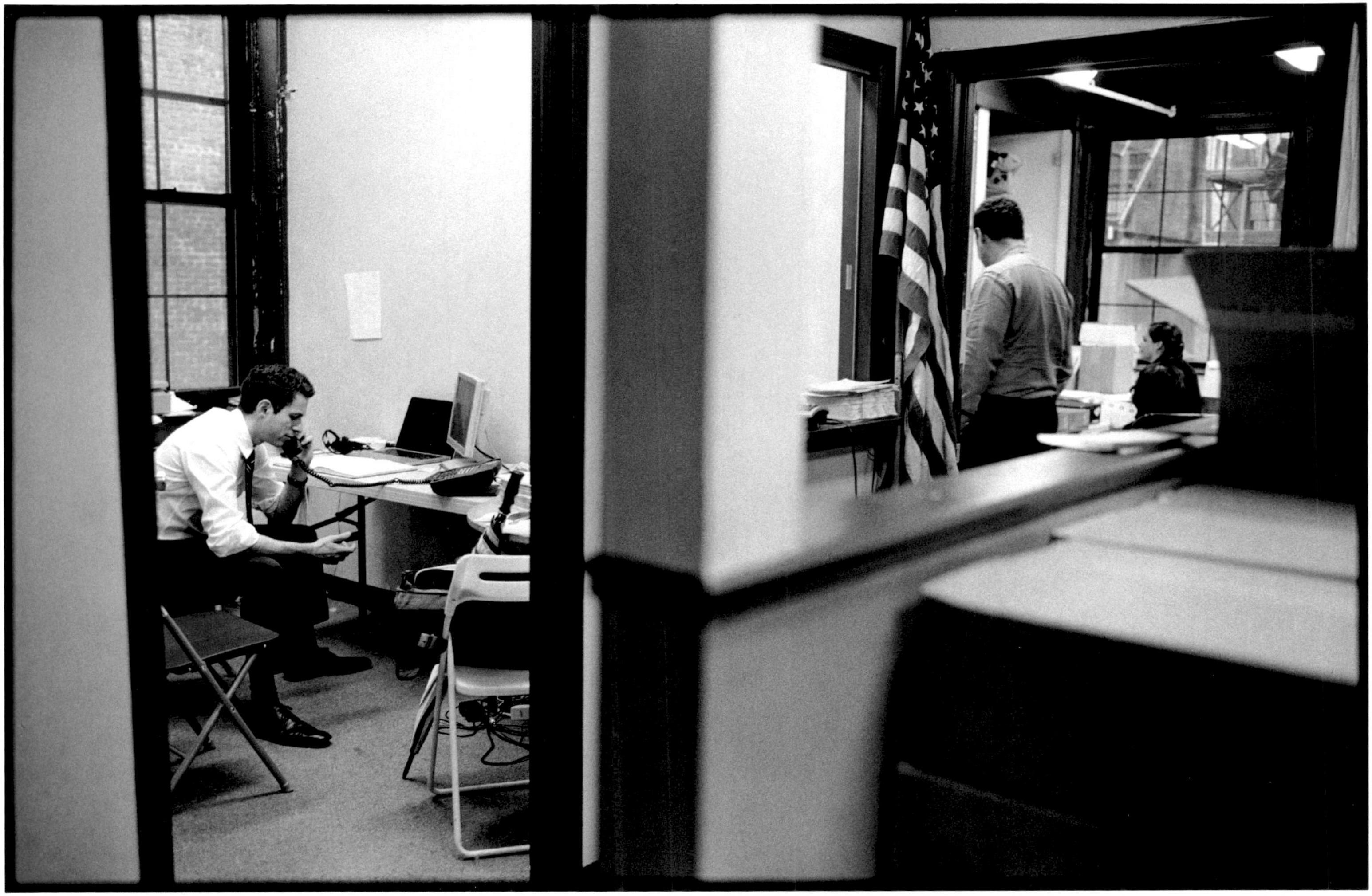

Tea Party Candidates Forum, Baruch College, Kips Bay, August 30, 2010

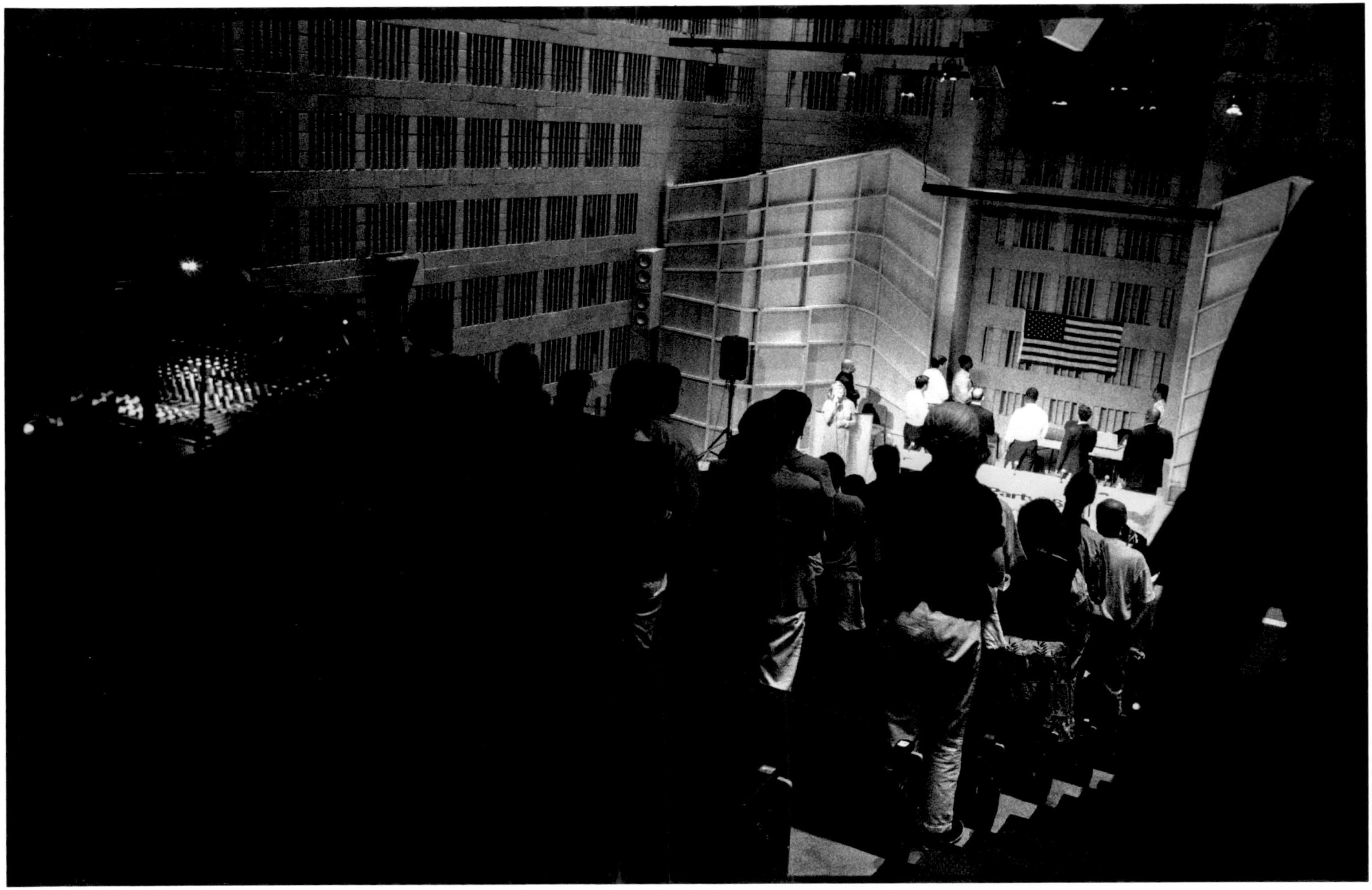

Get Out the Vote meeting, Metropolitan Republican Club, Upper East Side, October 28, 2010

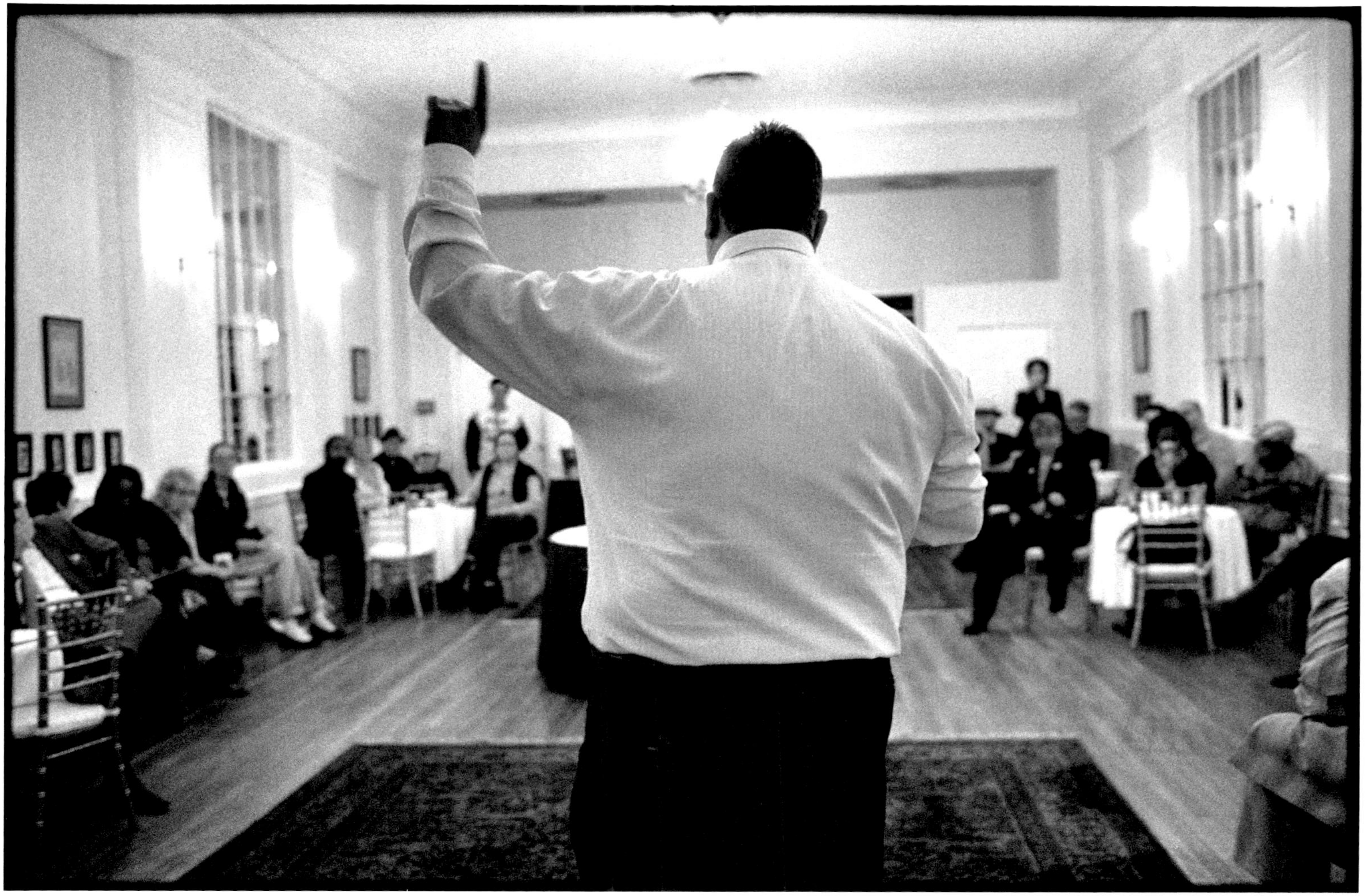

Watching a primary debate, Manhattan Republican Club, Upper East Side, December 15, 2015

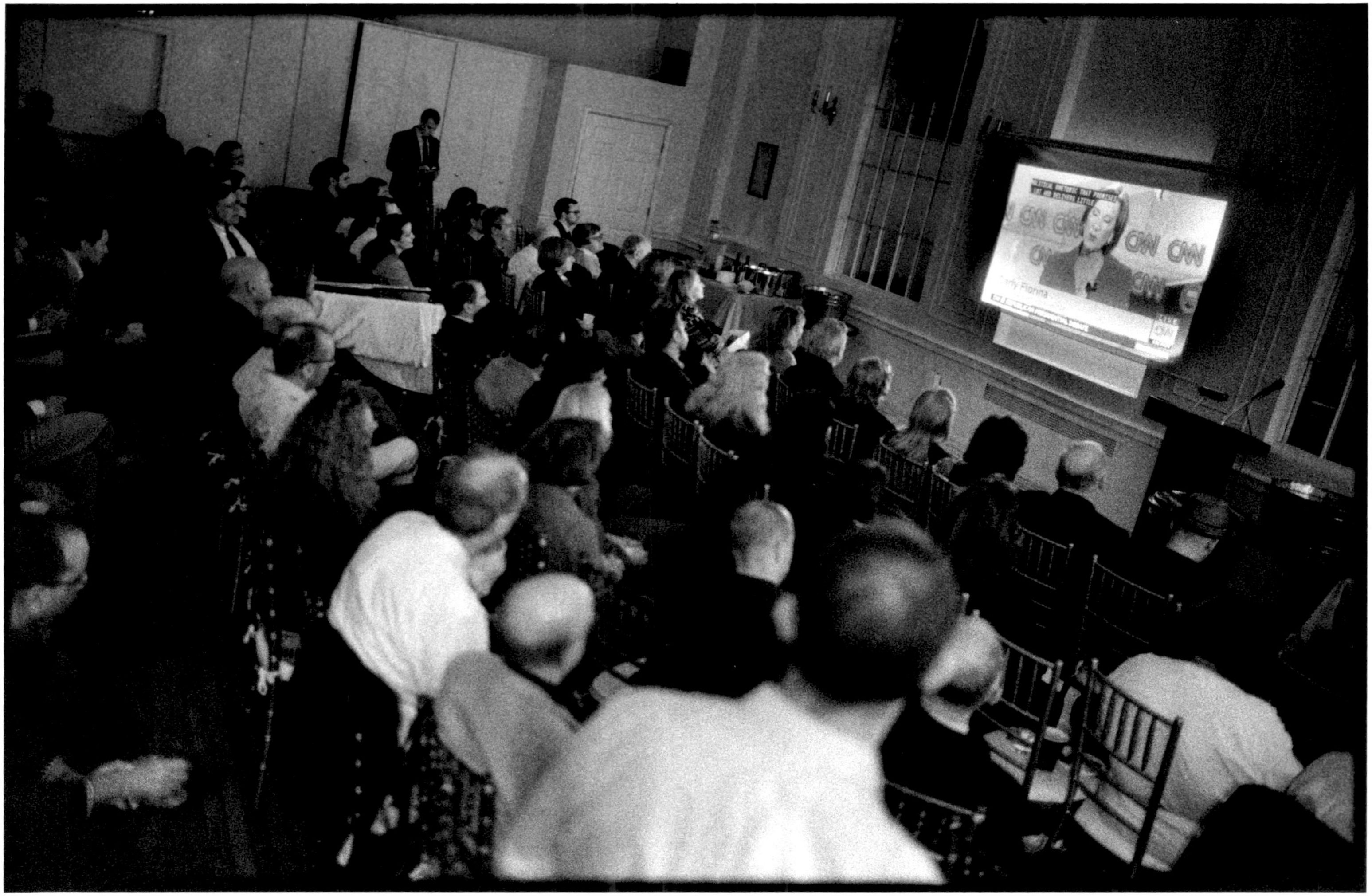
CNN

Campaign strategist, Midtown, September 28, 2010

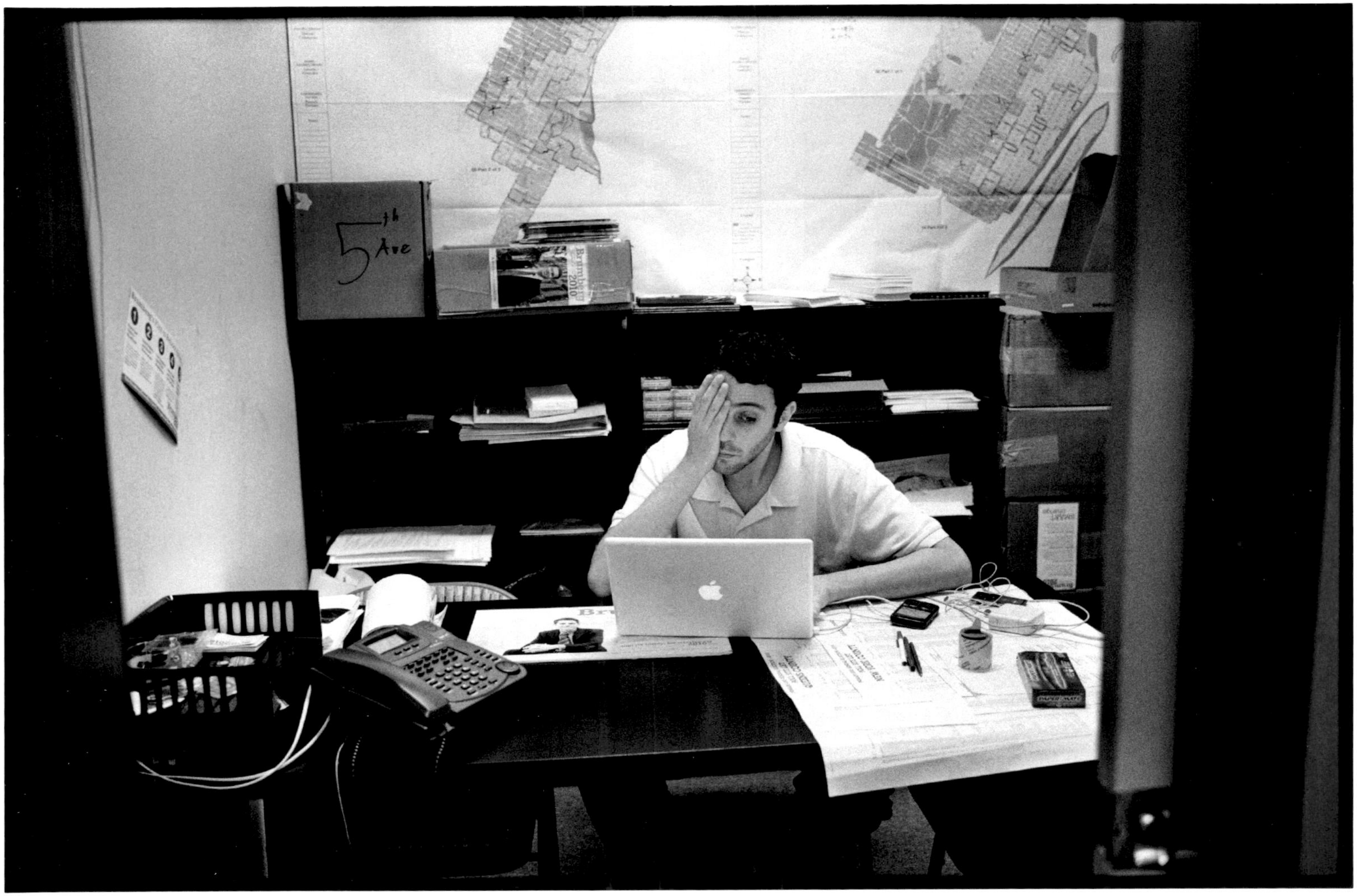
5th Ave
2010

Crackpot political posters, Broadway and 106th Street, Upper West Side, December 21, 2014

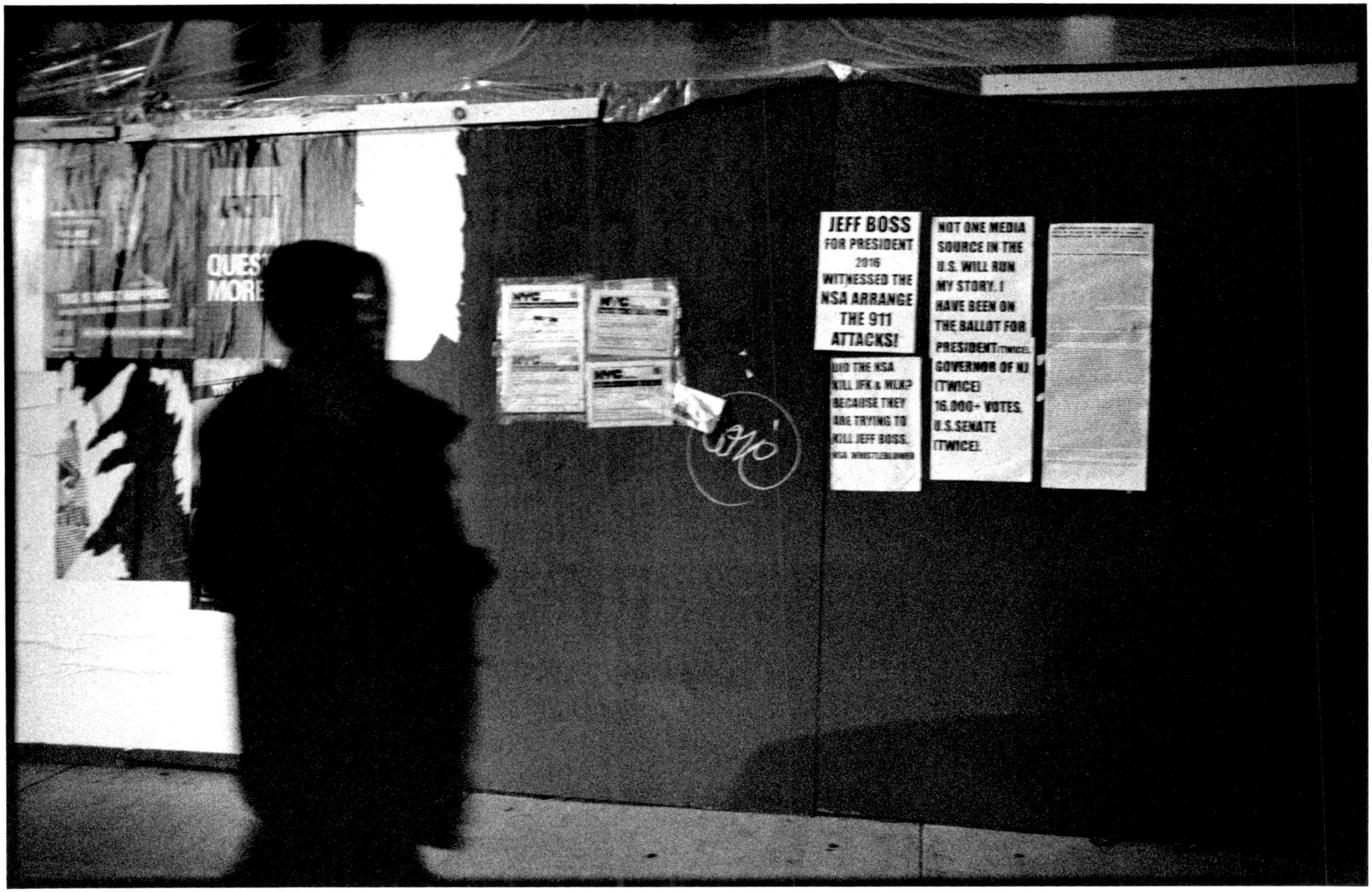
JEFF BOSS
FOR PRESIDENT
2016
WITNESSED THE
NSA ARRANGE
THE 911
ATTACKS!
NOT ONE MEDIA
SOURCE IN THE
U.S. WILL RUN
MY STORY. I
HAVE BEEN ON
THE BALLOT FOR
PRESIDENT(TWICE)
GOVERNOR OF NJ
(TWICE)
16,000+ VOTES.
U.S.SENATE
(TWICE).
DID THE NSA
KILL JFK & MLK?
BECAUSE THEY
ARE TRYING TO
KILL JEFF BOSS.
NSA WHISTLEBLOWER

Assigning poll watchers, 53 Duke Ellington Boulevard, Upper West Side, November 1, 2010

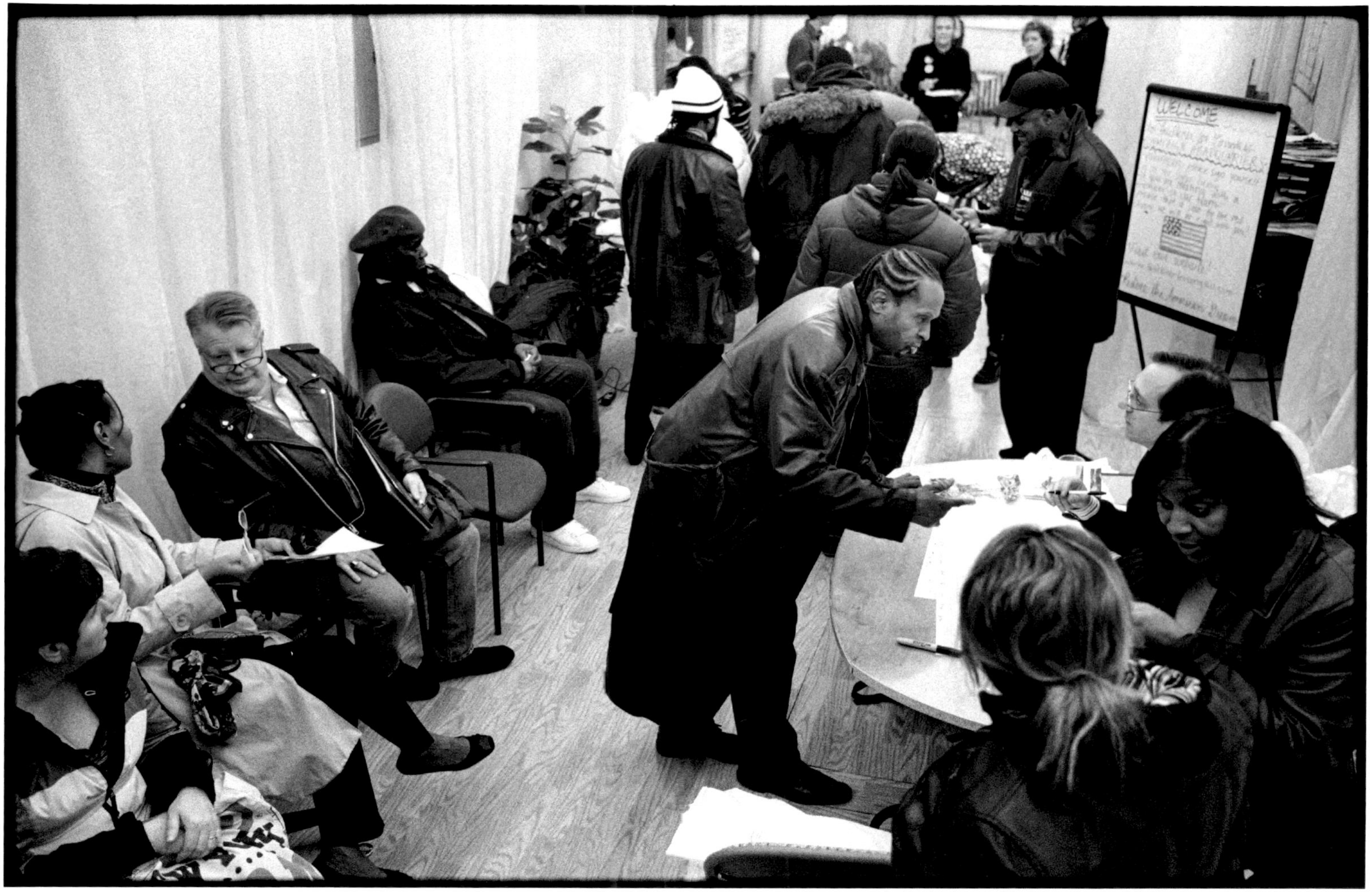
WELCOME

Store boarded up for Election Day, Broadway, Upper West Side, November 3, 2020

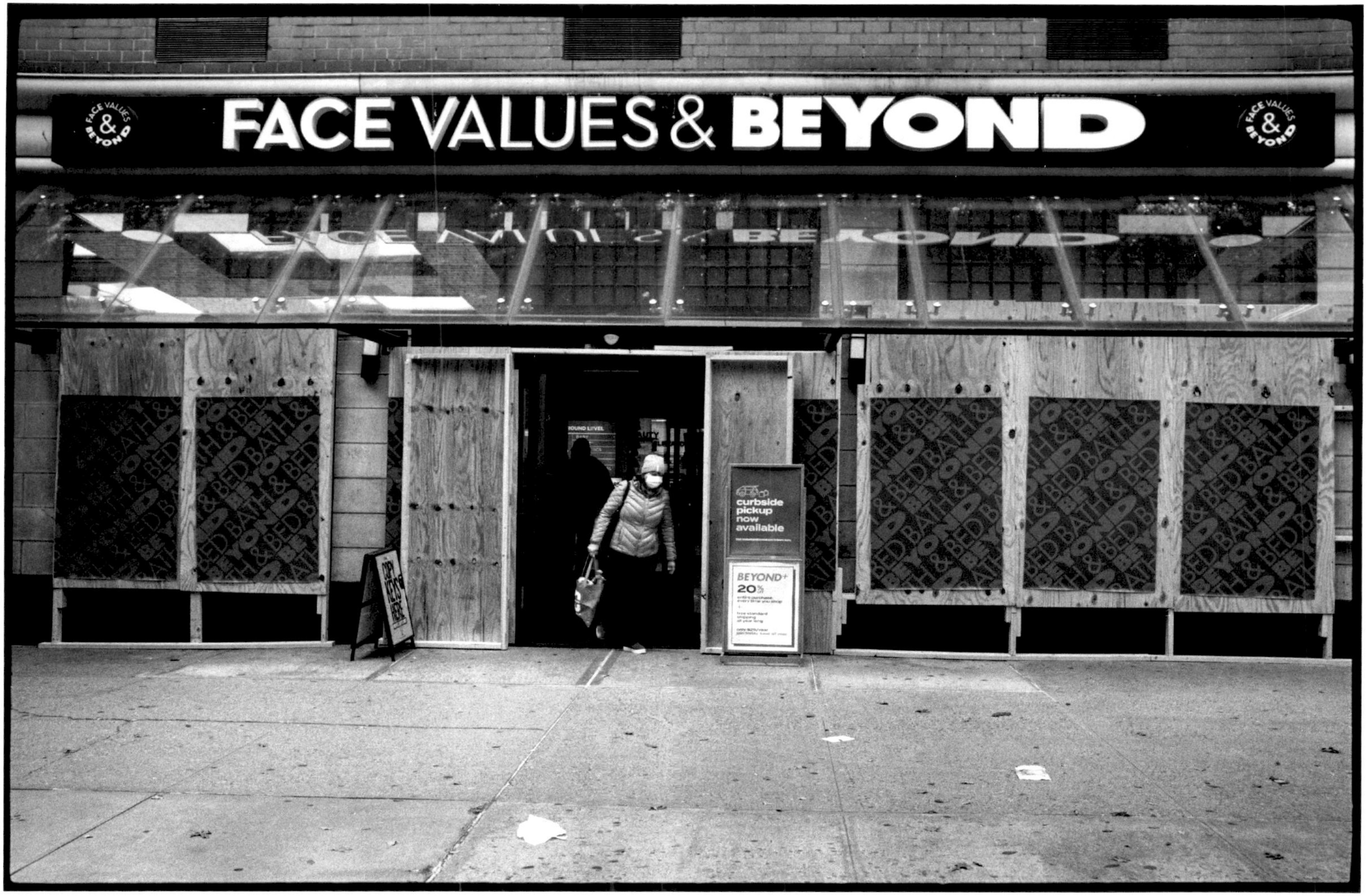
FACE VALUES & BEYOND
curbside pickup now available
BEYOND+
20%
COPY KEYS HERE
BED BATH & BEYOND

Entering a polling place, Upper West Side, November 2, 2010

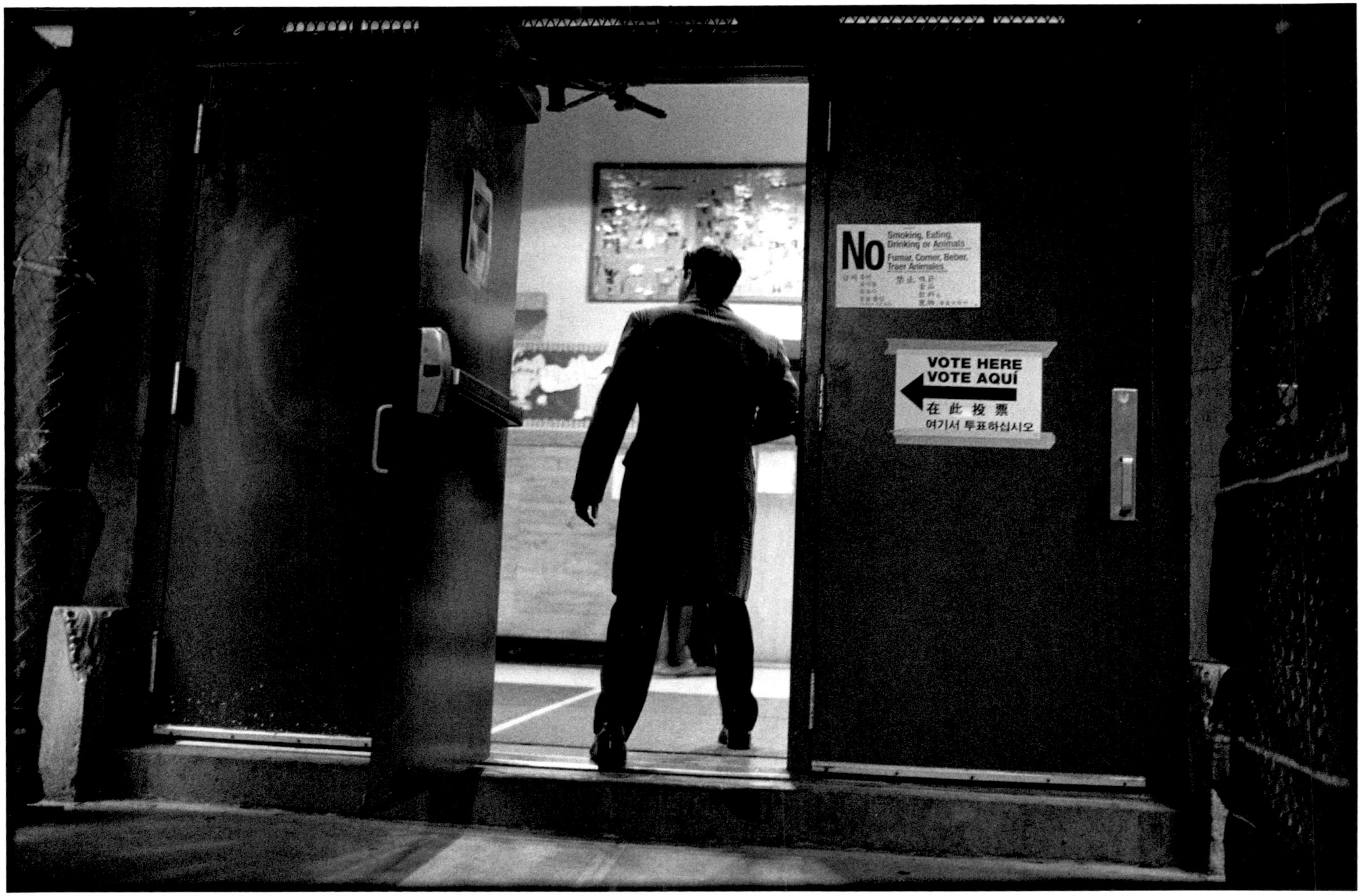
No
Smoking, Eating, Drinking or Animals
Fumar, Comer, Beber, Traer Animales
VOTE HERE
VOTE AQUÍ
在此投票
여기서 투표하십시오

Election night, Republican headquarters, Hilton hotel, Midtown, November 2, 2011

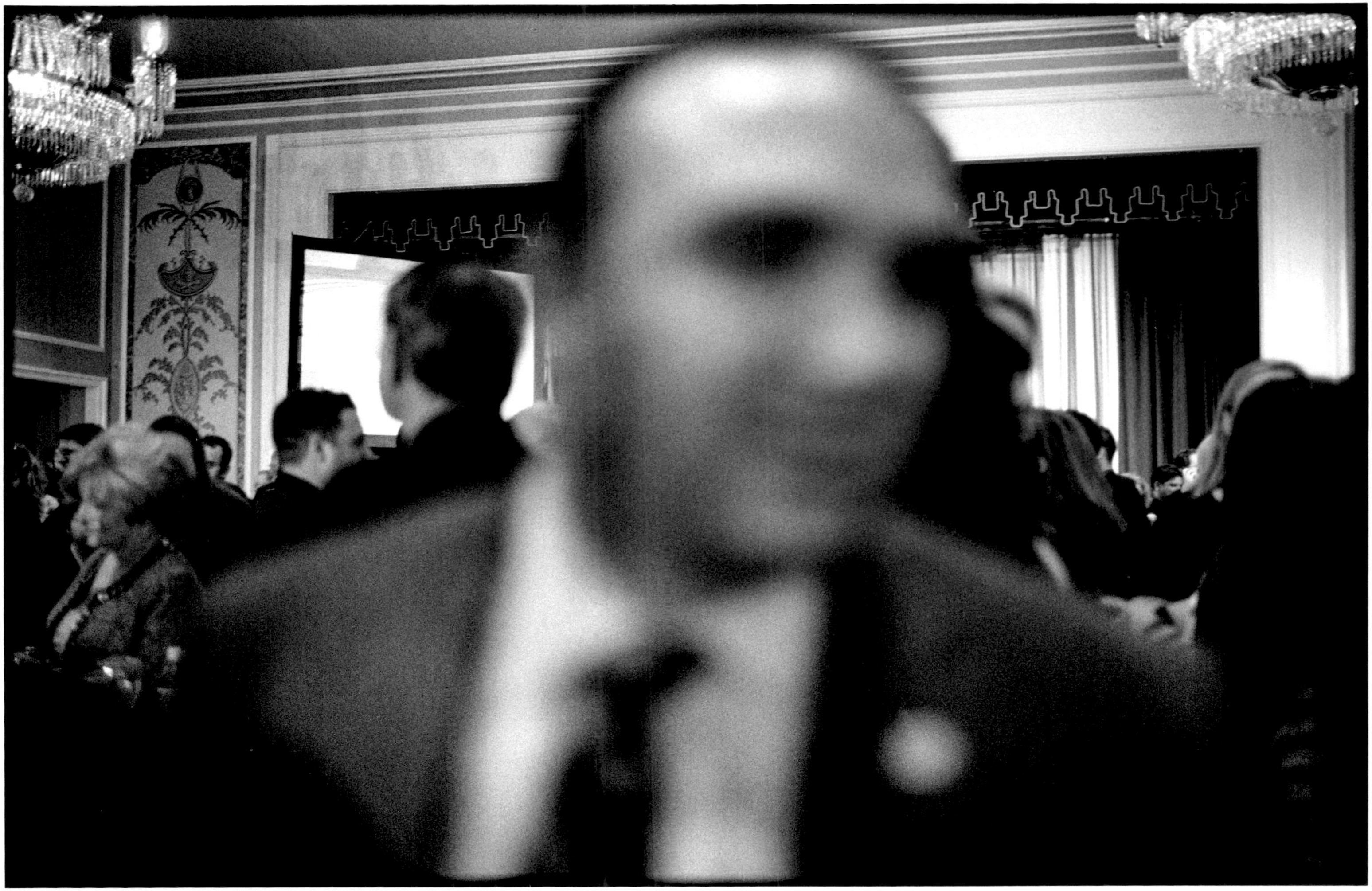

Election night, losing candidate's headquarters, Harlem, November 2, 2010

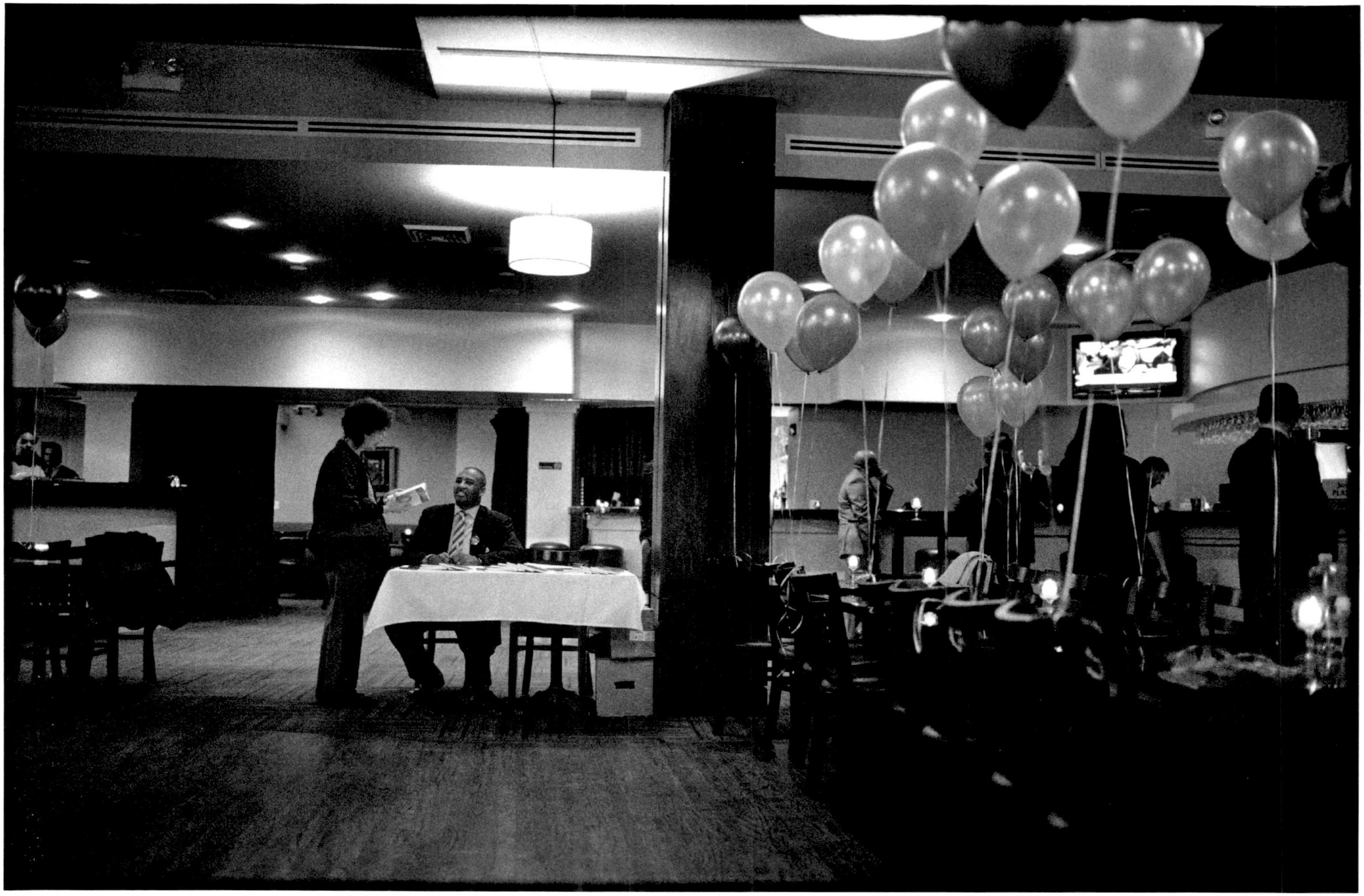

GOVERNANCE

Providing services, confronting problems

Democratic City Council member Helen Rosenthal, Open House, 6th District, Upper West Side, June 14, 2015

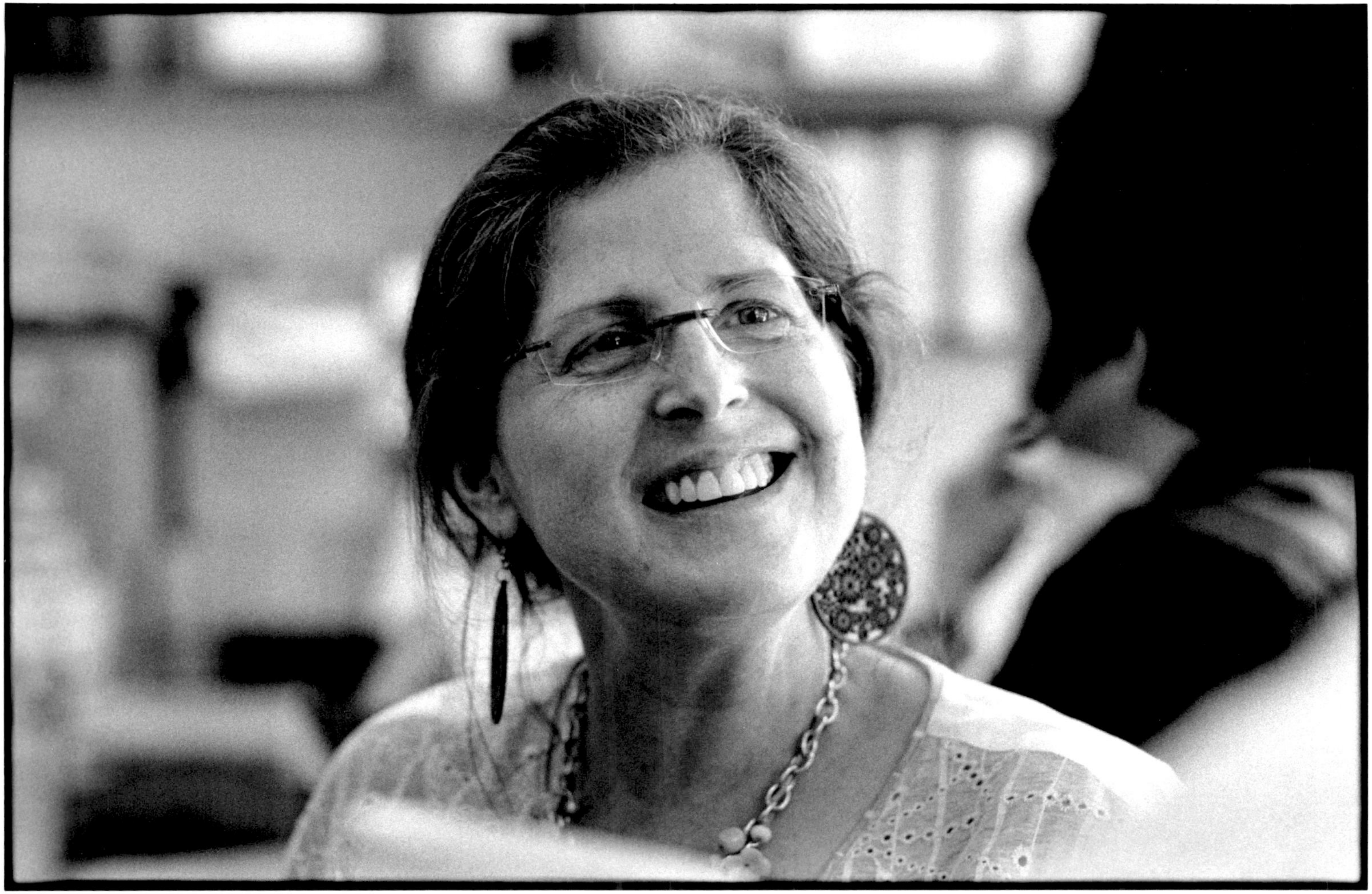

FDNY ambulance at a sledding accident, Riverside Park, January 27, 2015

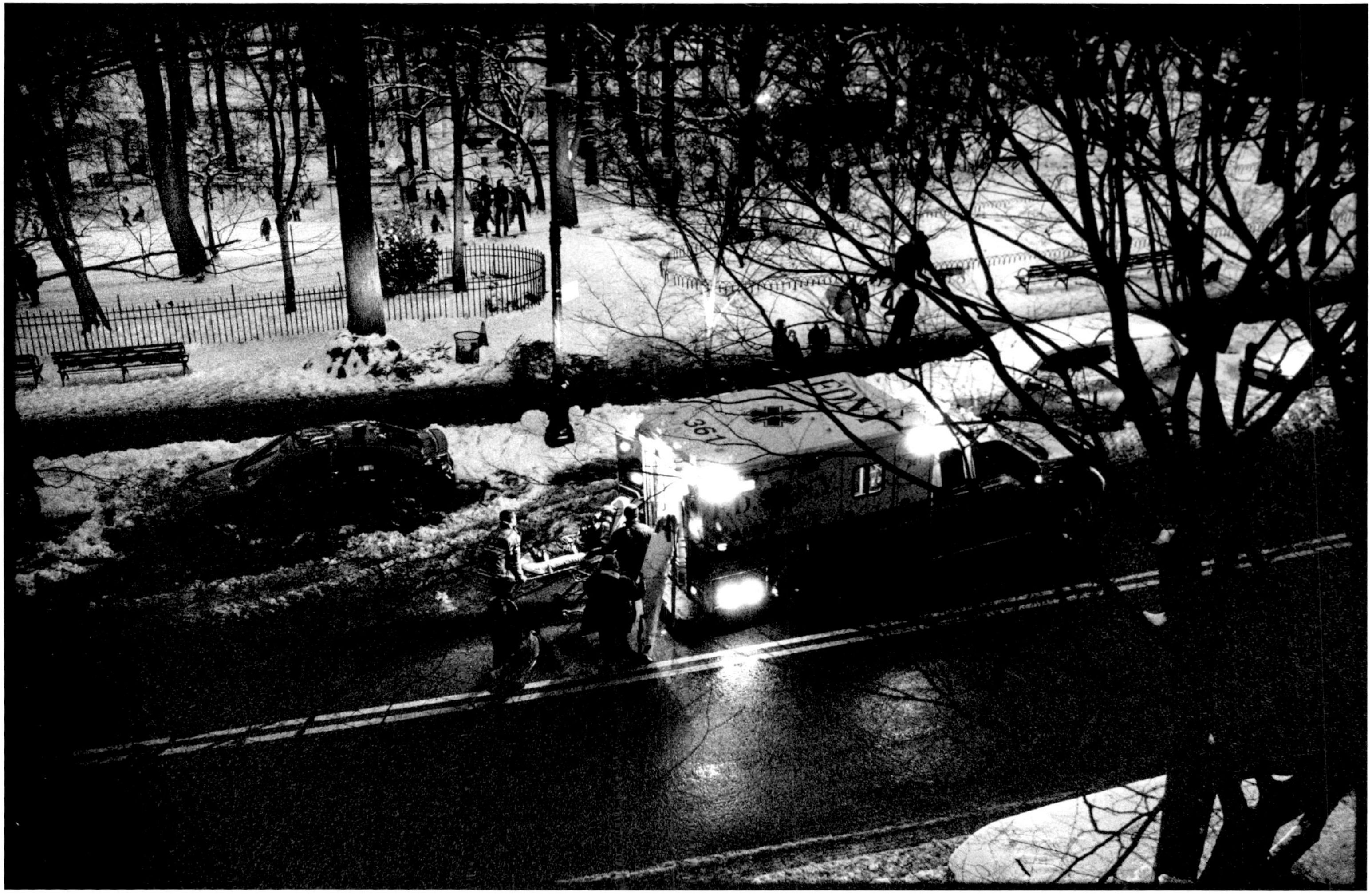

Citizenship test study group, St. Agnes Library, Upper West Side, November 19, 2019

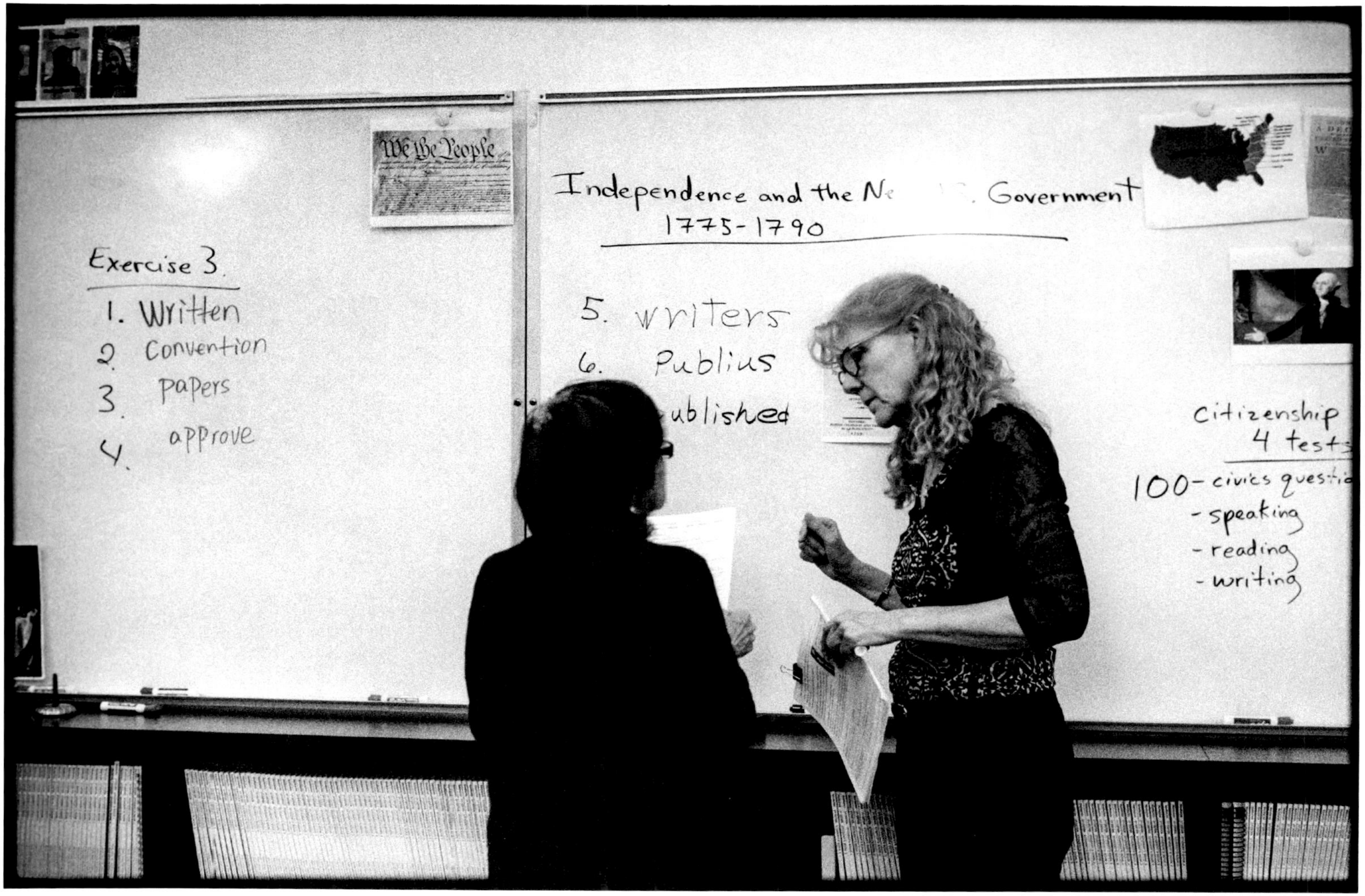
We the People
Independence and the Ne
Government
1775-1790
Exercise 3.
1. Written
2. convention
3. papers
4. approve
5. writers
6. Publius
Citizenship
- speaking
- reading
- writing

New York City Water Tunnel No. 3, Van Cortlandt Park Valve Chamber, Bronx, June 1991

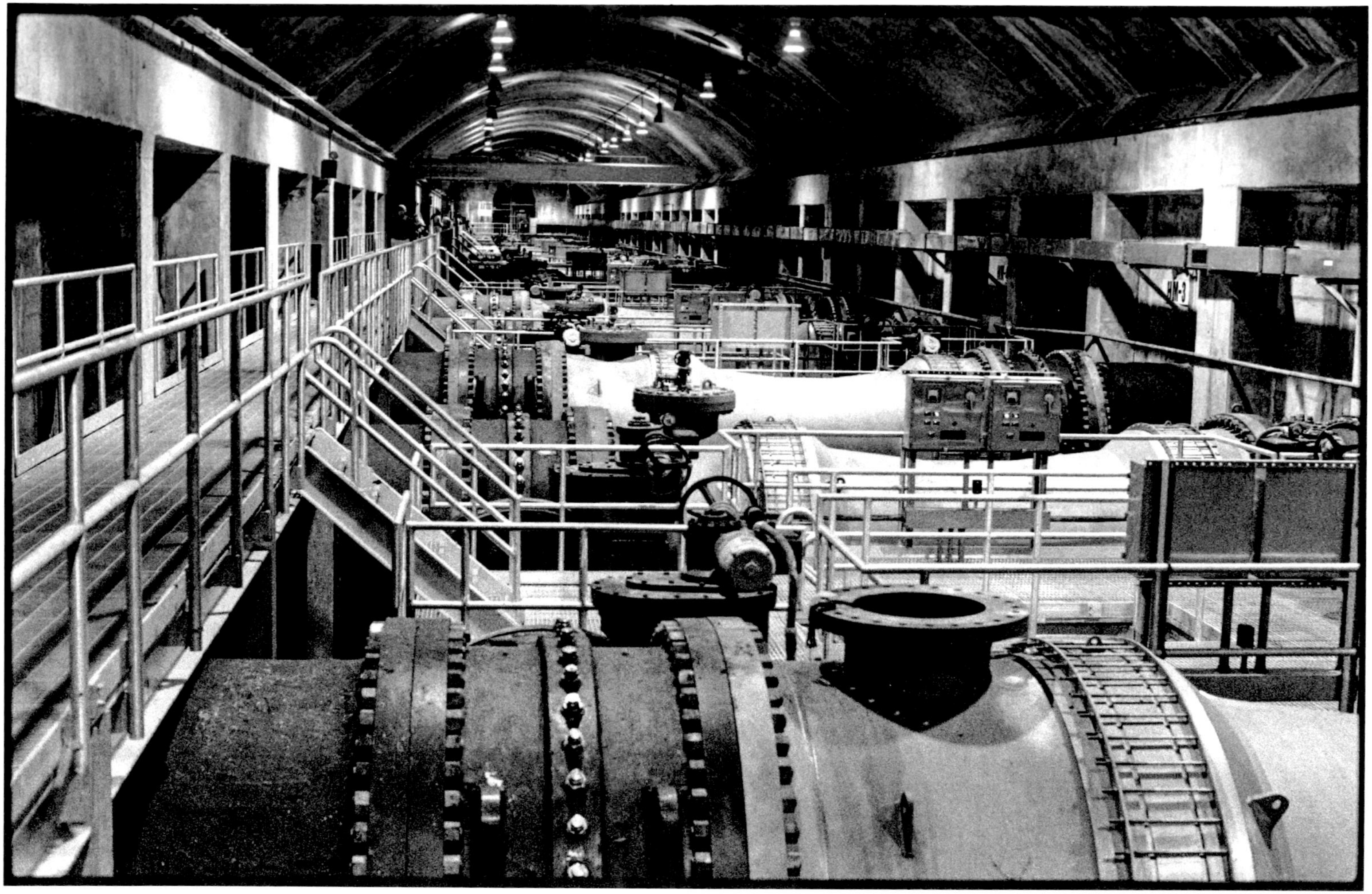

MTA bus driver, M86 bus, October 25, 2007

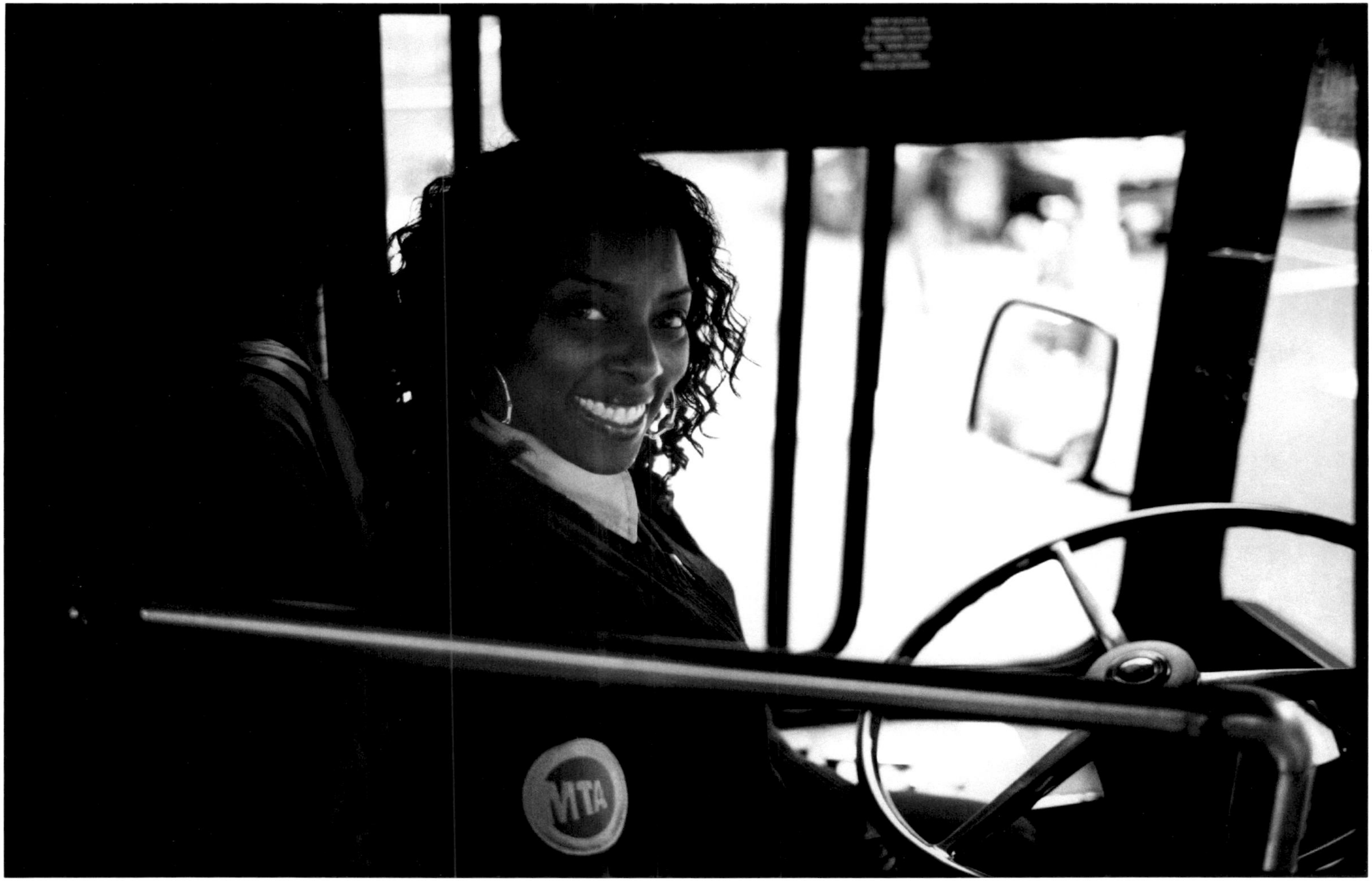

Commissioner Bitta Mostofi (right) in conference, Mayor's Office of Immigrant Affairs, Tribeca, June 6, 2018

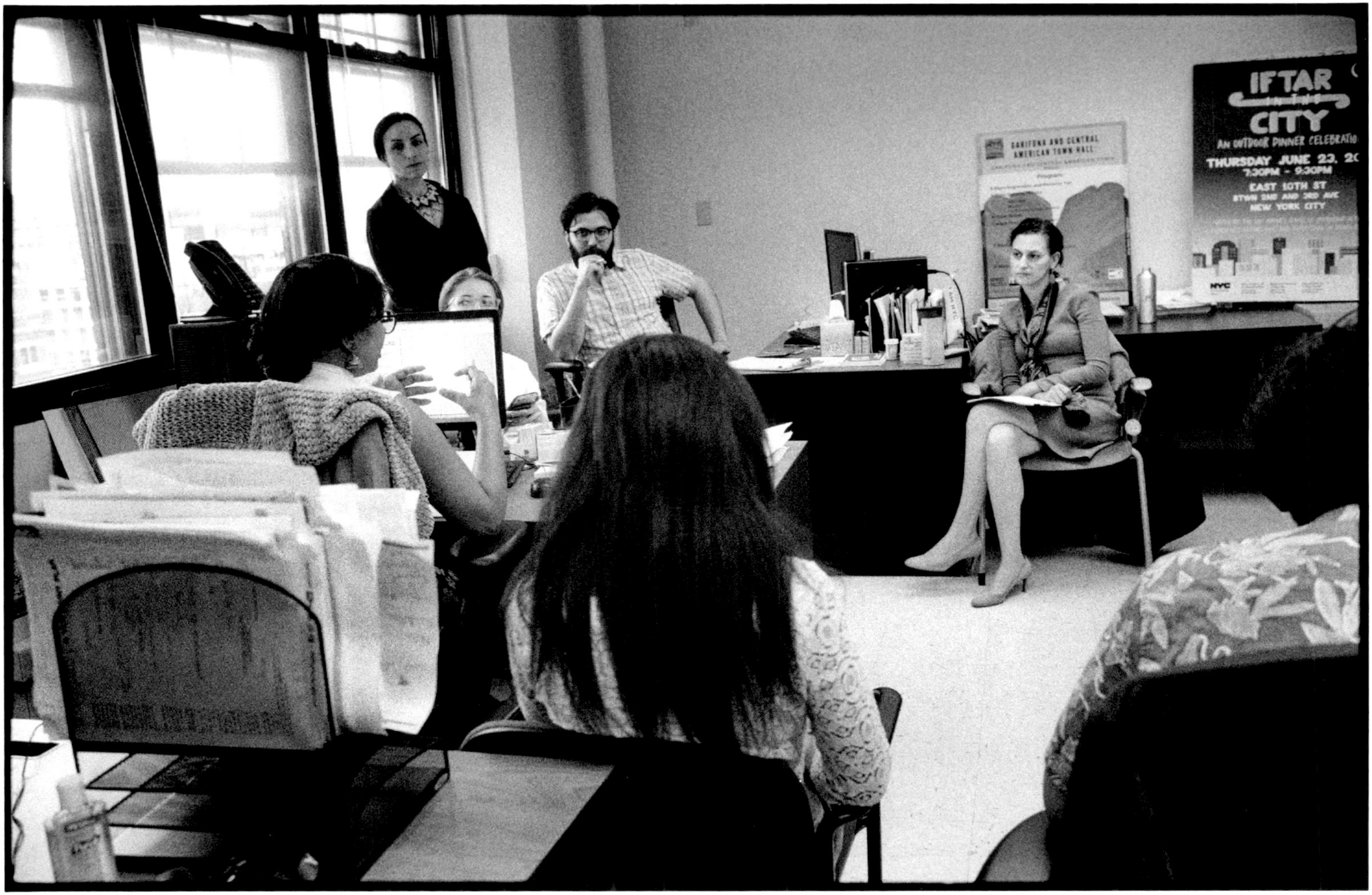
GARIFUNA AND CENTRAL
AMERICAN TOWN HALL
IFTAR
CITY
AN OUTDOOR DINNER CELEBRATIO
THURSDAY JUNE 23, 2
7:30PM - 9:30PM
EAST 10TH ST
BTWN 2ND AND 3RD AVE
NEW YORK CITY
NYC

New York Public Library, Fifth Avenue and 42nd Street, Midtown, December 2, 2007

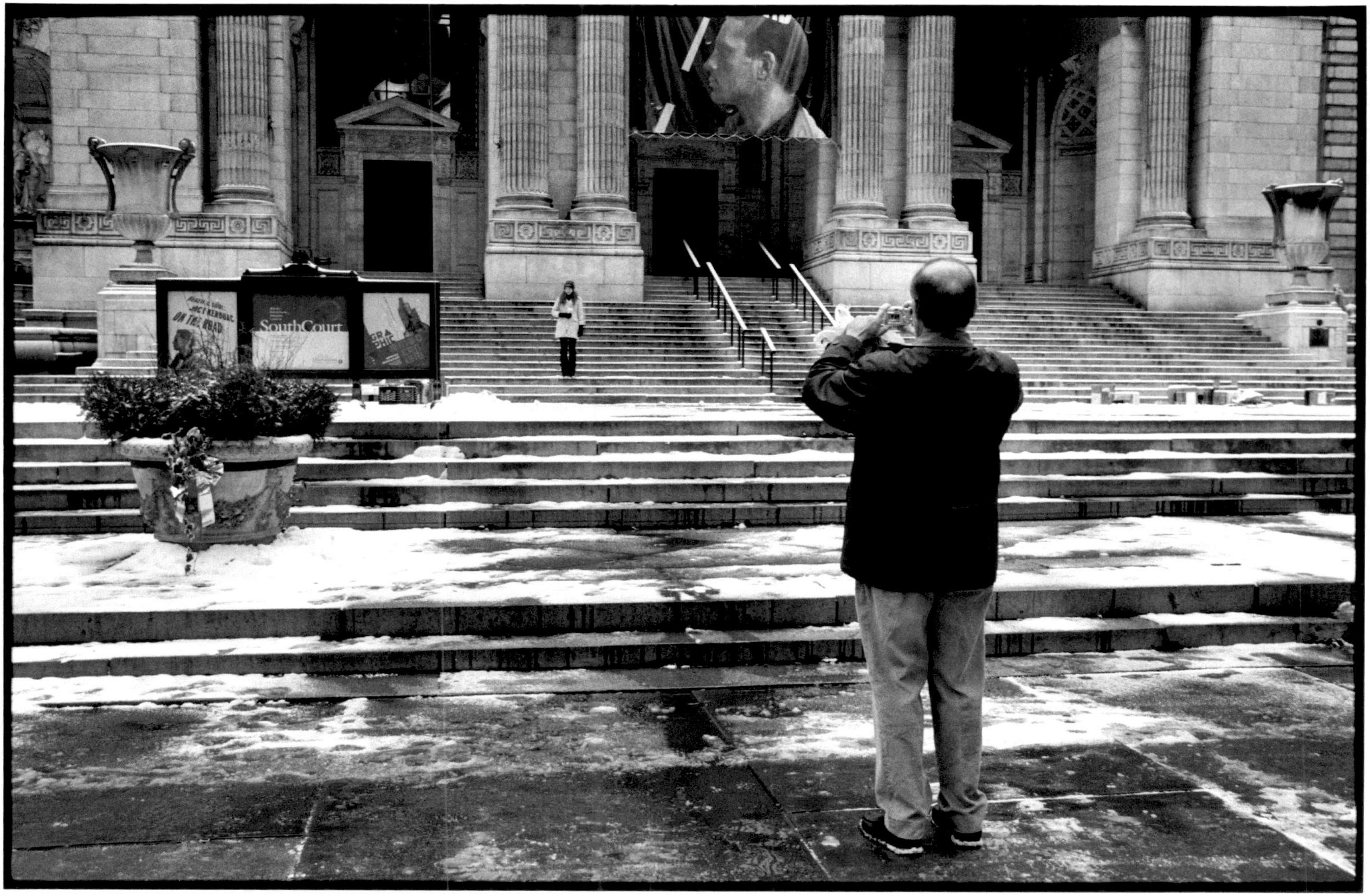
ON THE ROAD
SouthCourt

FDNY recruiting, 116th Street subway station, Harlem, February 21, 2017

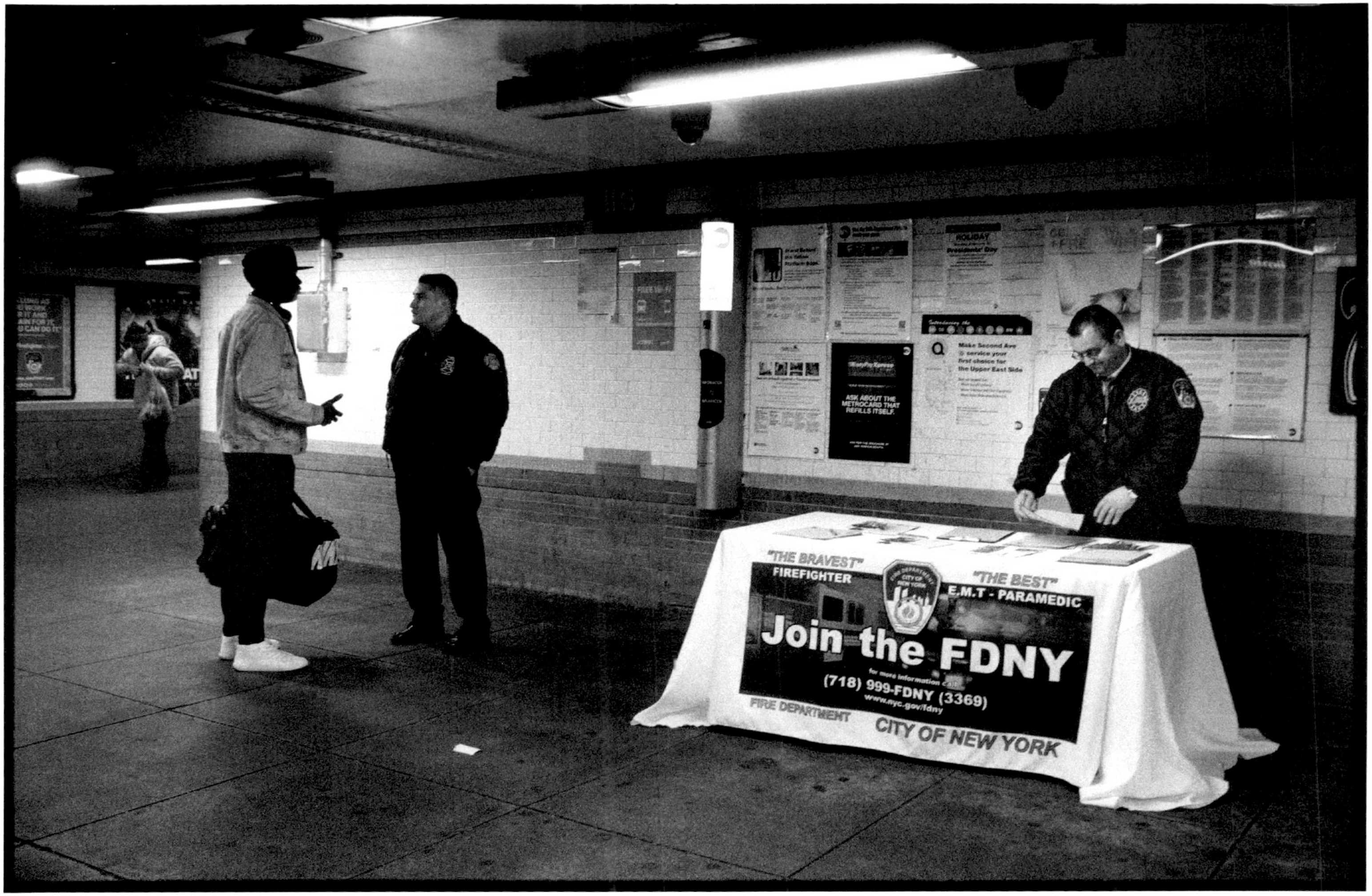
"THE BRAVEST"
FIREFIGHTER
"THE BEST"
E.M.T - PARAMEDIC
Join the FDNY
(718) 999-FDNY (3369)
www.nyc.gov/fdny
FIRE DEPARTMENT
CITY OF NEW YORK
ASK ABOUT THE METROCARD THAT REFILLS ITSELF.

Assistant District Attorney Joseph Abrams, 1 Hogan Place, Civic Center, January 23, 2026

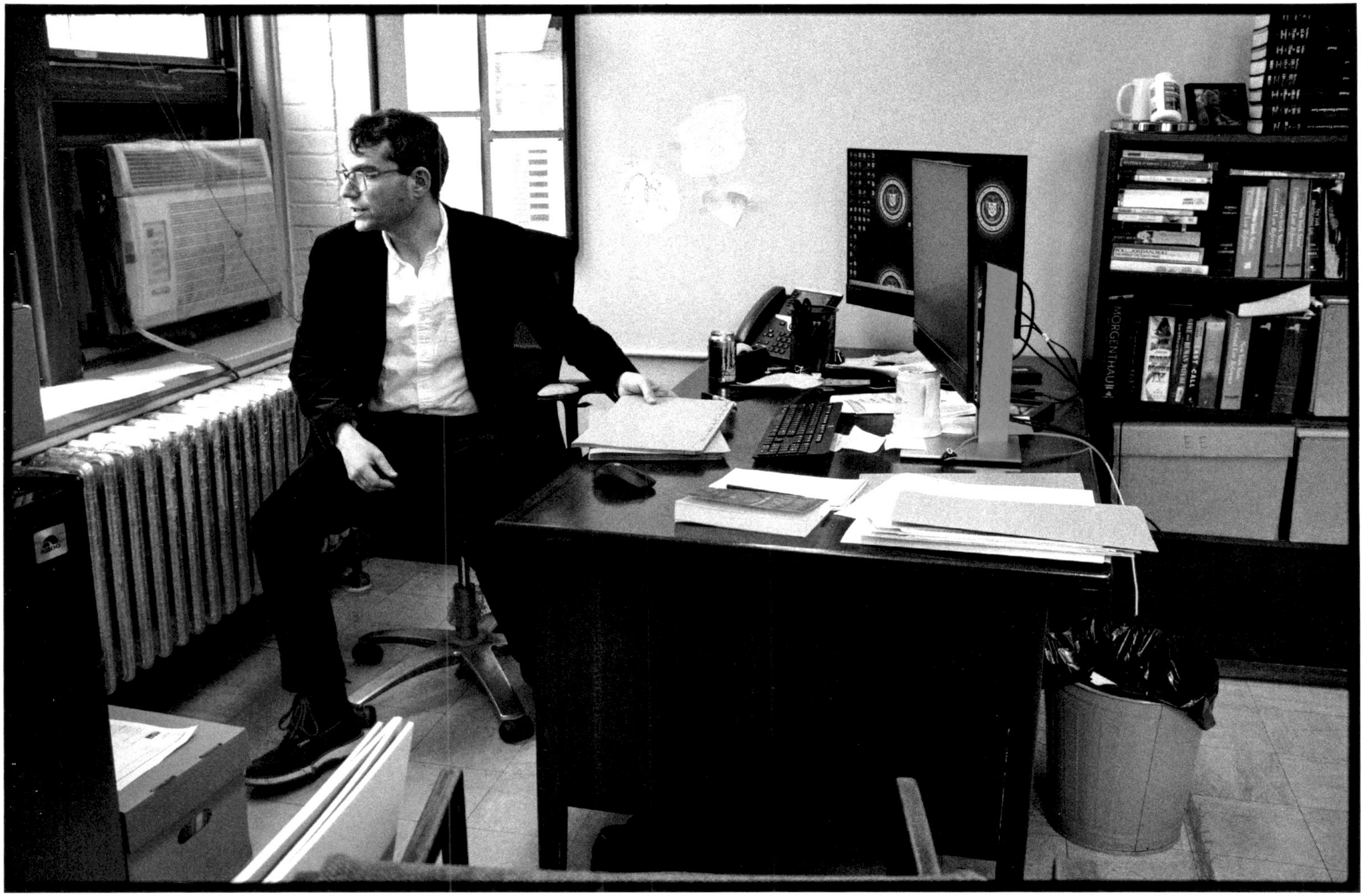
MORGENTHAU

3333 Broadway, constructed under the Mitchell-Lama program, Harlem, April 10, 2019

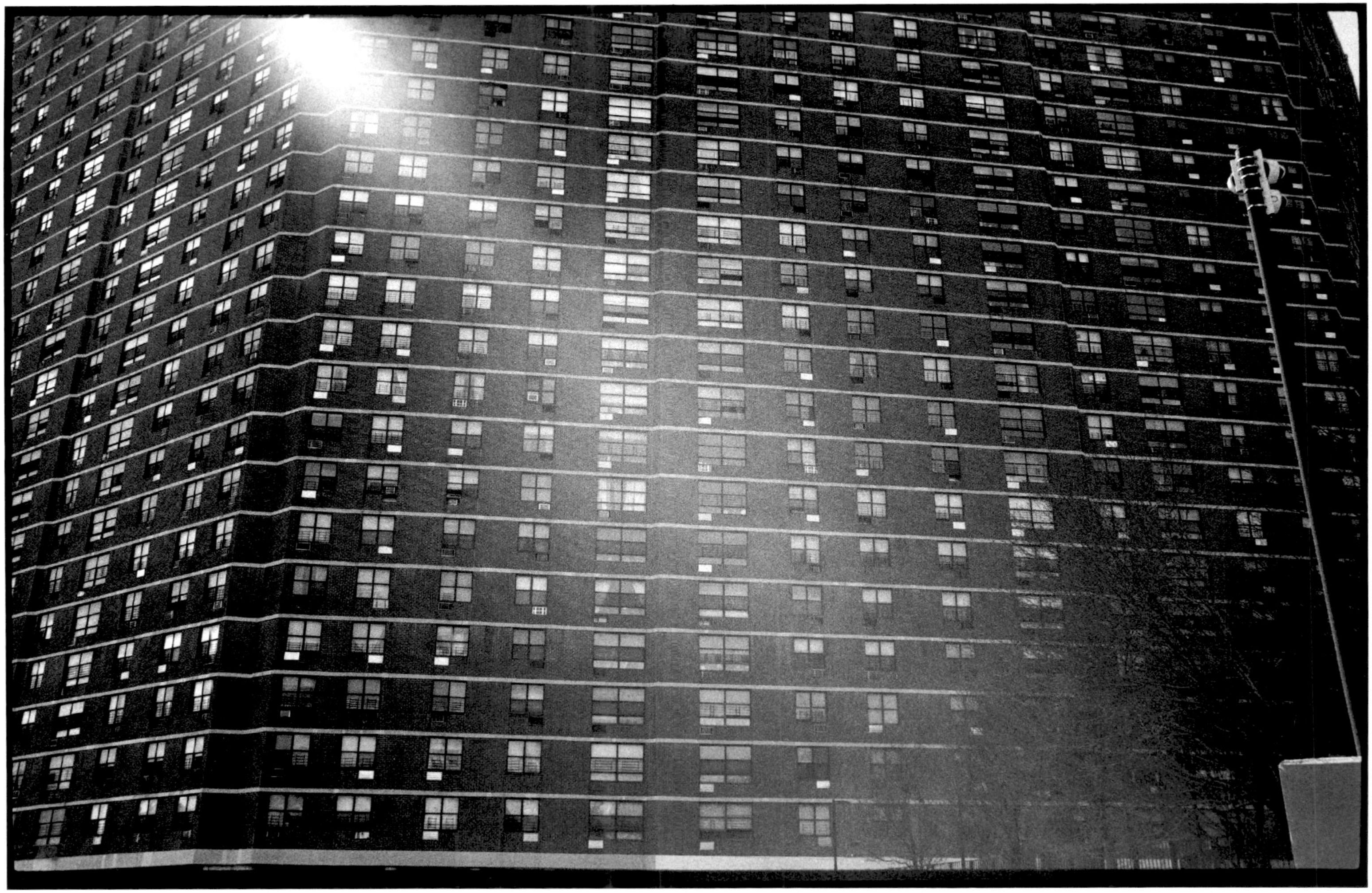

Manhattan Marriage Bureau, Louis J. Lefkowitz State Office Building, Civic Center, August 23, 2018

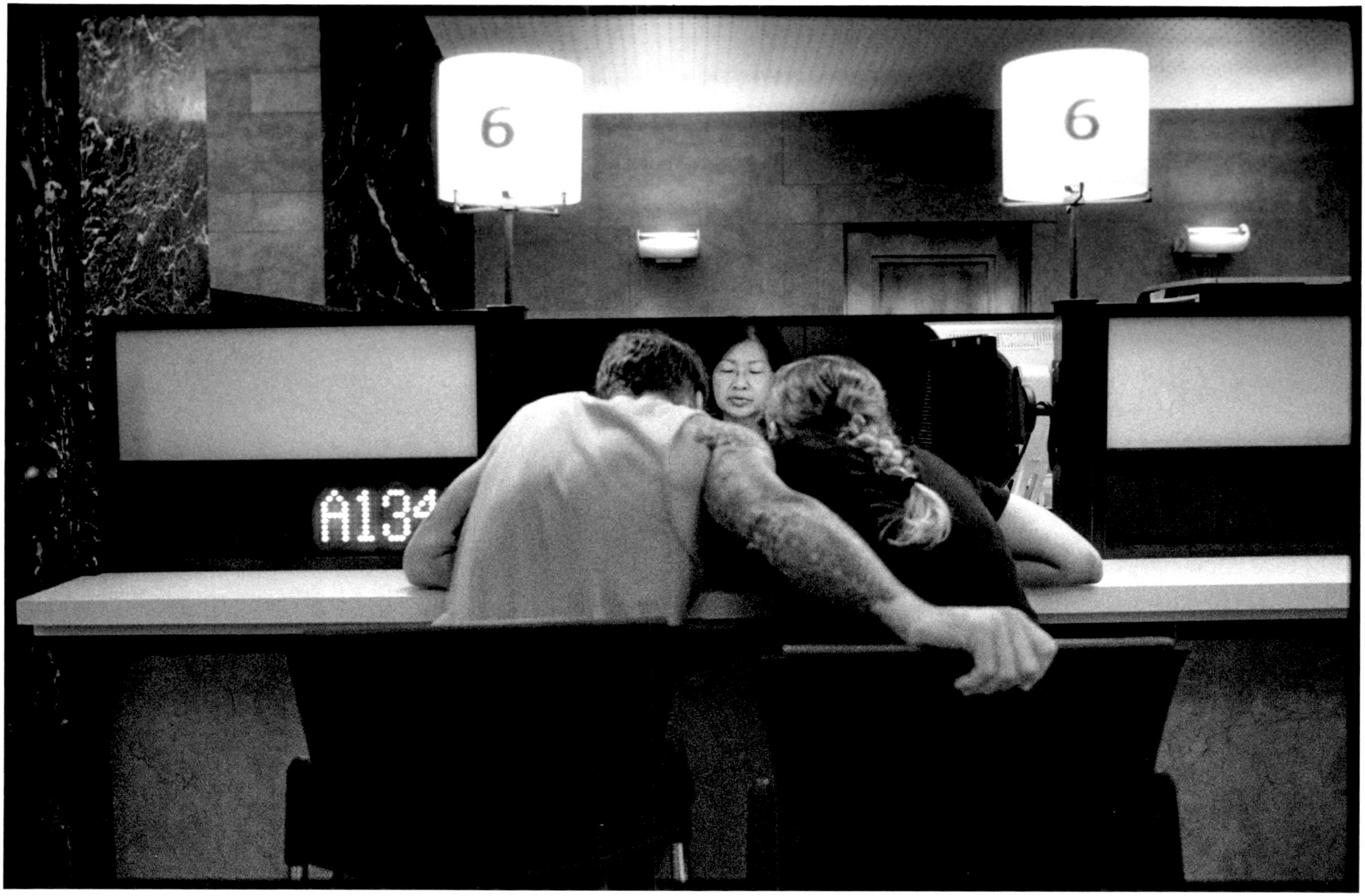
6
6
A13

Justice Shirley Kornreich (left), New York County Supreme Court, Civil Term, and clerks, Civic Center, January 8, 2015

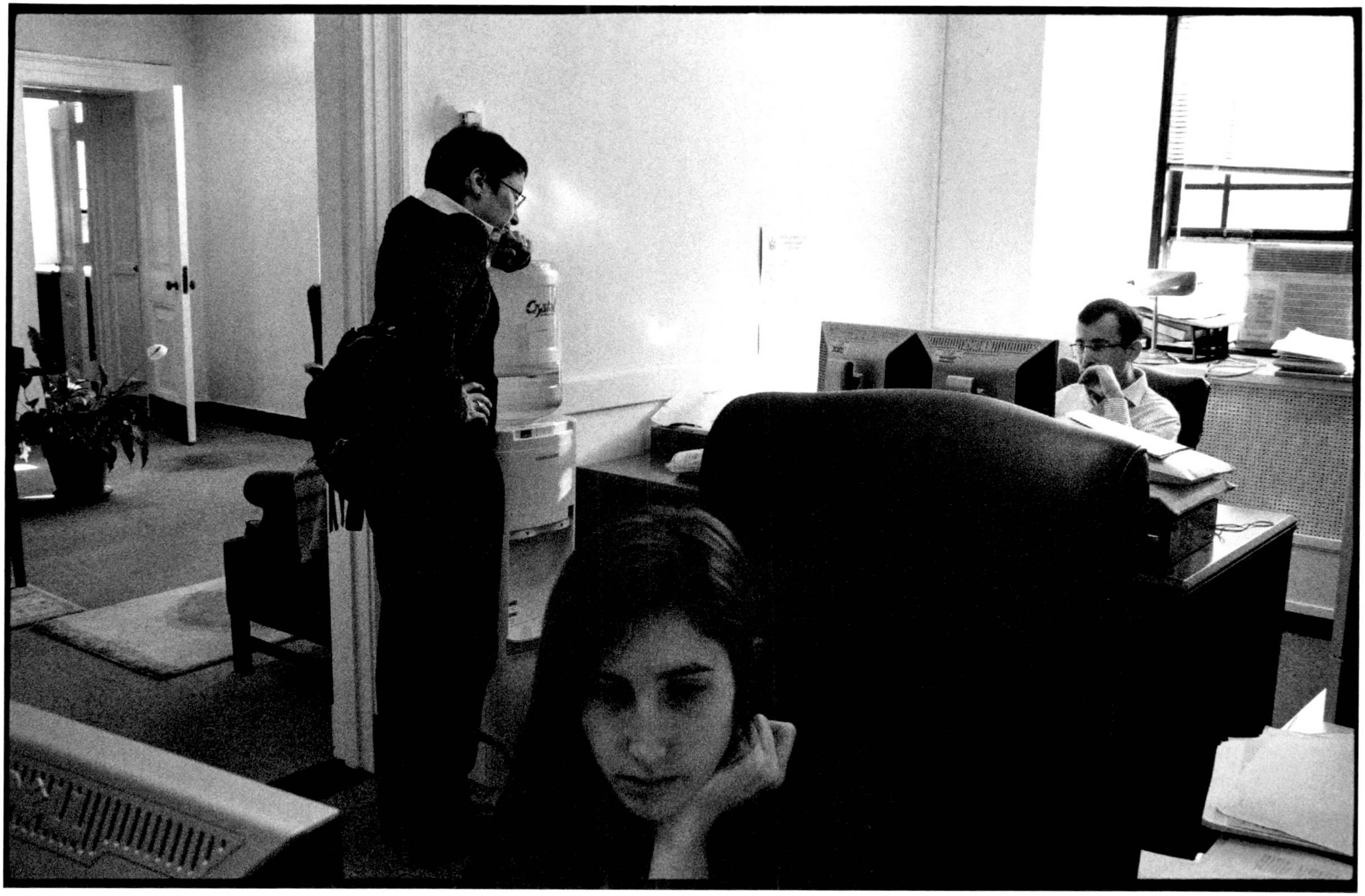

A USPS post office, Concourse Village, Bronx, January 22, 1999

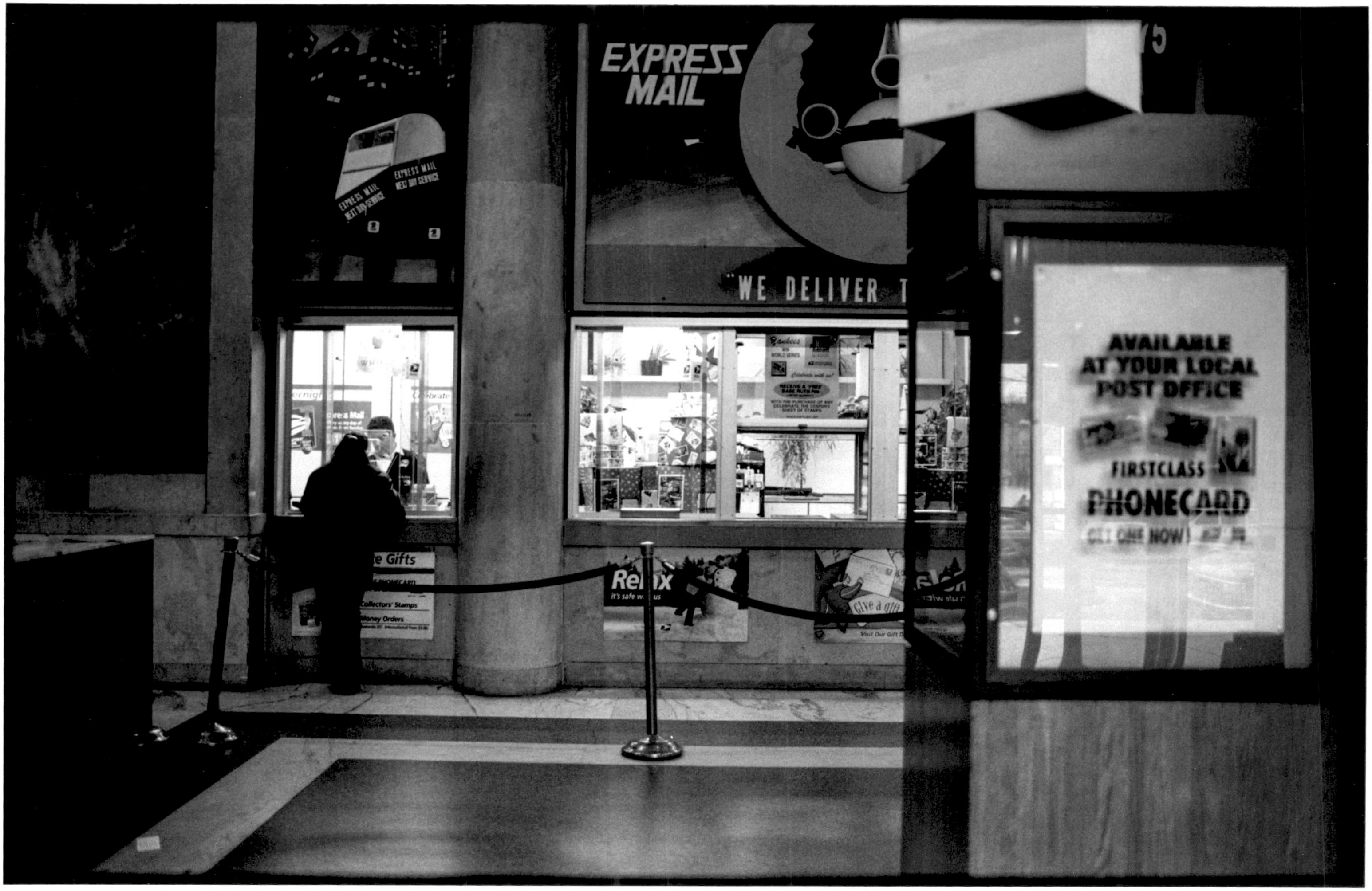
EXPRESS MAIL
EXPRESS MAIL NEXT DAY SERVICE
"WE DELIVER T
AVAILABLE AT YOUR LOCAL POST OFFICE
FIRSTCLASS
PHONECARD

City Council hearing, City Hall, Civic Center, August 8, 2017

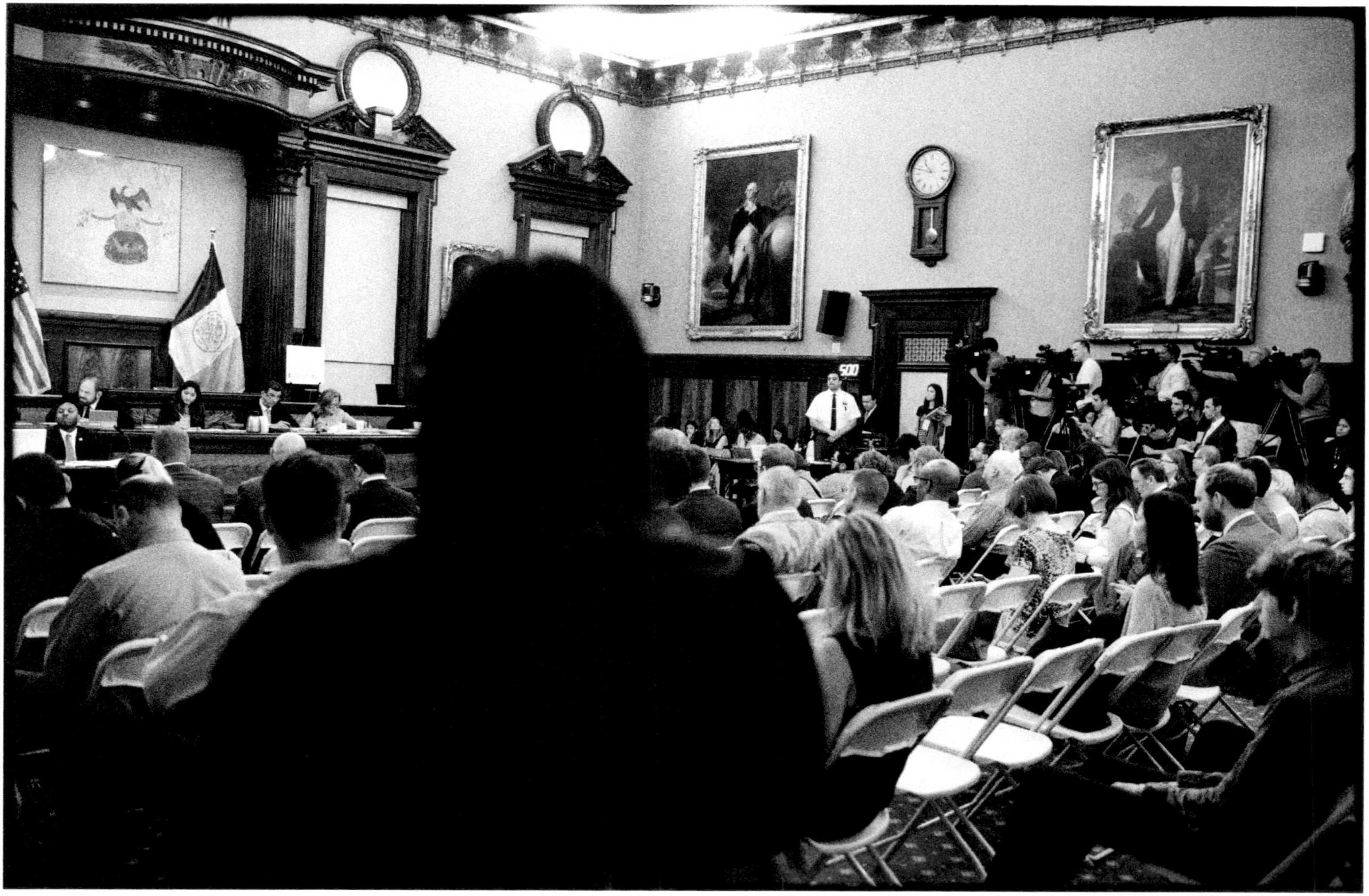

Homelessness, Broadway, Upper West Side, November 25, 2017

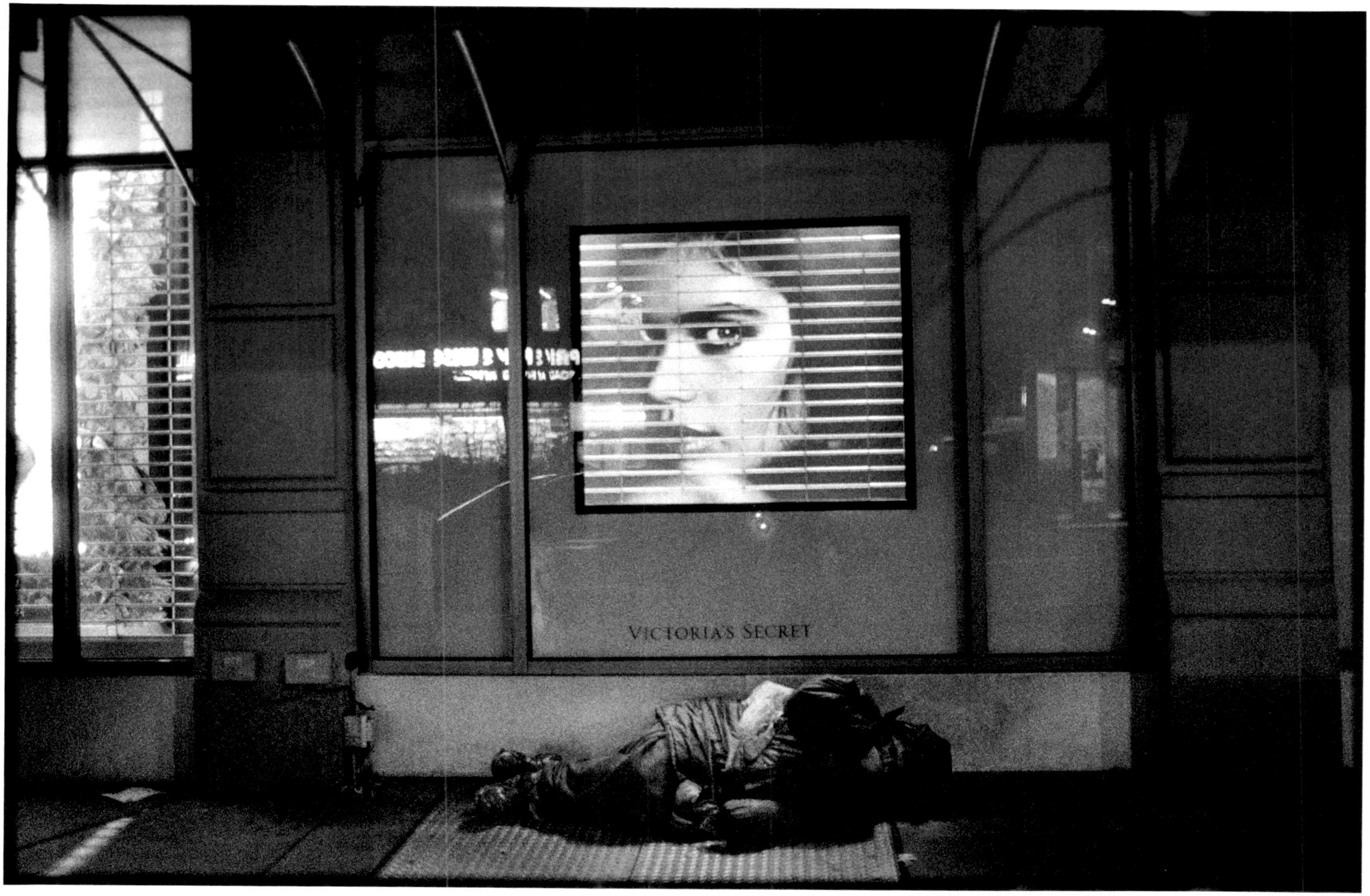
VICTORIA'S SECRET

COVID-19 pandemic dining protocol, Amsterdam Avenue, Upper West Side, October 5, 2020

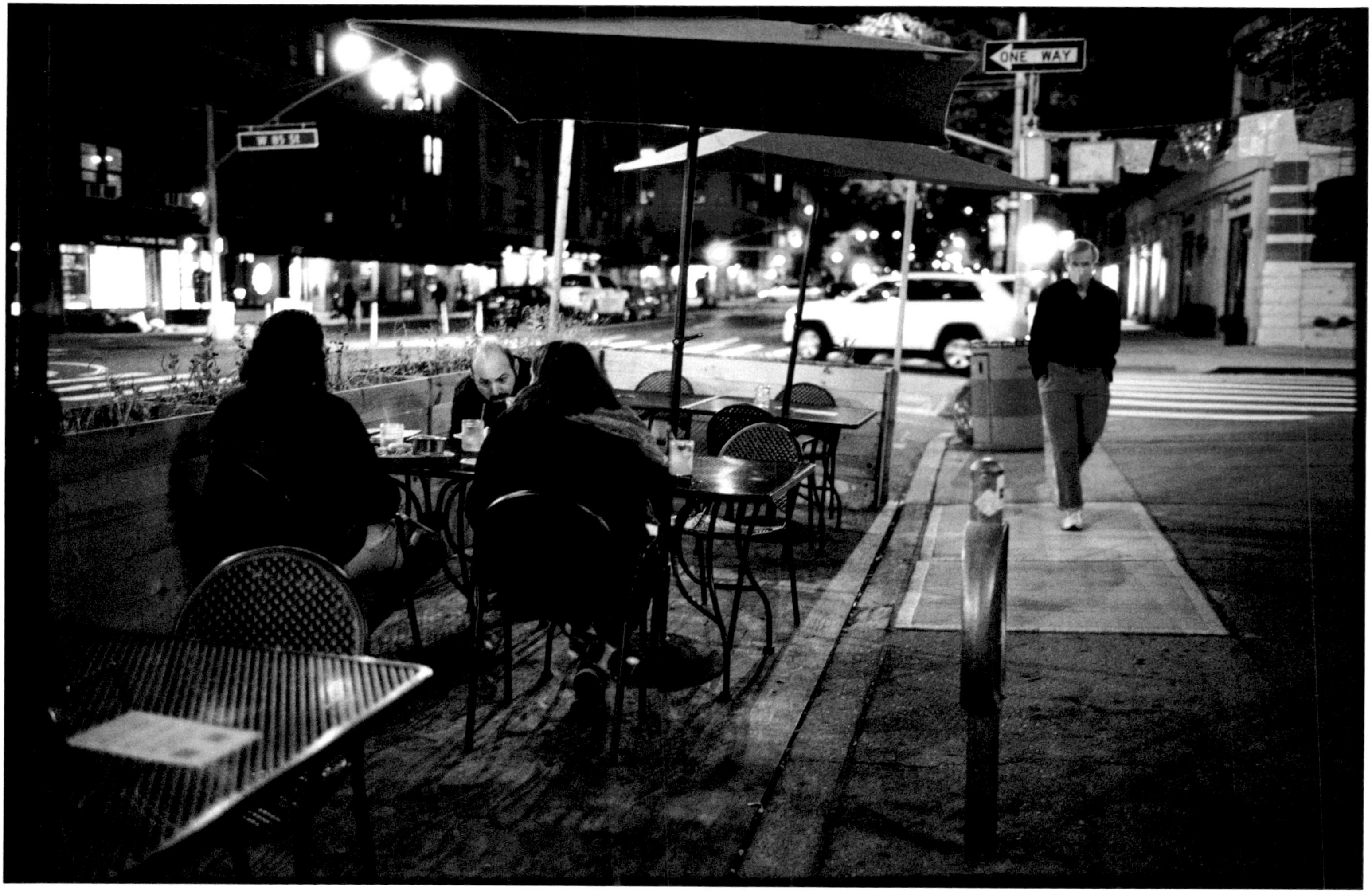
ONE WAY

Housing Preservation and Development walk-through at a construction site, Sheepshead Bay, Brooklyn, March 3, 2016

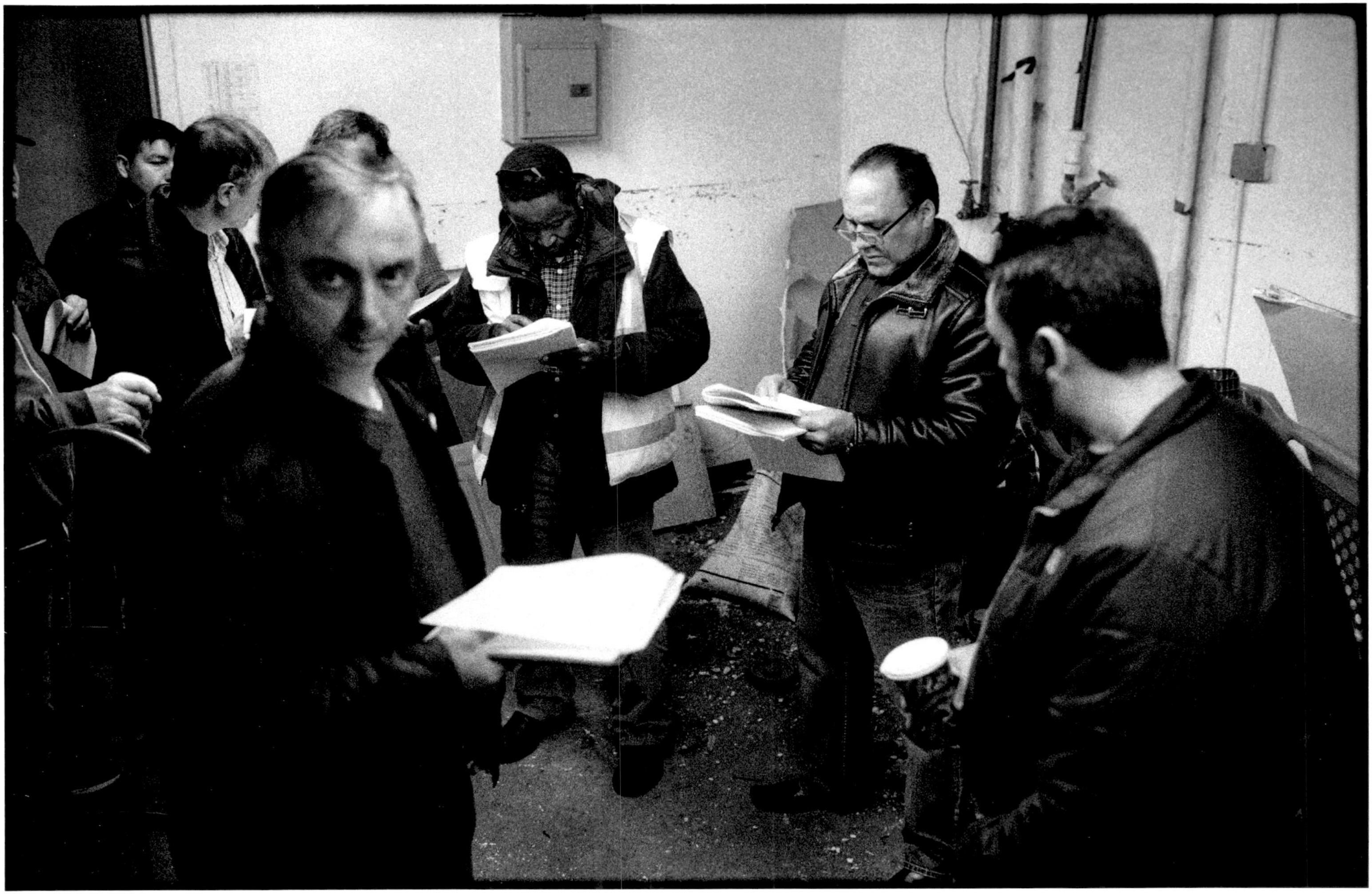

Third Annual Iftar hosted by the Mayor's Office of Immigrant Affairs, Jackson Heights, Queens, May 31, 2018

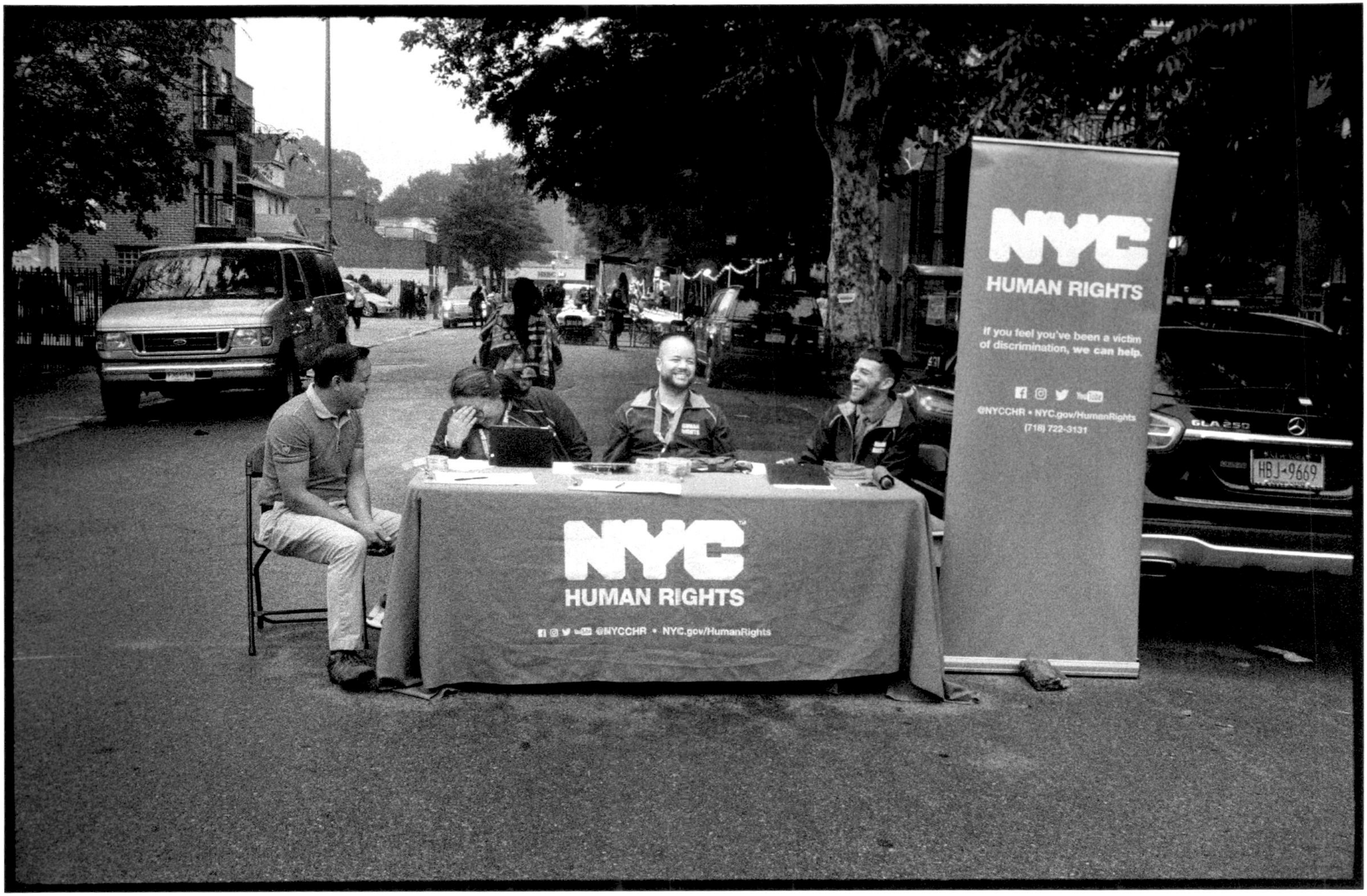
NYC
HUMAN RIGHTS
@NYCCHR • NYC.gov/HumanRights
NYC
HUMAN RIGHTS
If you feel you've been a victim of discrimination, we can help.
@NYCCHR • NYC.gov/HumanRights
(718) 722-3131

Department of City Planning, Urban Design Office, 120 Broadway, Financial District, May 11, 2016

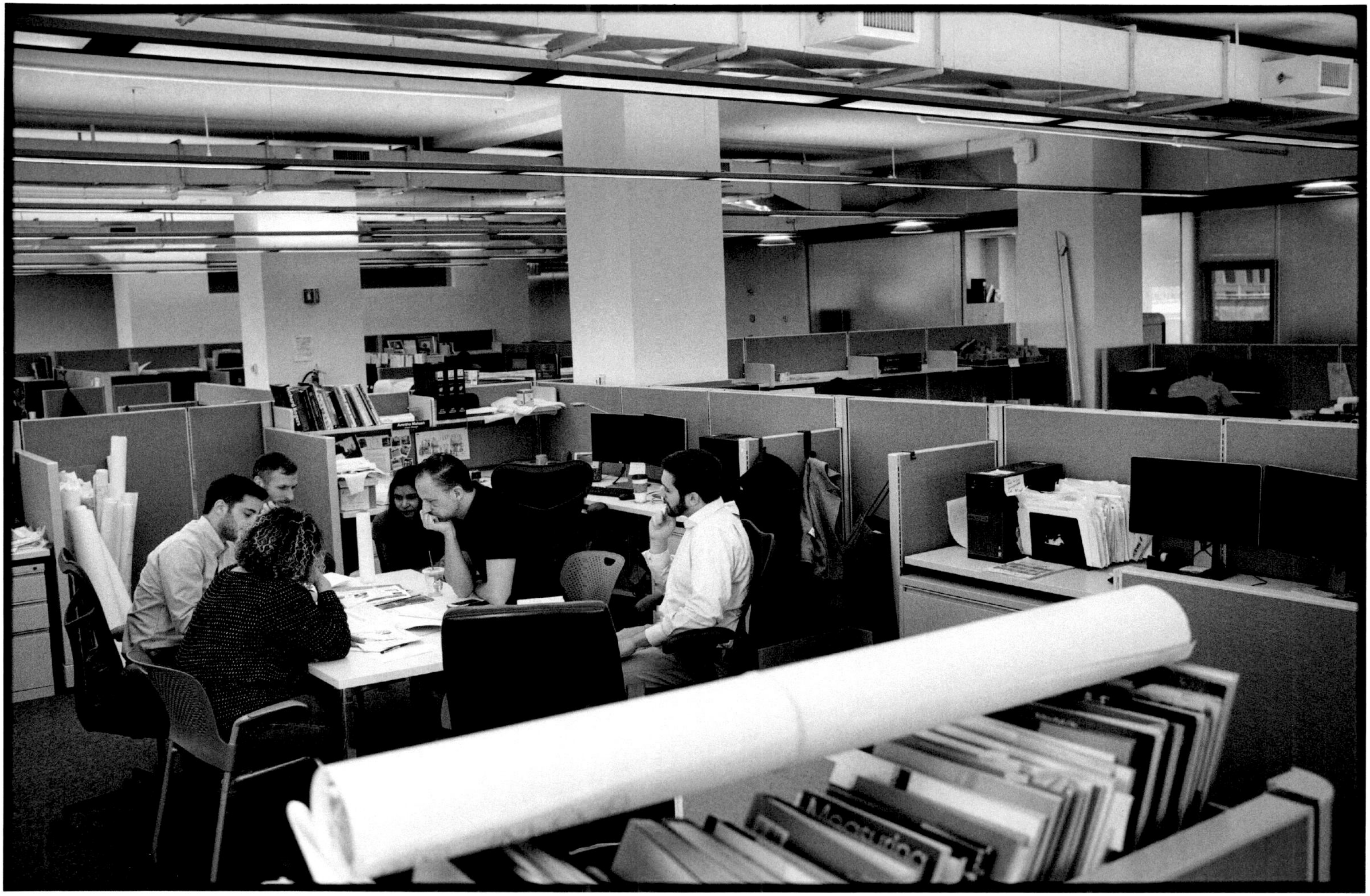

Rat, Jacqueline Kennedy Onassis Reservoir, Central Park, October 10, 2010

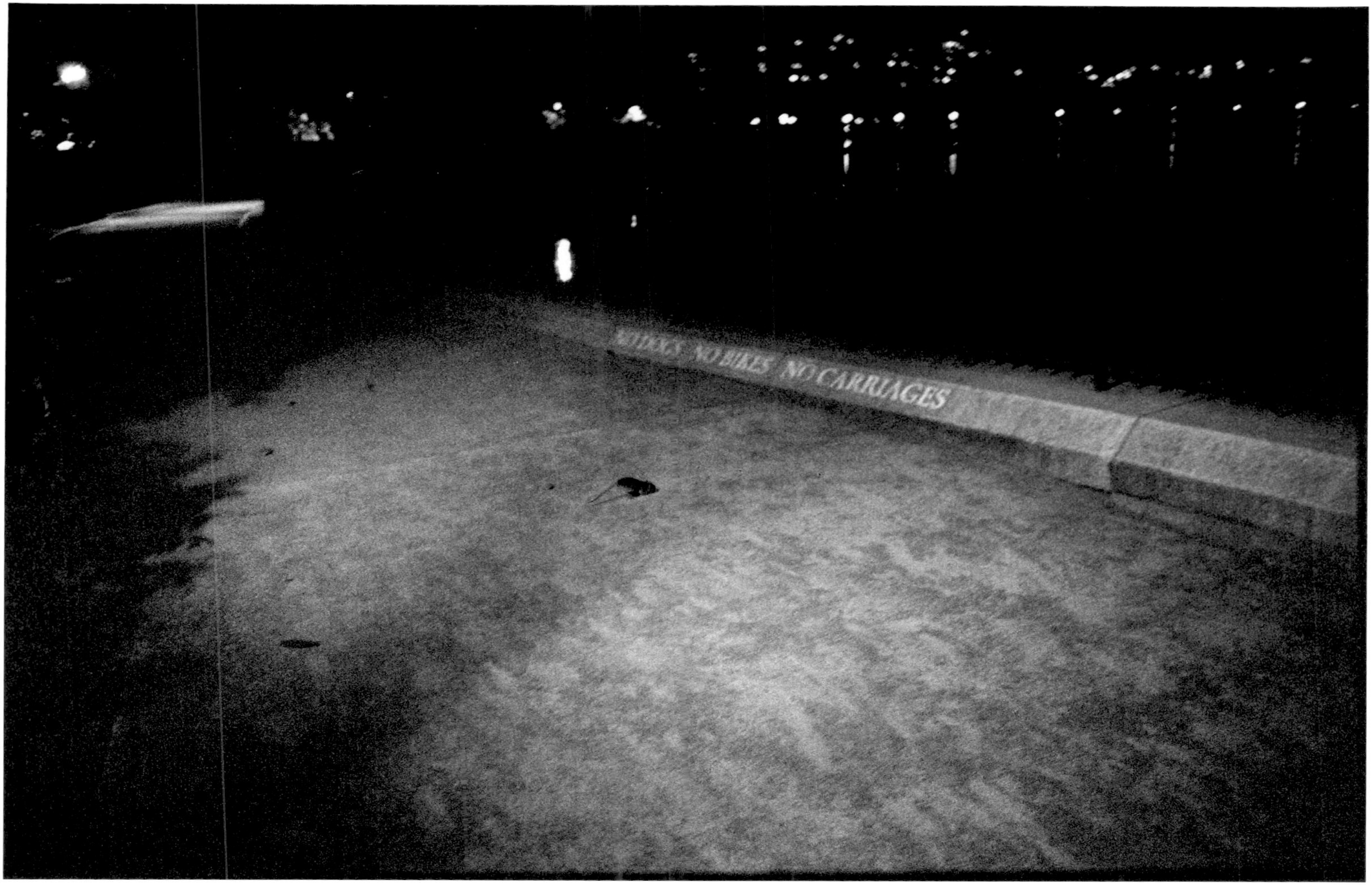
NO BIKES NO CARRIAGES

Department of Sanitation worker and truck, Upper West Side, July 9, 2020

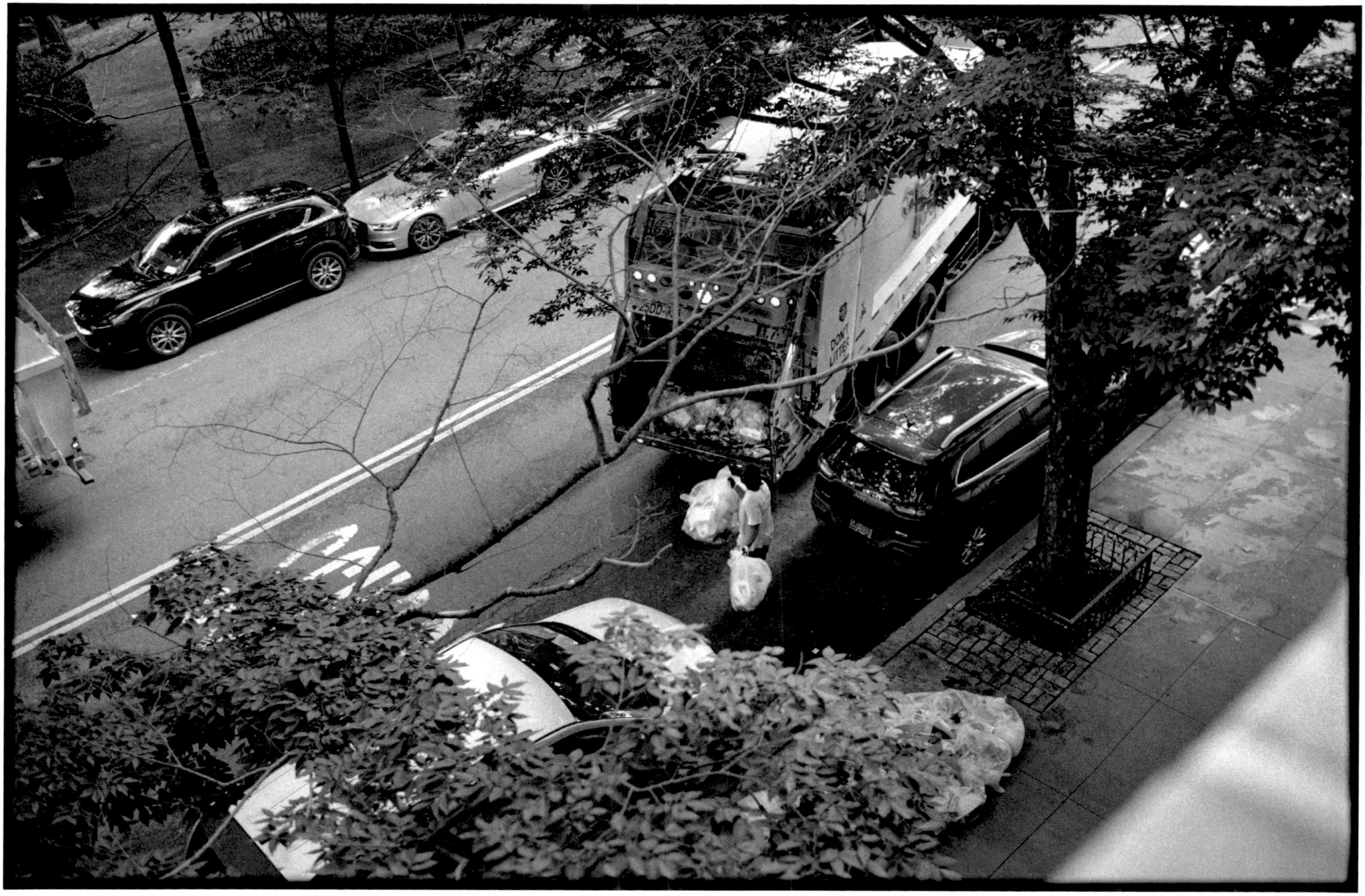

Public school principal, Morrisania, Bronx, June 29, 2000

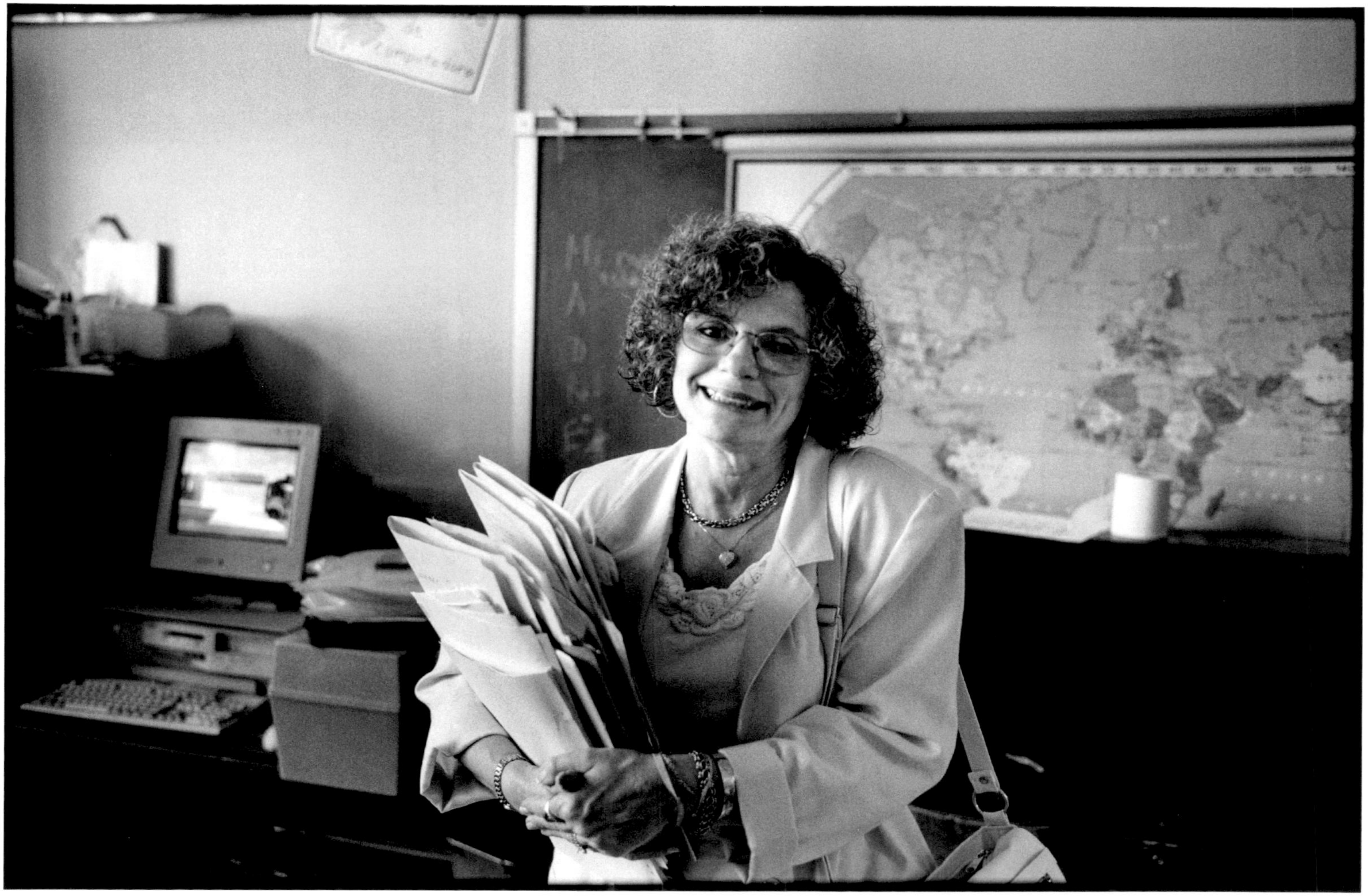

Suspect detained by police, SoHo, February 12, 2018

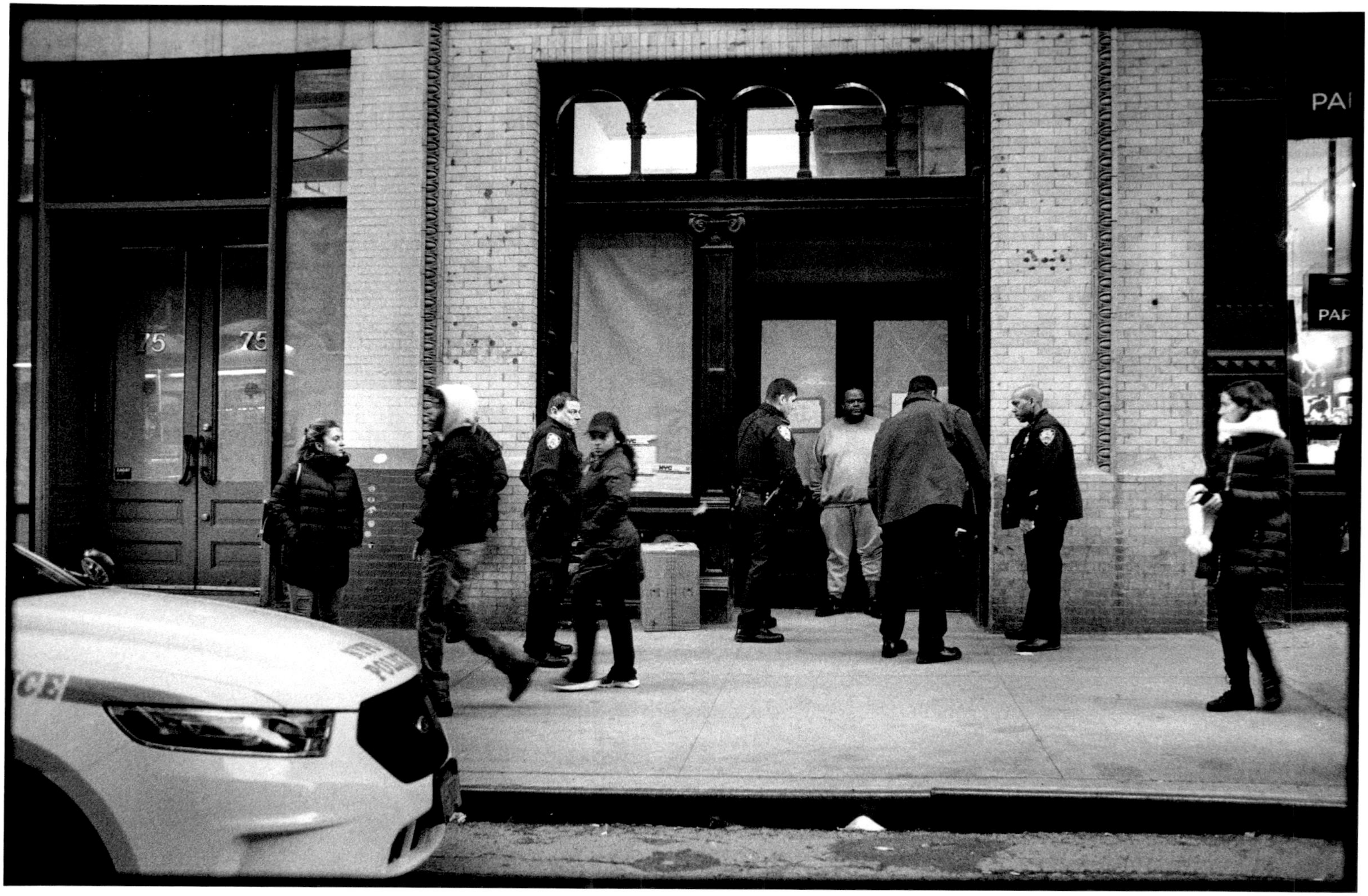
75
75

Department of Education yellow school buses, Co-op City, Bronx, February 4, 1999

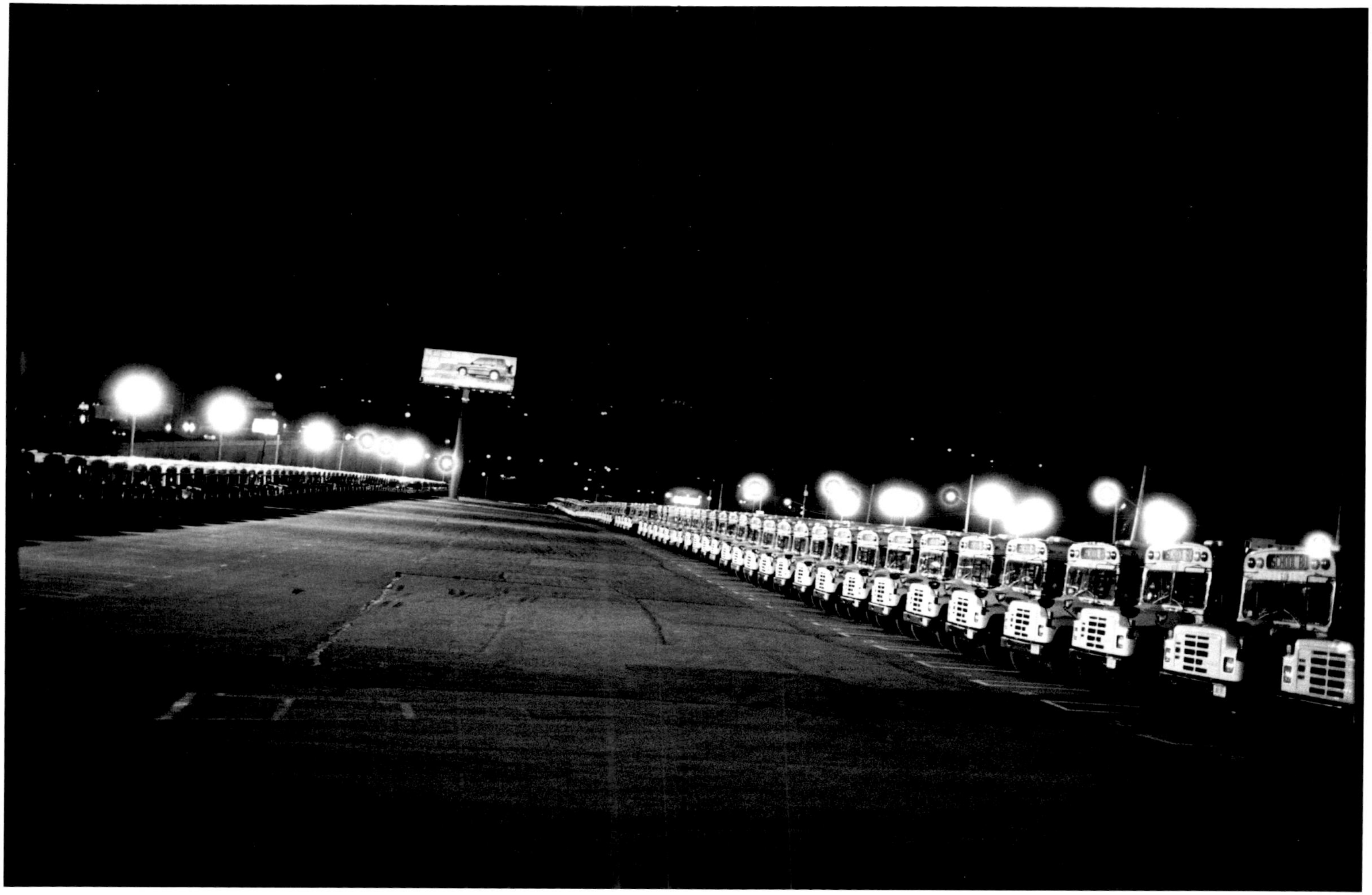

Infrastructure repair, West End Avenue, Upper West Side, November 3, 2020

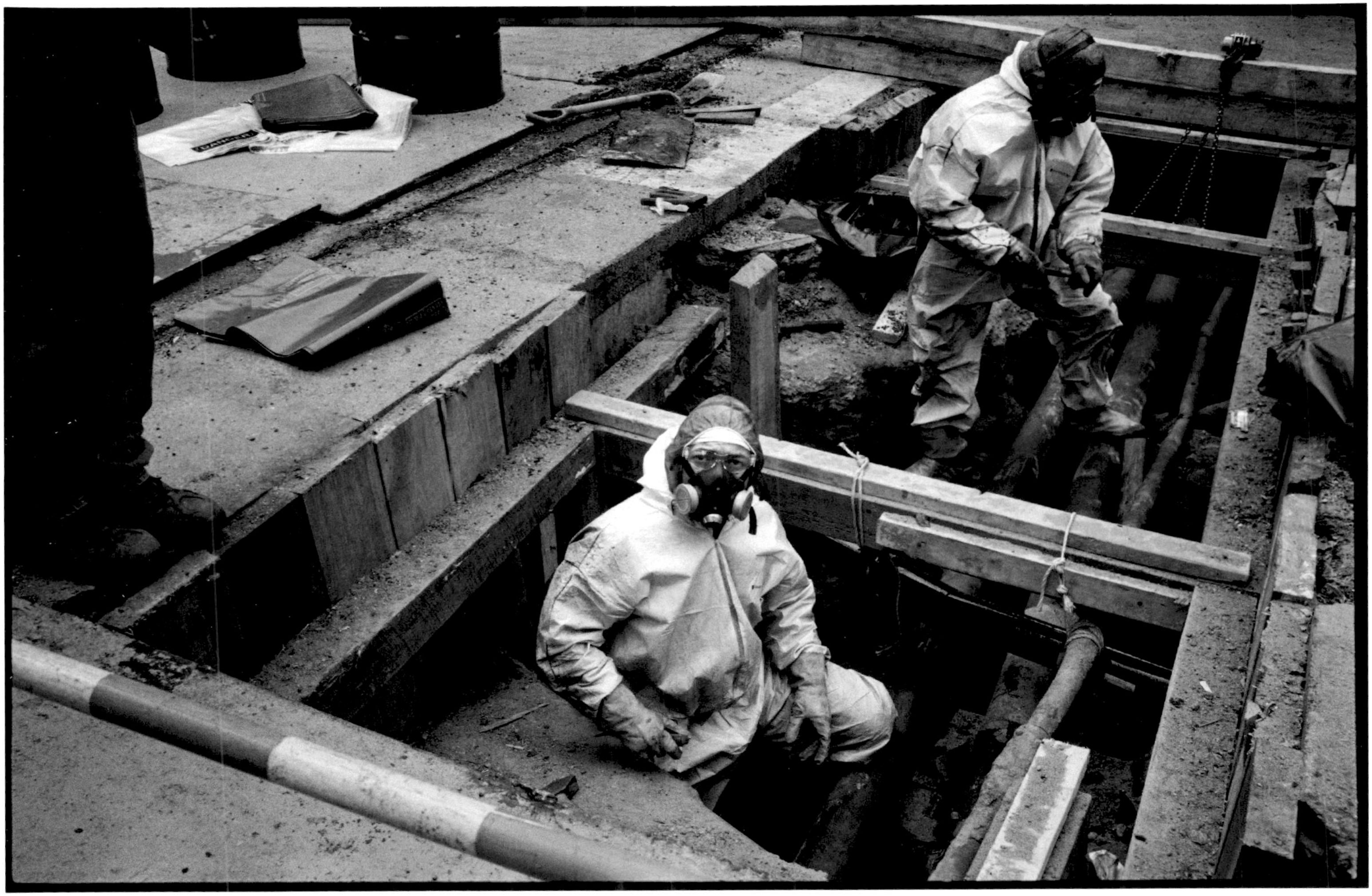

Photo of President Barack Obama, US Mission to the United Nations, First Avenue, Turtle Bay, July 28, 2014

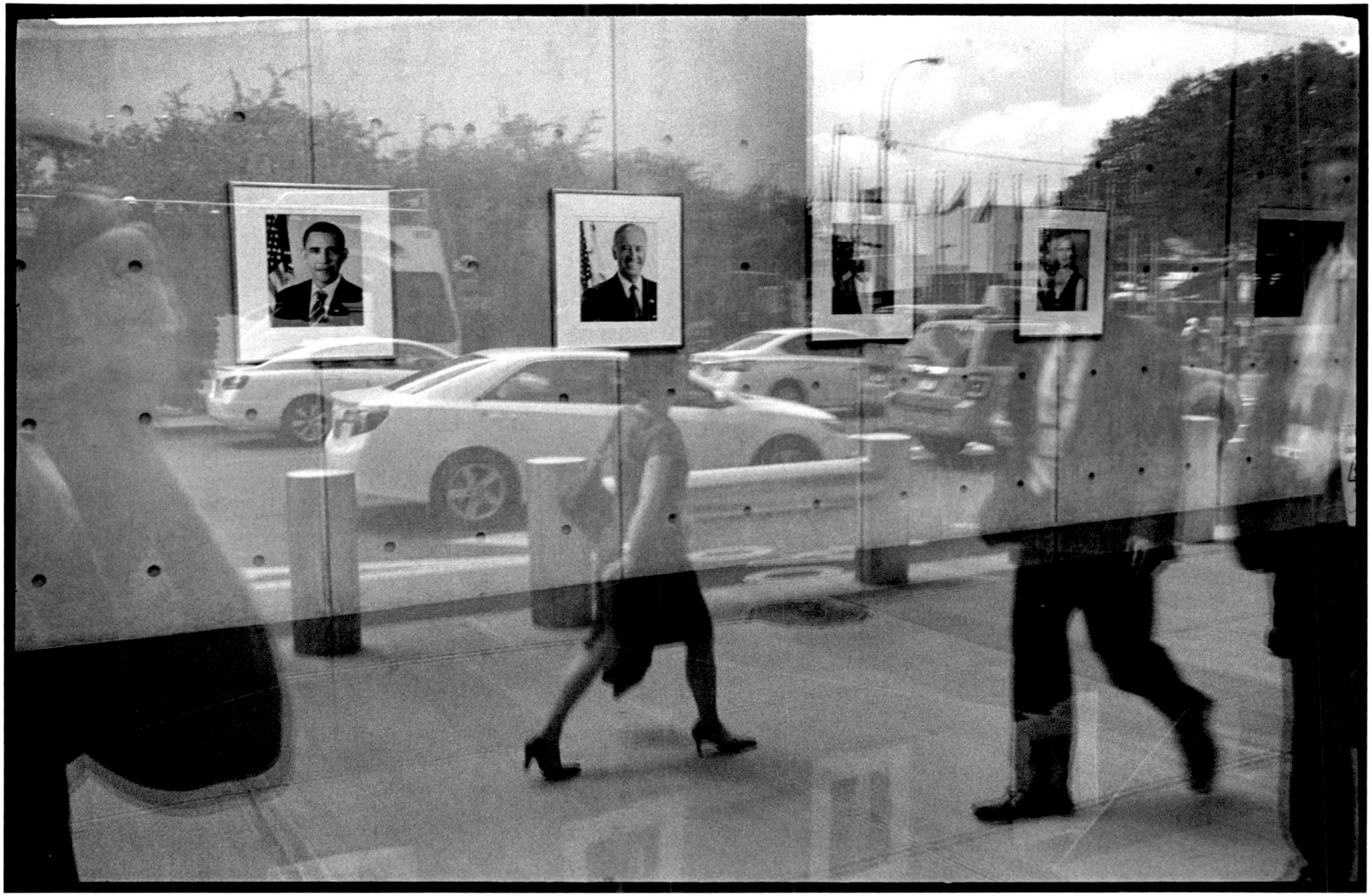

The National Anthem, police promotions ceremony, 1 Police Plaza, Civic Center, June 29, 2012

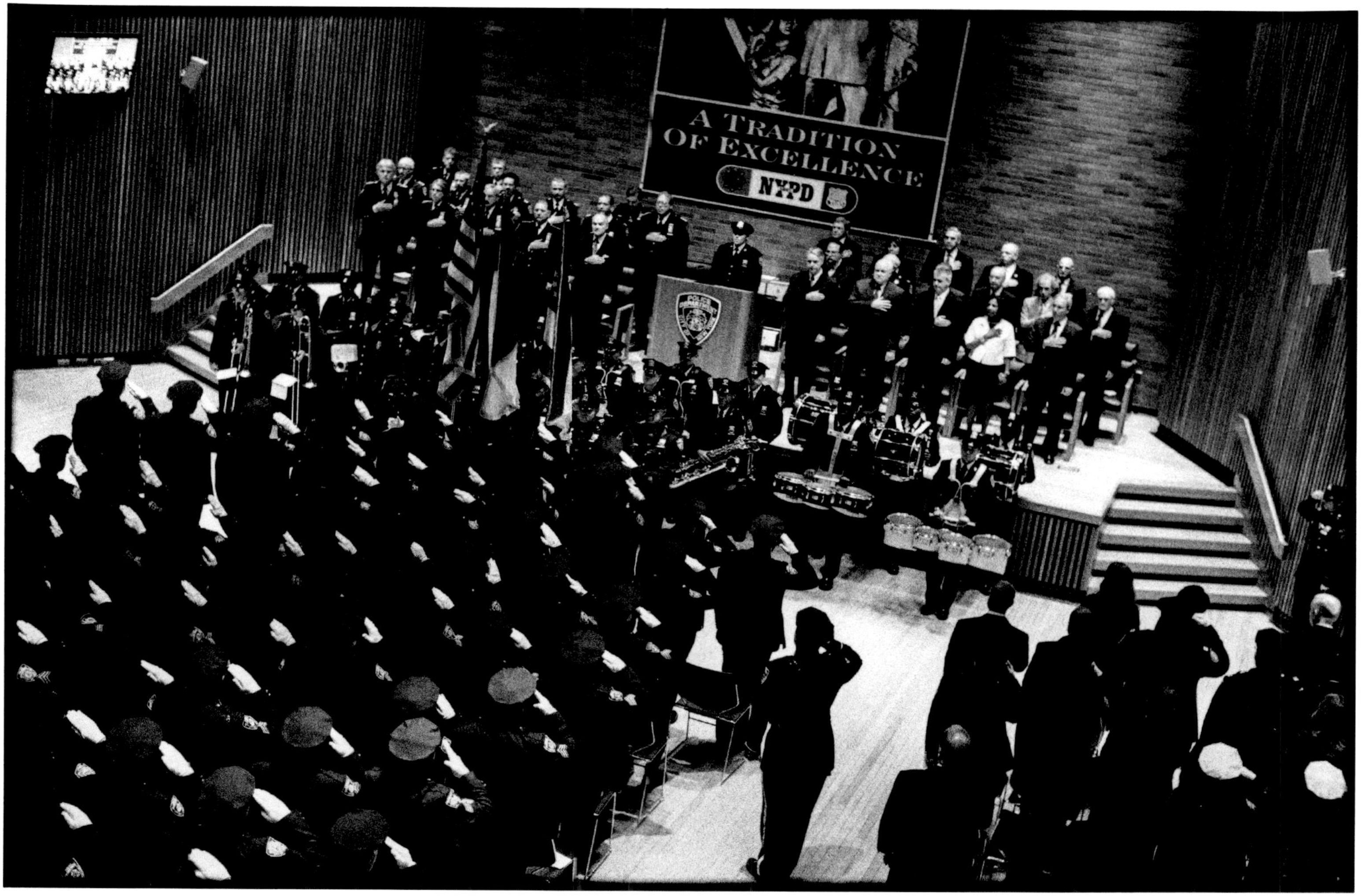
A TRADITION
OF EXCELLENCE
NYPD

DEMONSTRATIONS

Protests, grievances, raising public awareness

Occupy Wall Street, Zuccotti Park, Financial District, October 6, 2011

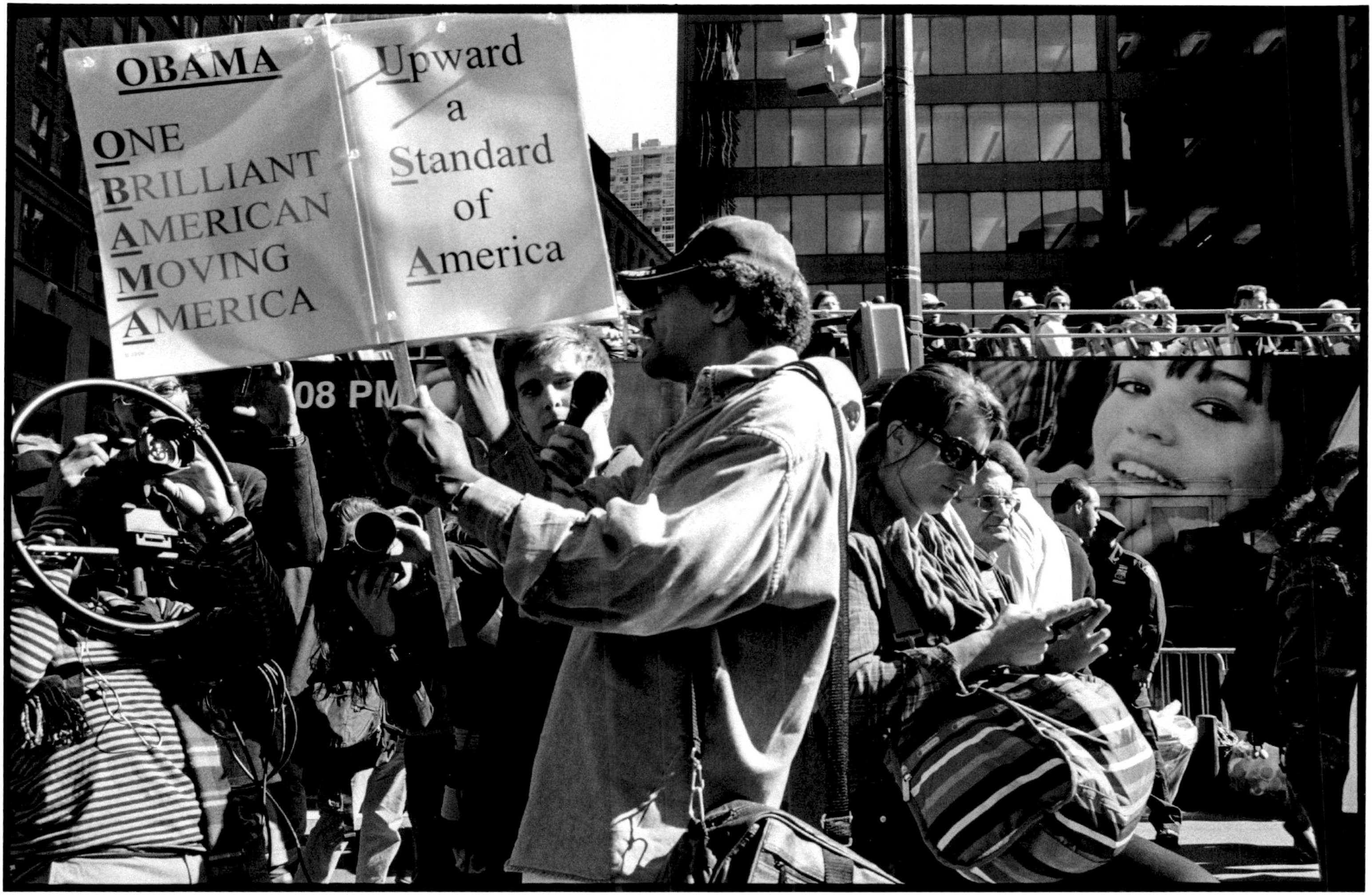
OBAMA
ONE
BRILLIANT
AMERICAN
MOVING
AMERICA
Upward
a
Standard
of
America
08 PM

Tea Party 365 demonstration, Eighth Avenue, Midtown, April 15 (Tax Day), 2010

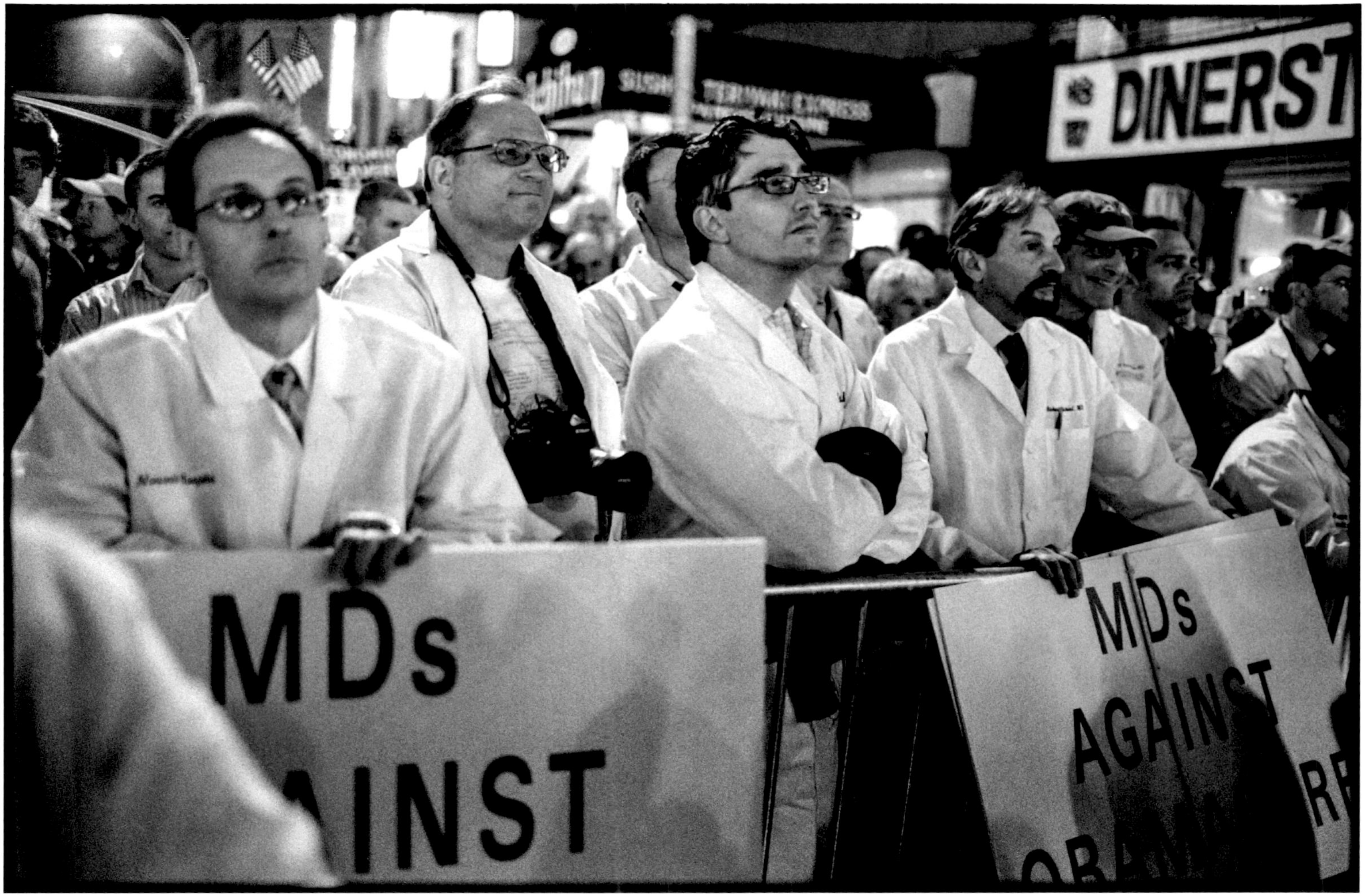
DINERST
MDs
AINST
MDs
AGAINST

AIDS Walk New York, Riverside Drive, May 15, 2011

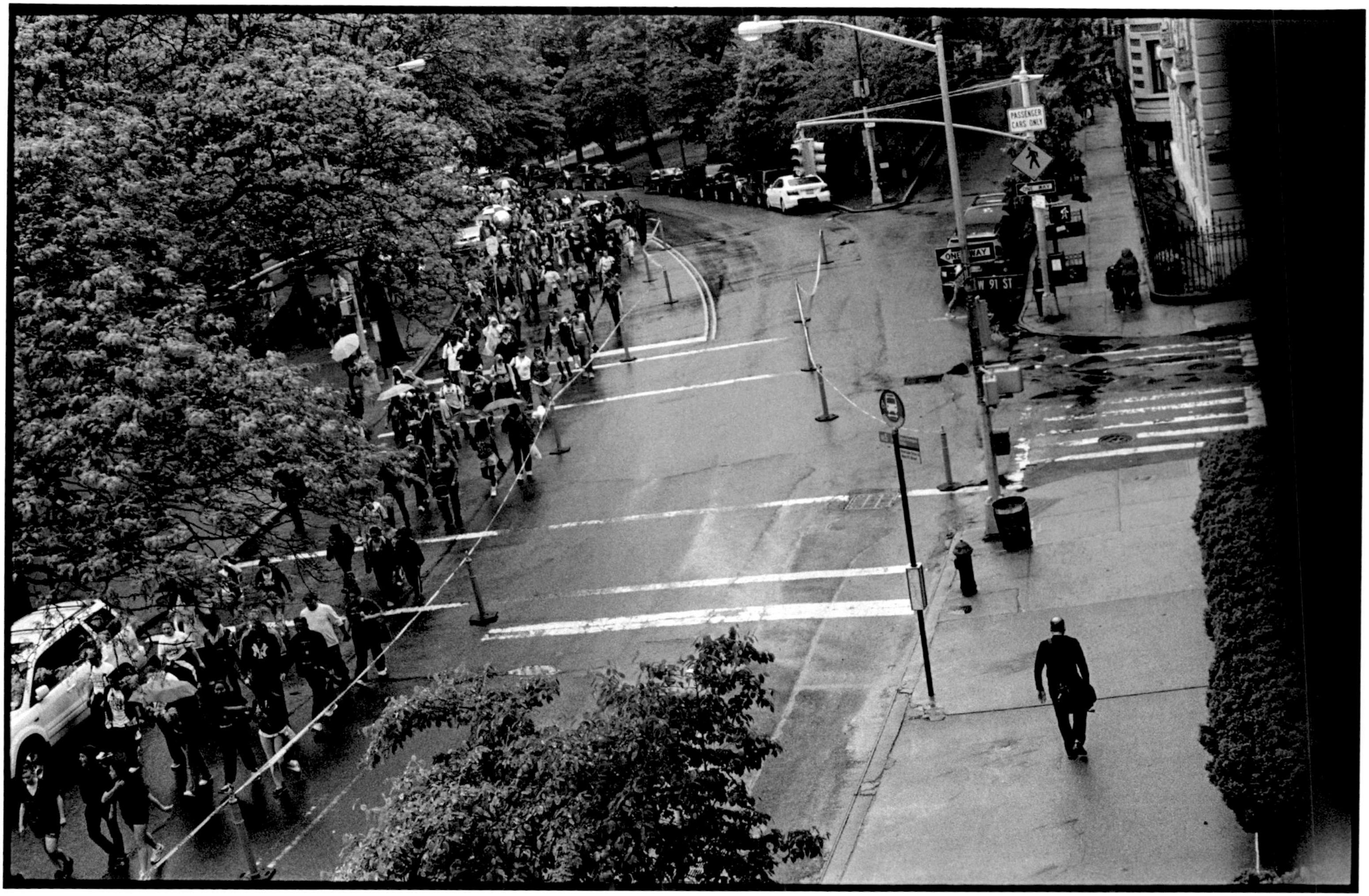
PASSENGER
CARS ONLY
ONE WAY
W 91 ST

Union rat, Madison Avenue, Midtown, January 26, 2011

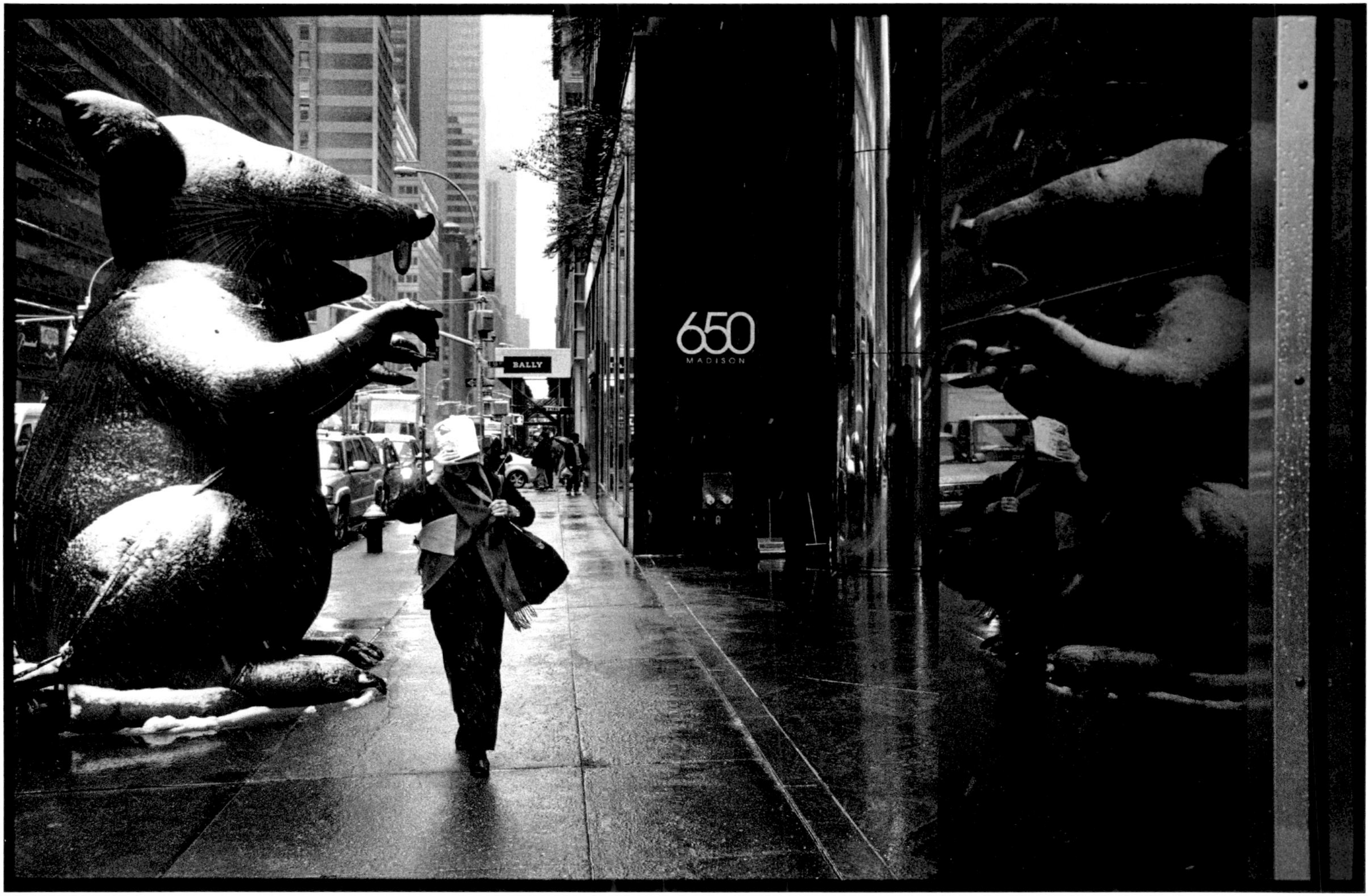
650
MADISON
BALLY

Leaders of a rally for a Ground Zero mosque, St. Peter's Roman Catholic Church, Financial District, September 12, 2010

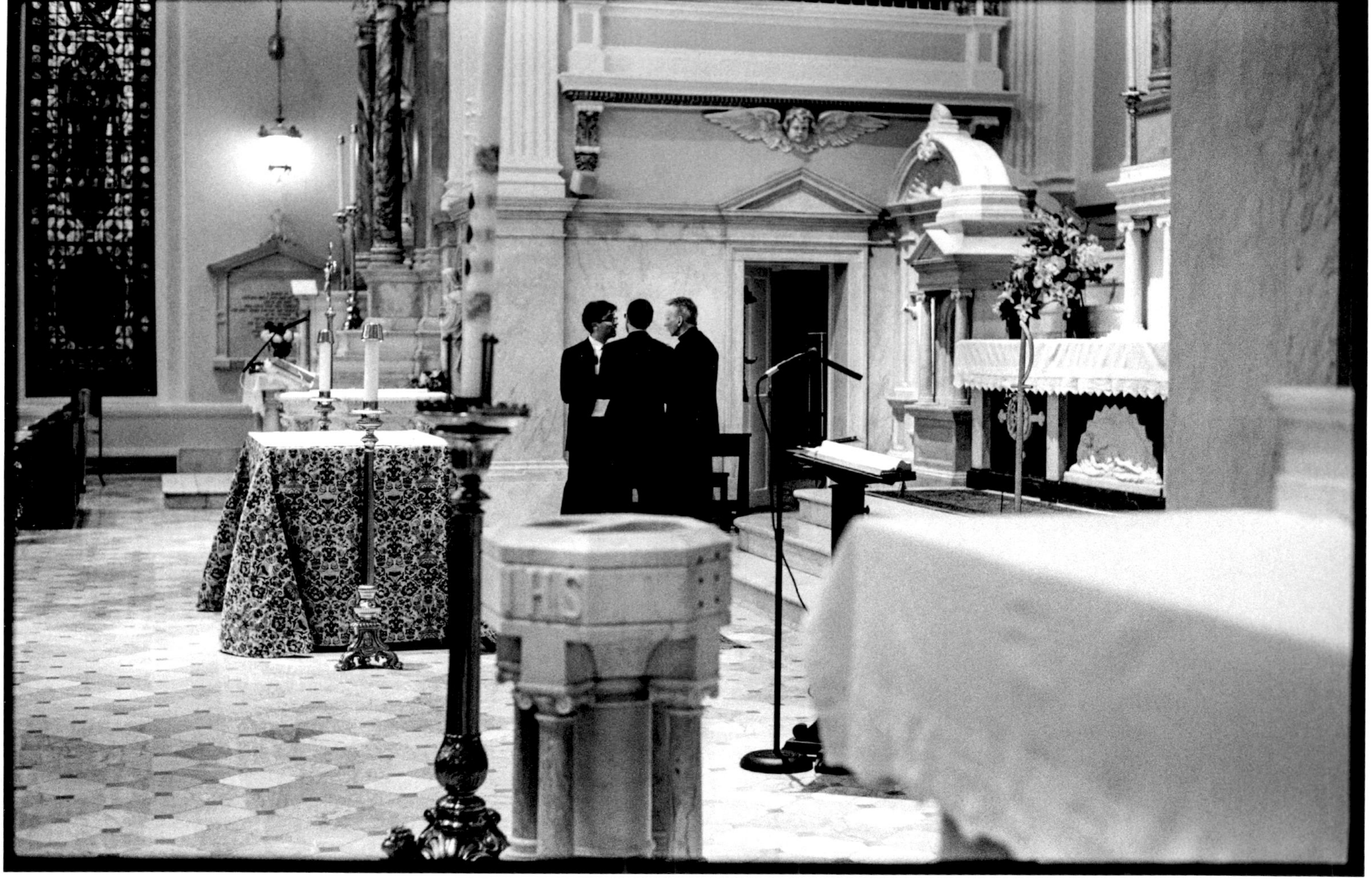
IHS

Black Lives Matter protest, Broadway and 96th Street, Upper West Side, November 20, 2020

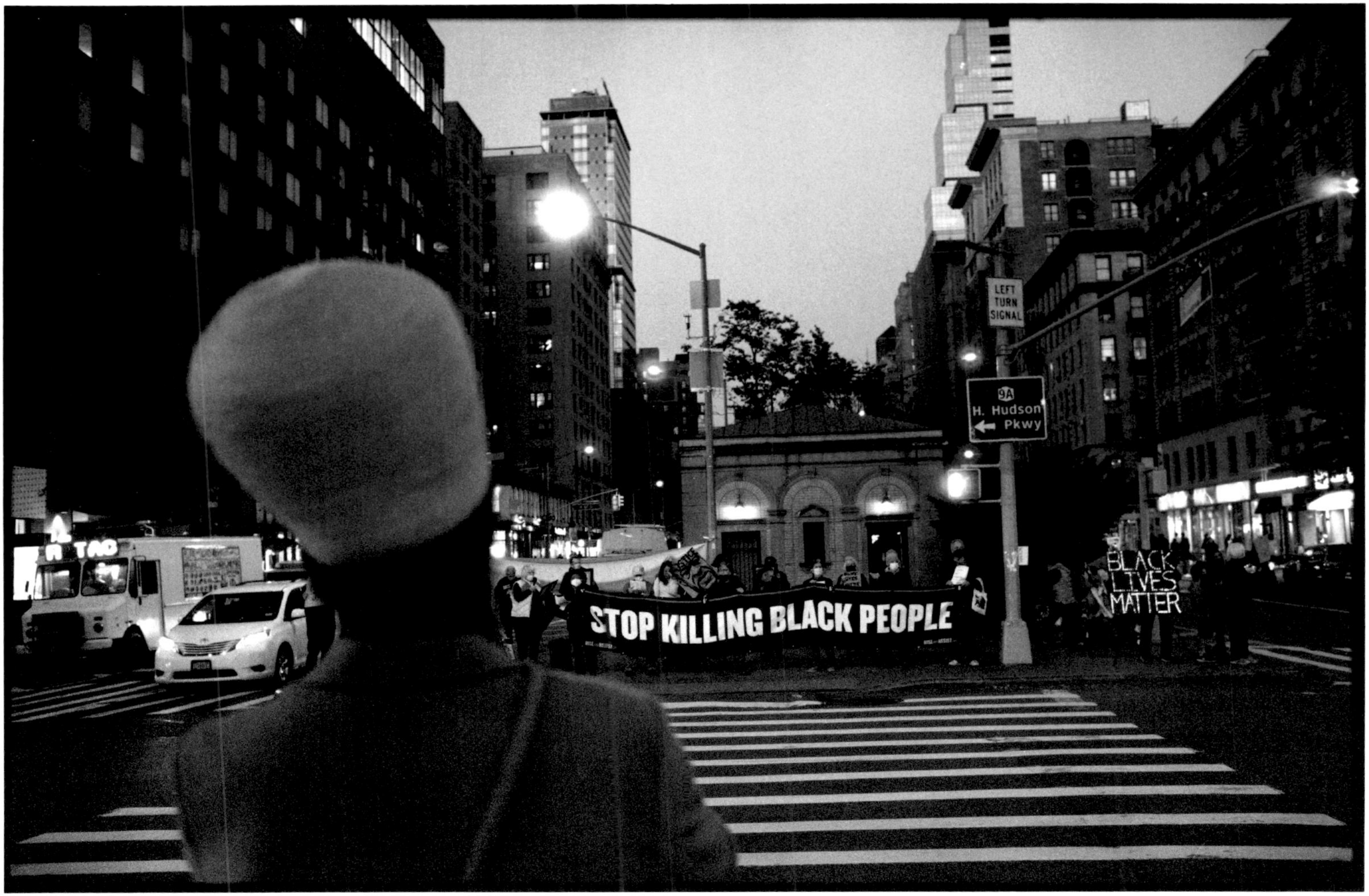
LEFT
TURN
SIGNAL
9A
H. Hudson
Pkwy
STOP KILLING BLACK PEOPLE
BLACK
LIVES
MATTER

Westboro Baptist Church rally, Second Avenue and 42nd Street, Murray Hill, September 24, 2009

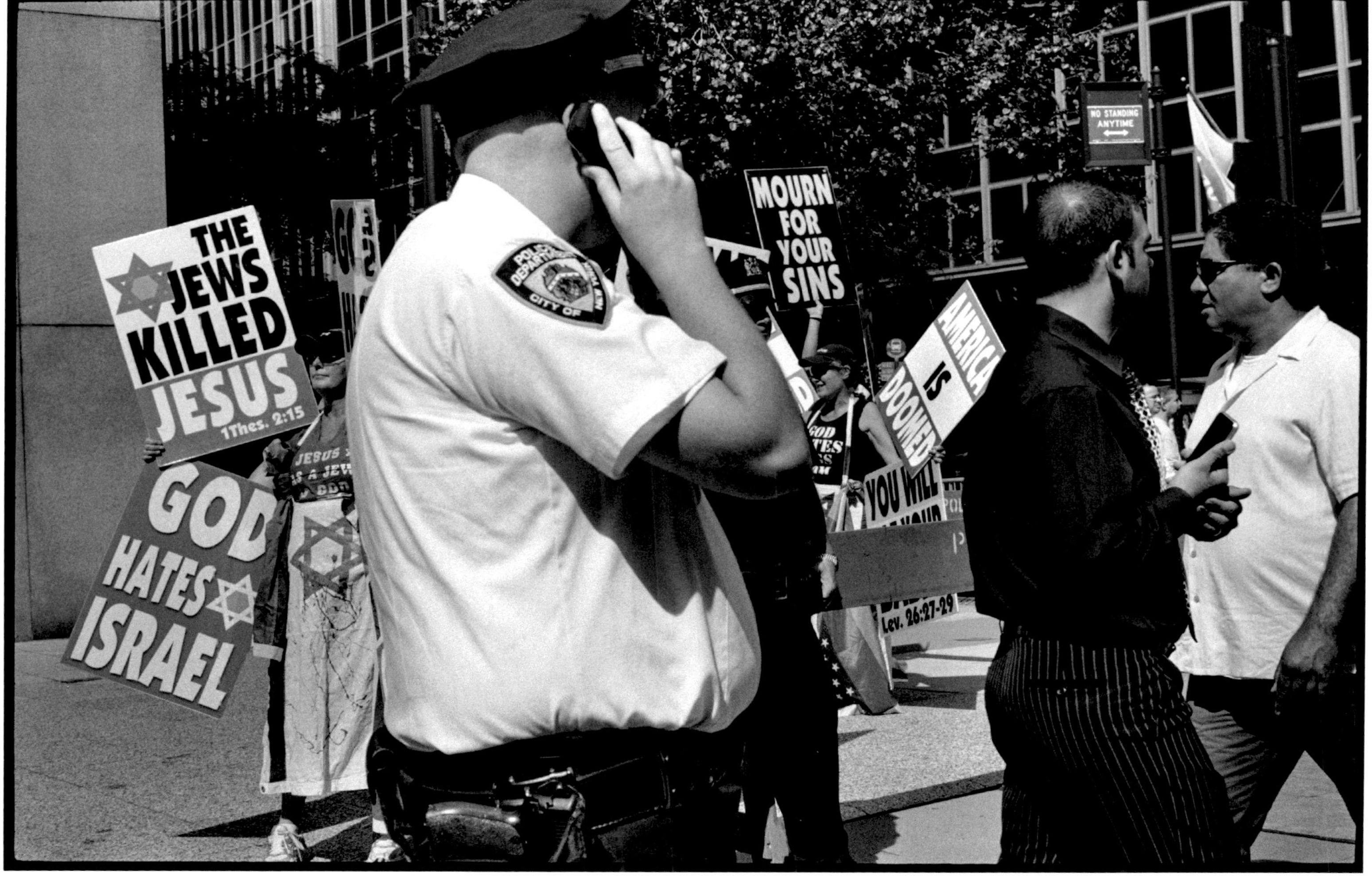
THE JEWS KILLED JESUS
1Thes. 2:15
GOD HATES ISRAEL
MOURN FOR YOUR SINS
NO STANDING ANYTIME
AMERICA IS DOOMED
YOU WILL
Lev. 26:27-29

Anti-Iran Nuclear Deal rally, Second Avenue and 48th Street, Turtle Bay, September 1, 2015

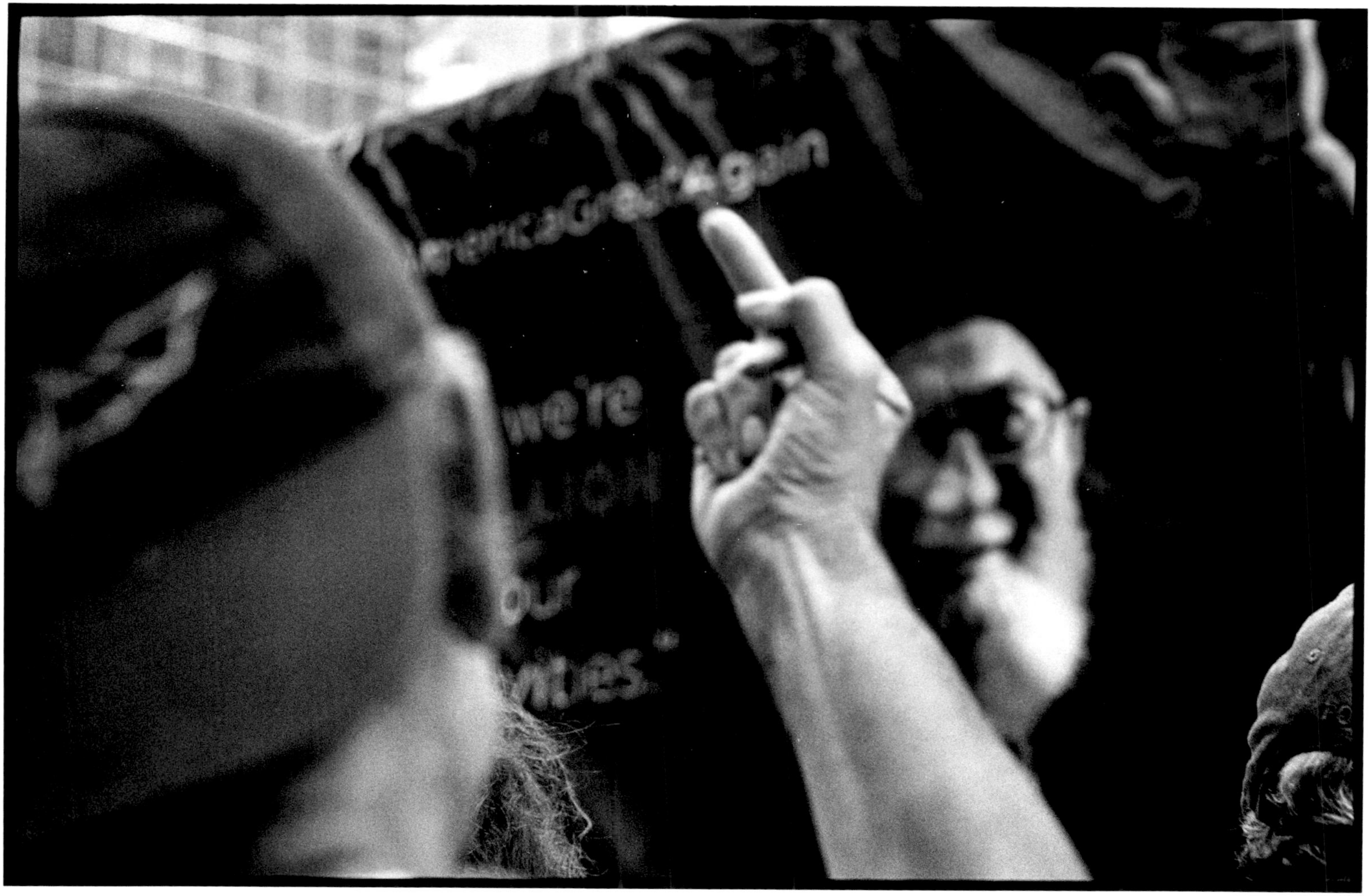
we're

People's Climate March, Central Park, September 21, 2014

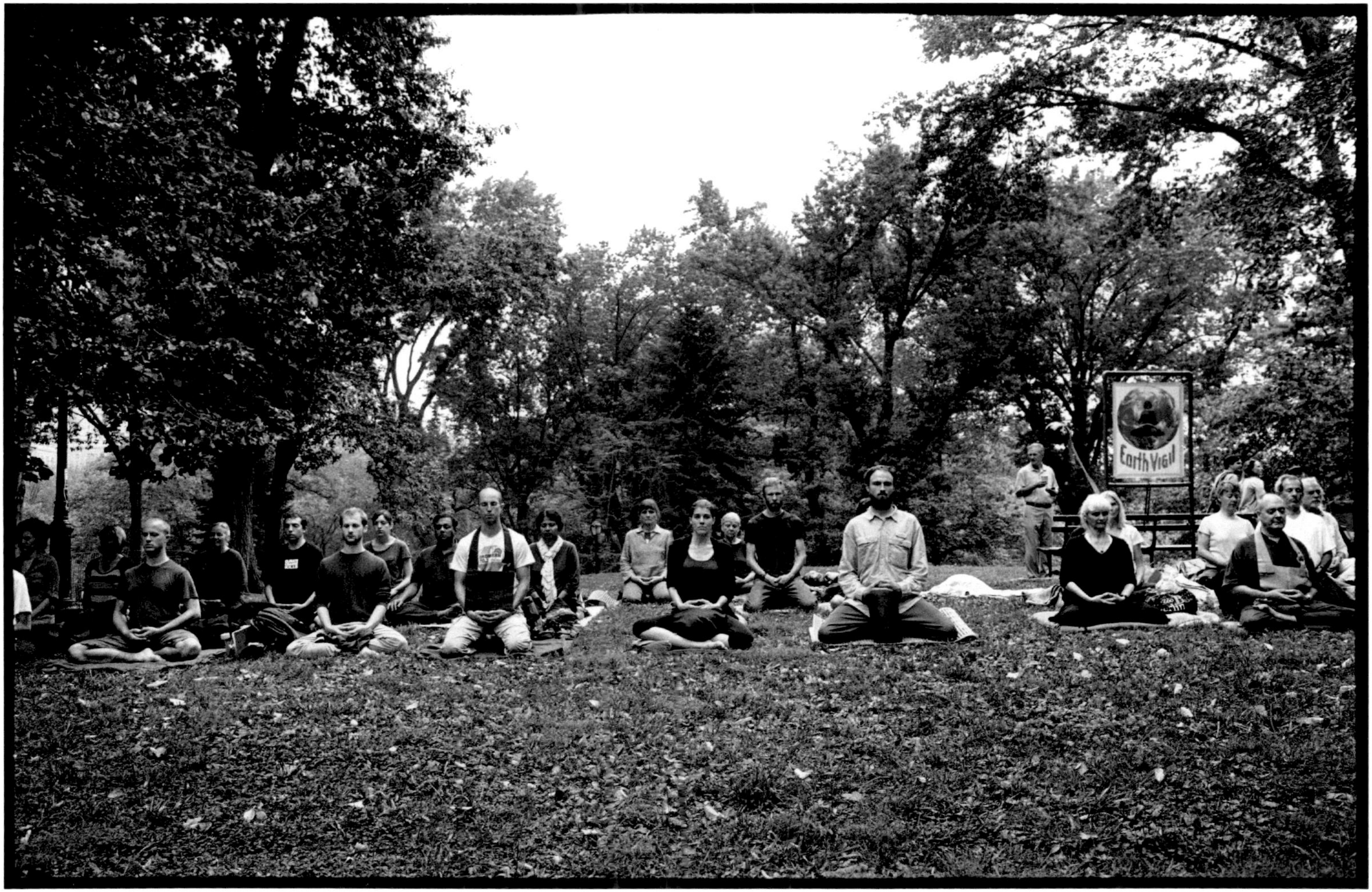
Earth Vigil

Protest against antisemitism, The New School, Greenwich Village, November 28, 2017

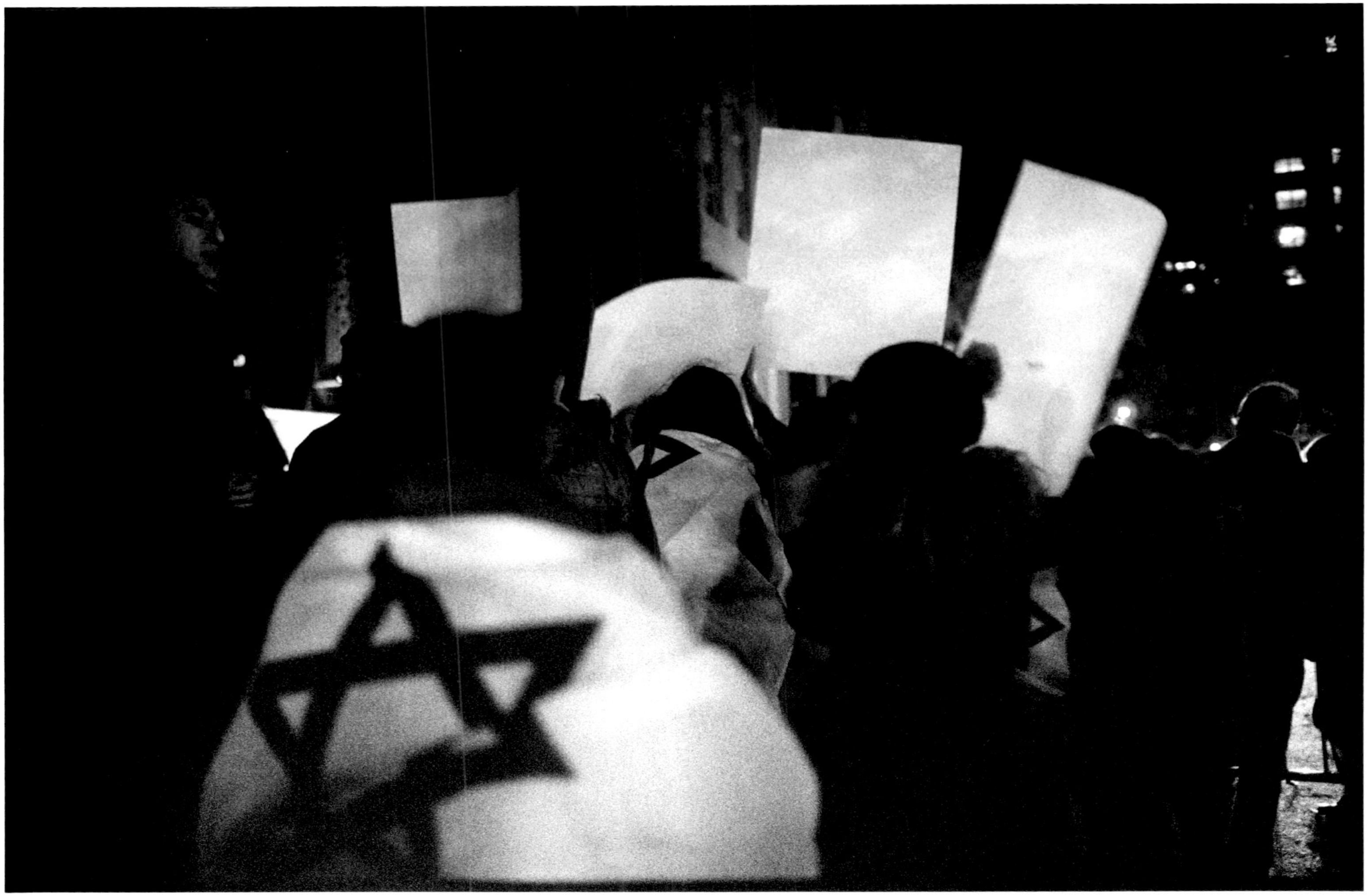

Rally in favor of a Ground Zero mosque, Financial District, August 22, 2010

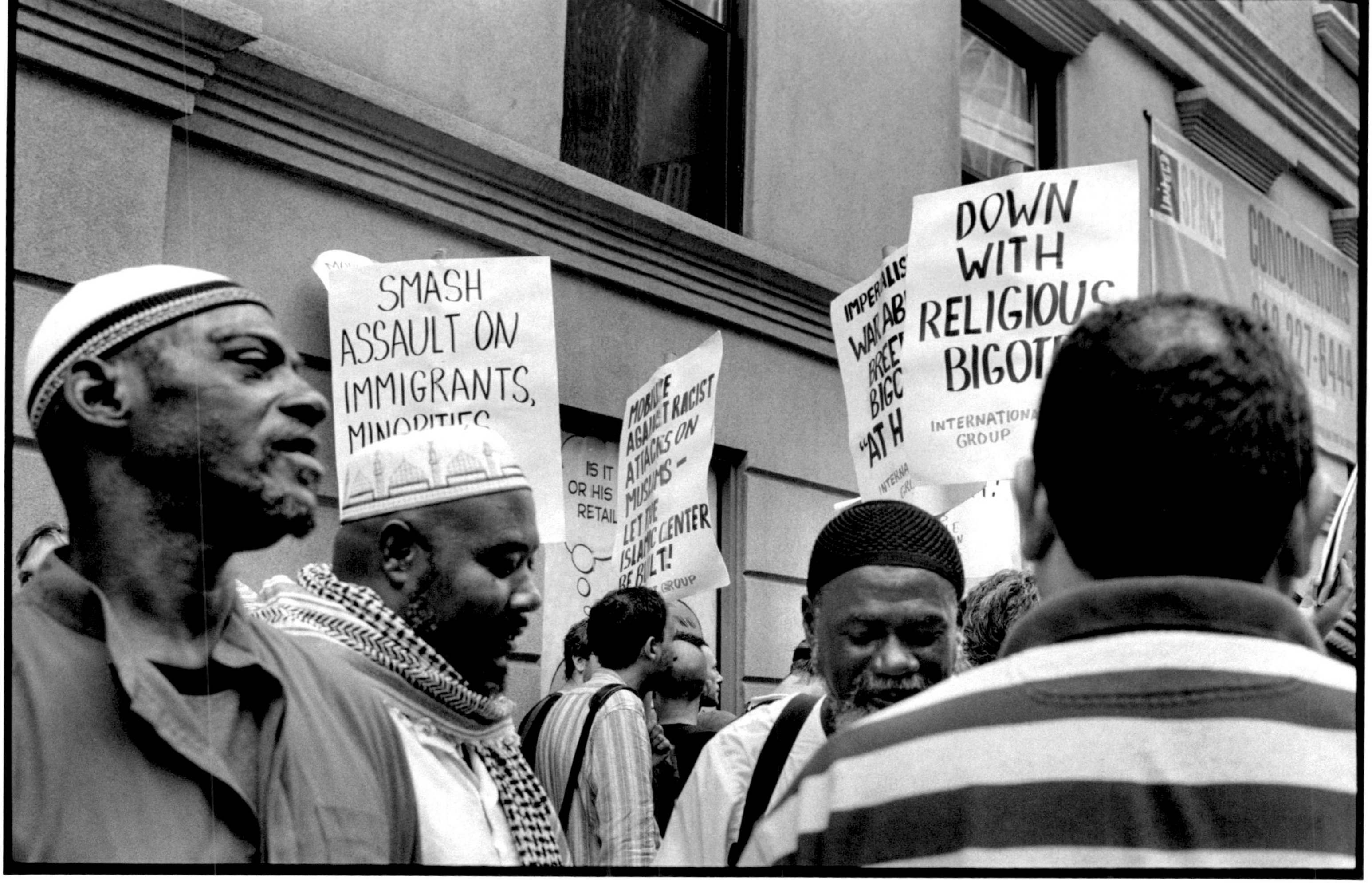
SMASH
ASSAULT ON
IMMIGRANTS,
ATTACKS ON
DOWN
WITH
RELIGIOUS
GROUP
CONDOMINIUMS

Signing petitions, Public Forum: Speak Out on Hydrofracking, Upper West Side, November 2, 2011

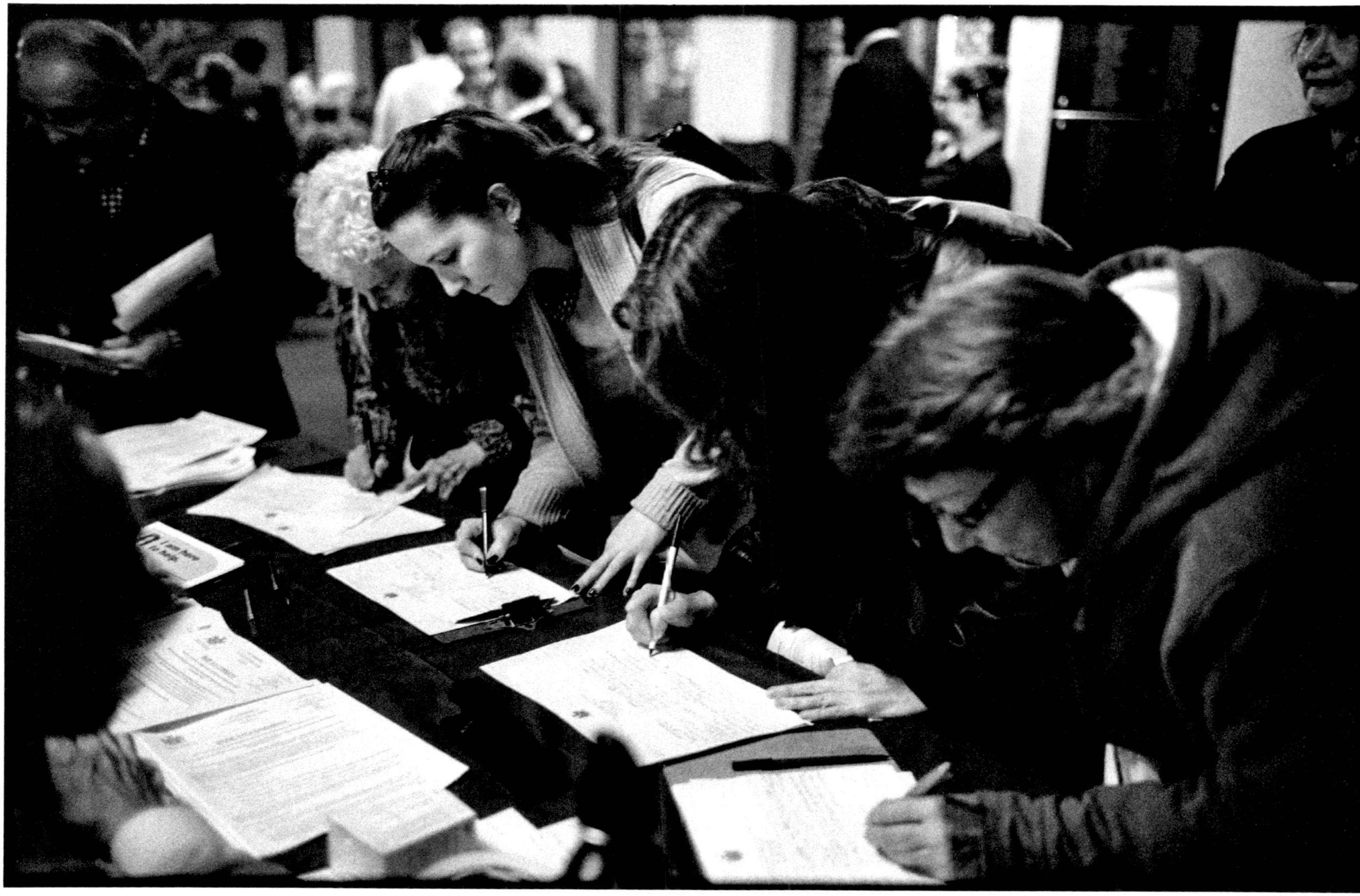

Support Our Troops Day, Congregation Ramath Orah, Morningside Heights, March 27, 2011

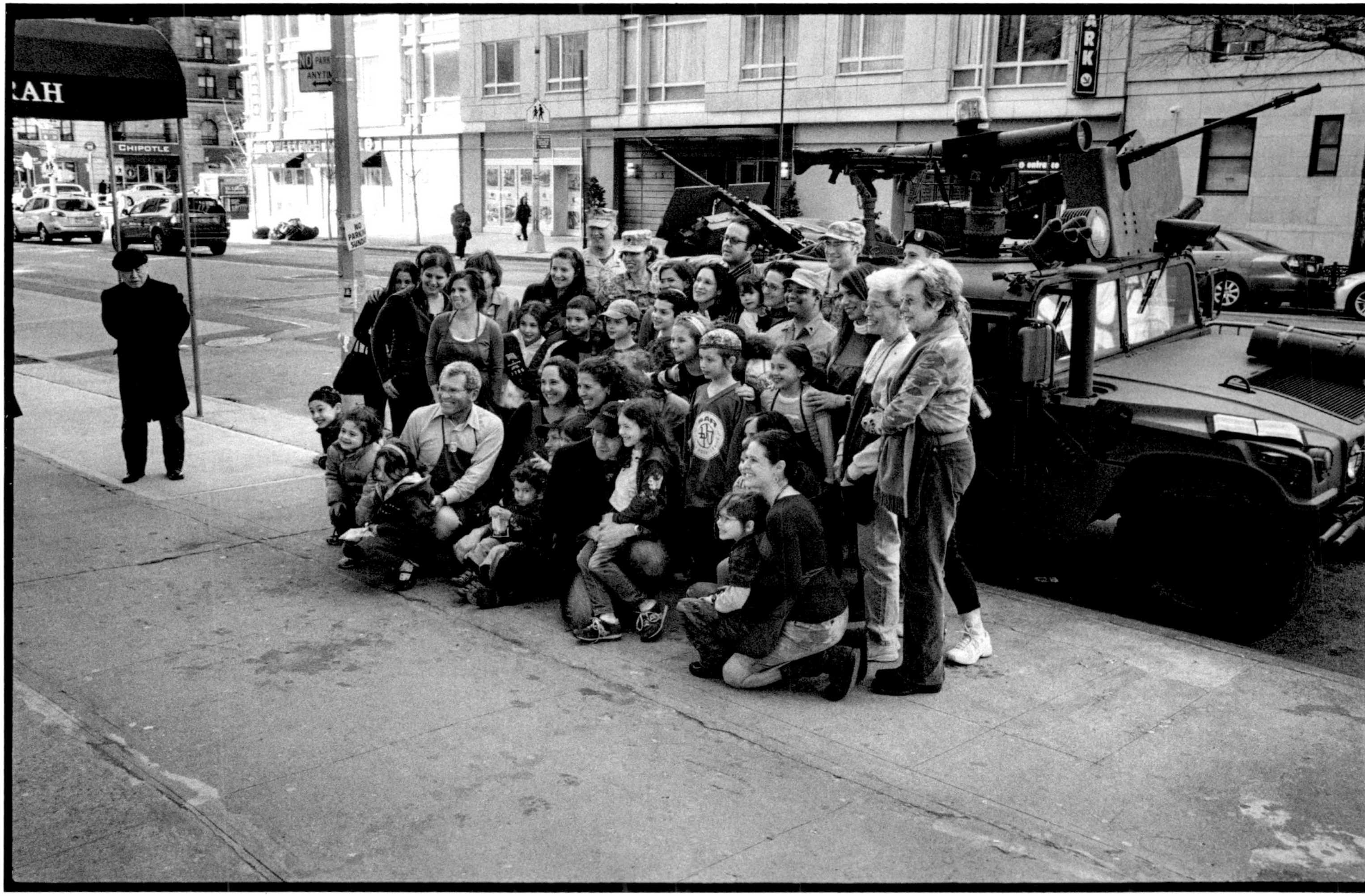
RAH
CHIPOTLE

1199SEIU healthcare union's demonstration at Rite Aid, Eighth Avenue and 52nd Street, Midtown, November 22, 2016

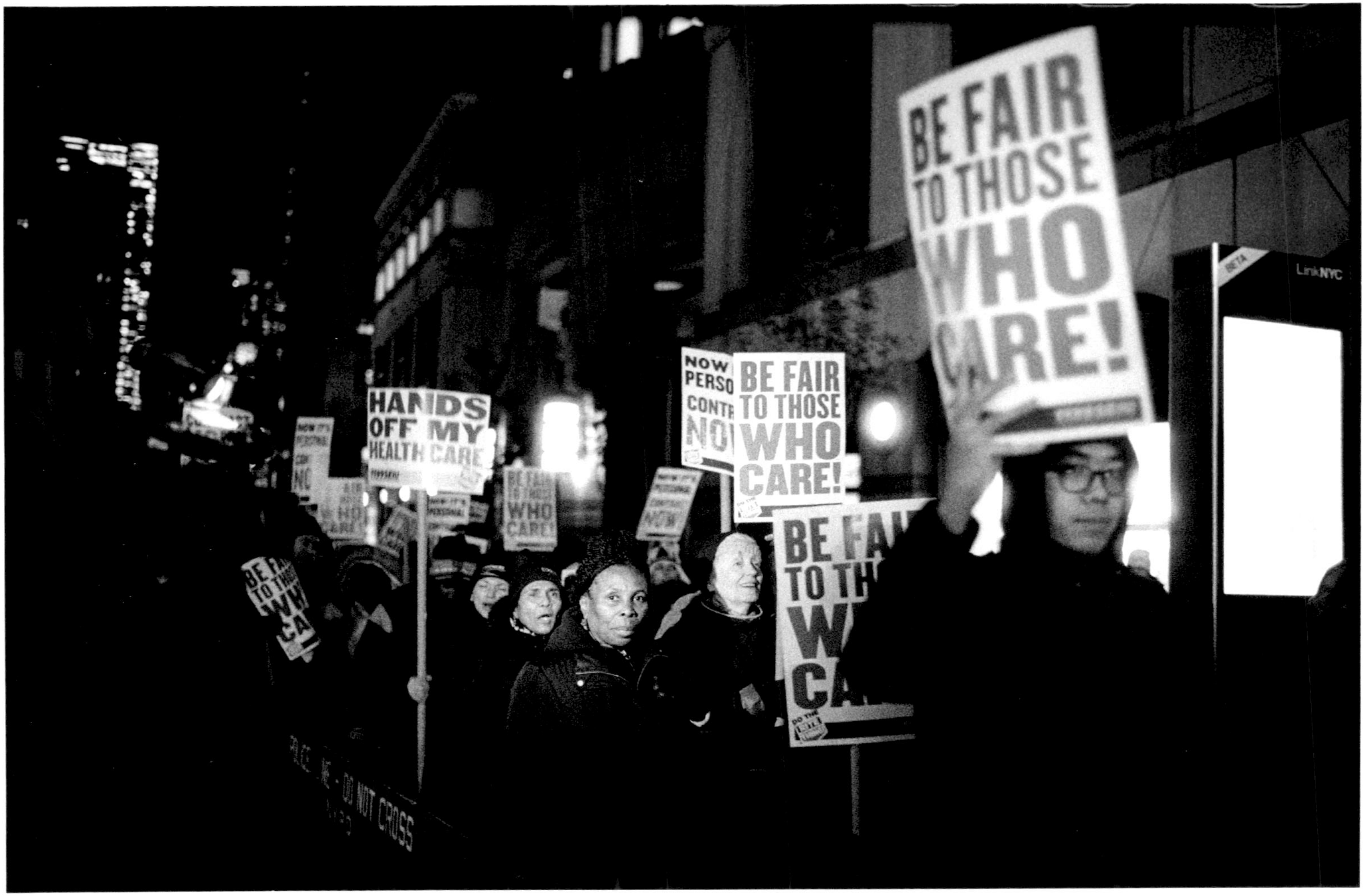
BE FAIR TO THOSE WHO CARE!
HANDS OFF MY HEALTH CARE
BE FAIR TO THOSE WHO CARE!
LinkNYC
DO NOT CROSS

Falun Gong demonstration, Dag Hammarskjöld Plaza, Turtle Bay, September 24, 2009

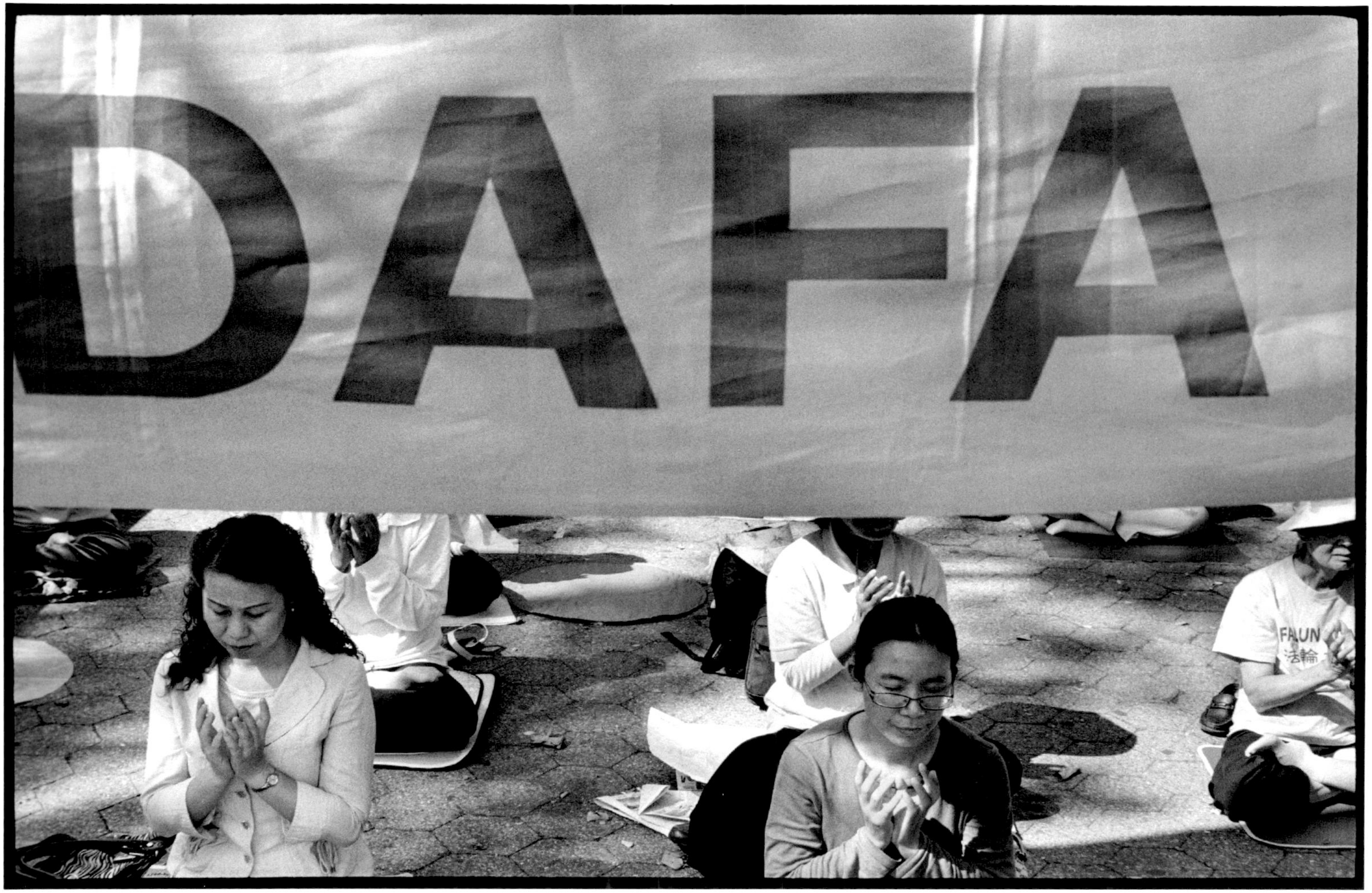
DAFA

Synagogue, Upper West Side, August 2, 2020

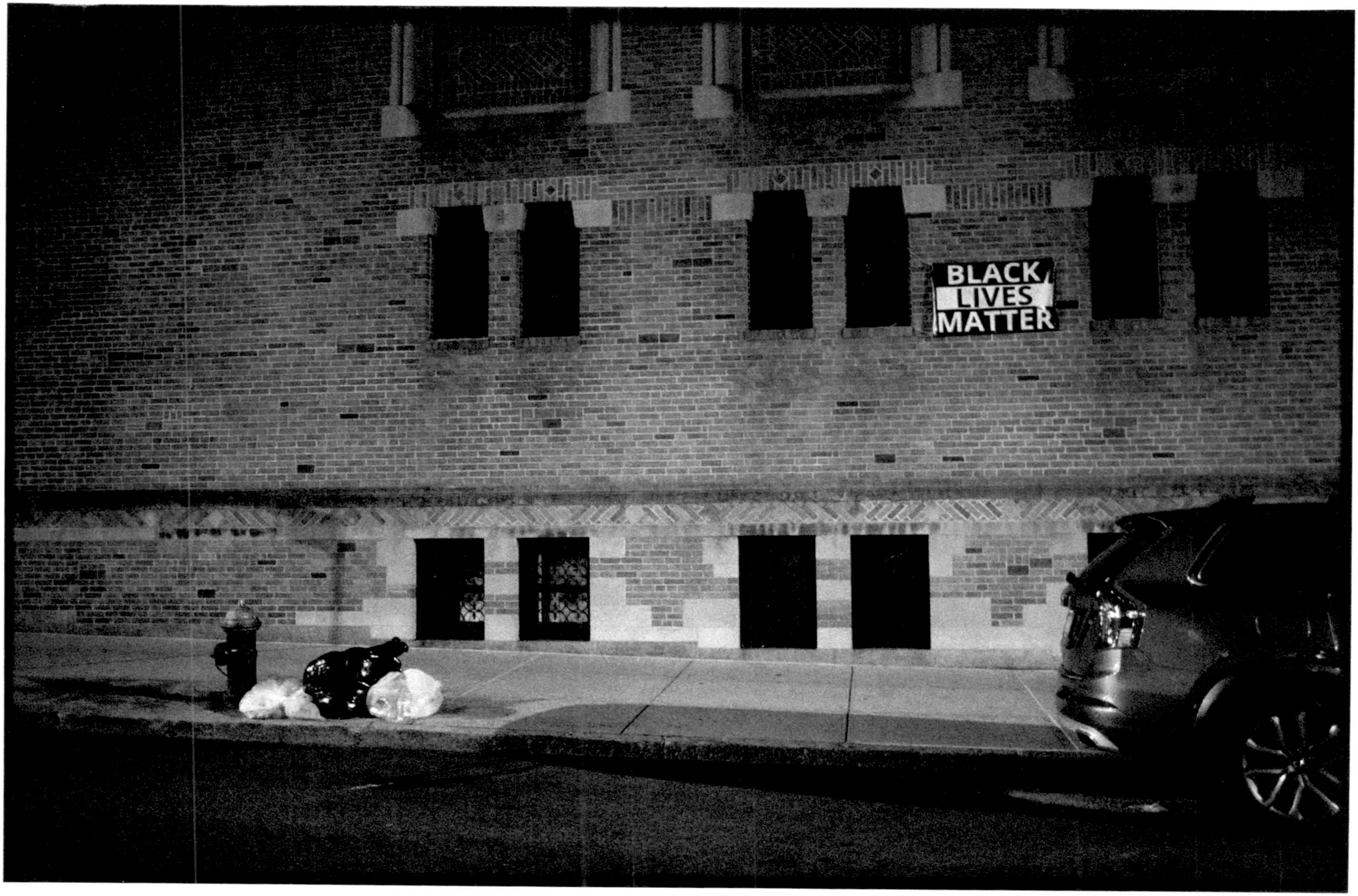
BLACK
LIVES
MATTER

PRESS

Informing the public

Newsrocm, New York *Daily News*, Financial District, March 19, 2015

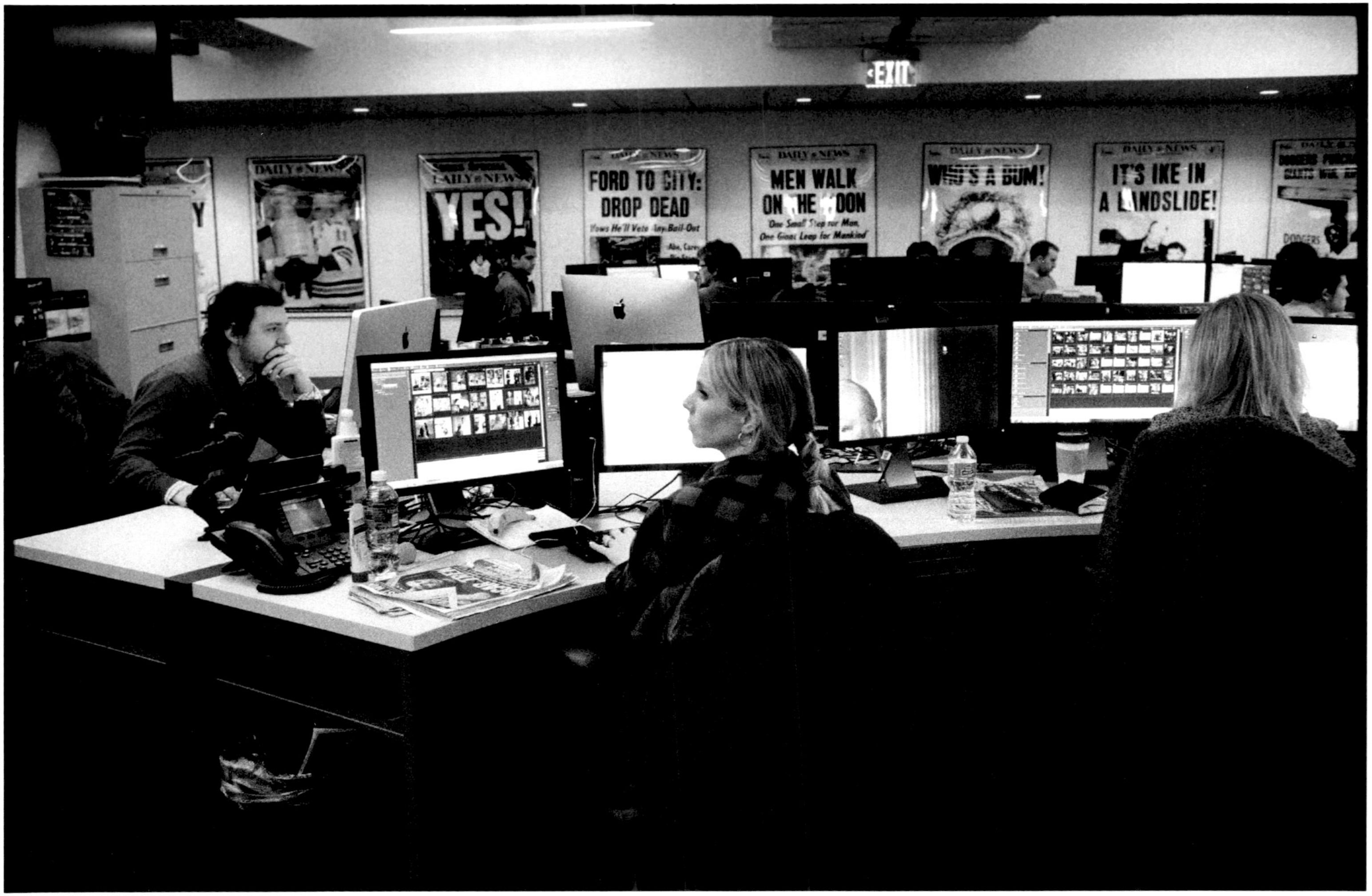
EXIT
DAILY NEWS
YES!
FORD TO CITY:
DROP DEAD
Vows He'll Veto Any Bail-Out
MEN WALK
'One Small Step for Man,
One Giant Leap for Mankind'
IT'S IKE IN

Reporter with Democratic Congresswoman Carolyn Maloney, Sutton Place Synagogue, October 26, 2010

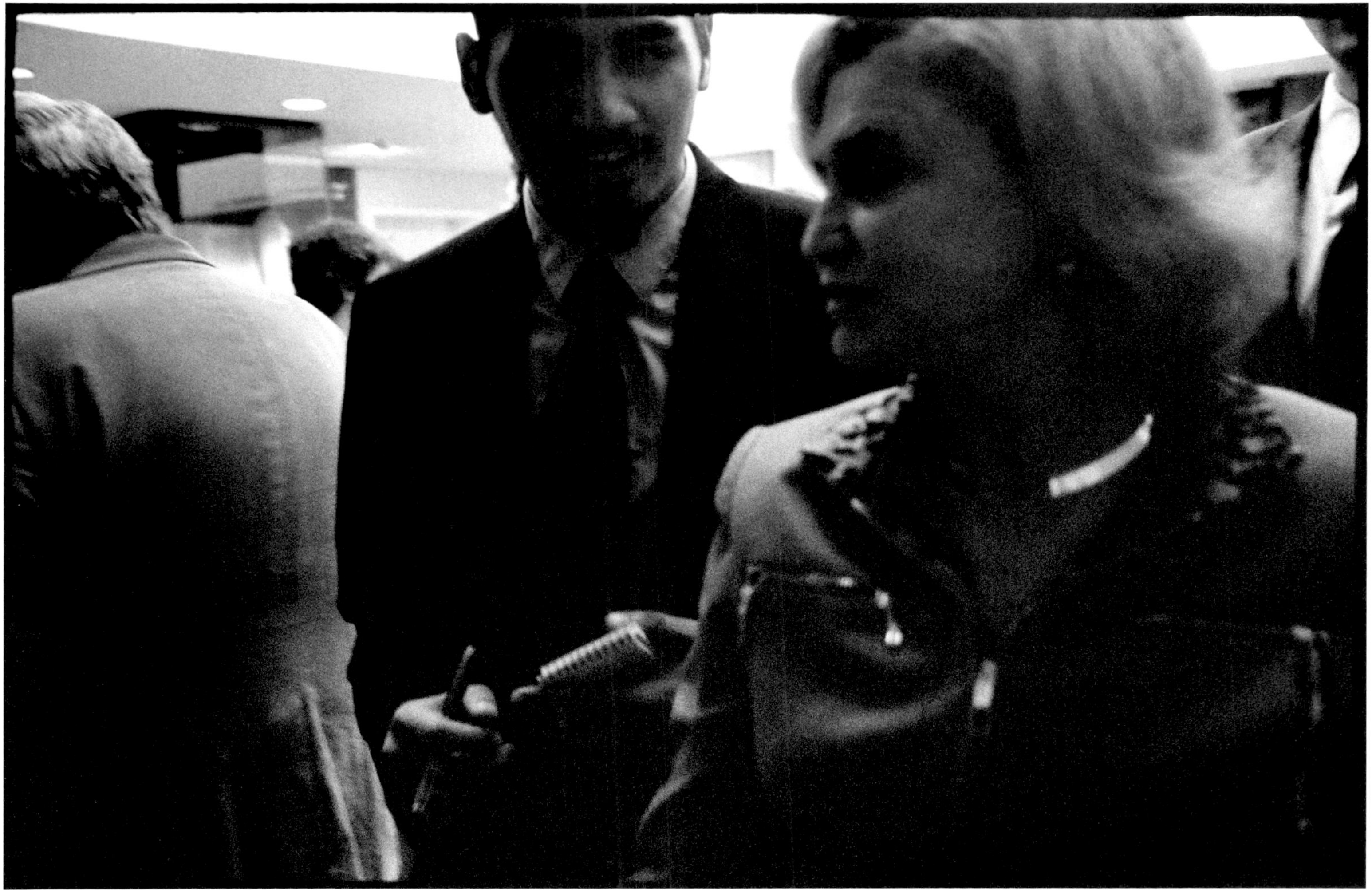

Interviewing the candidate, Tribeca, August 22, 2010

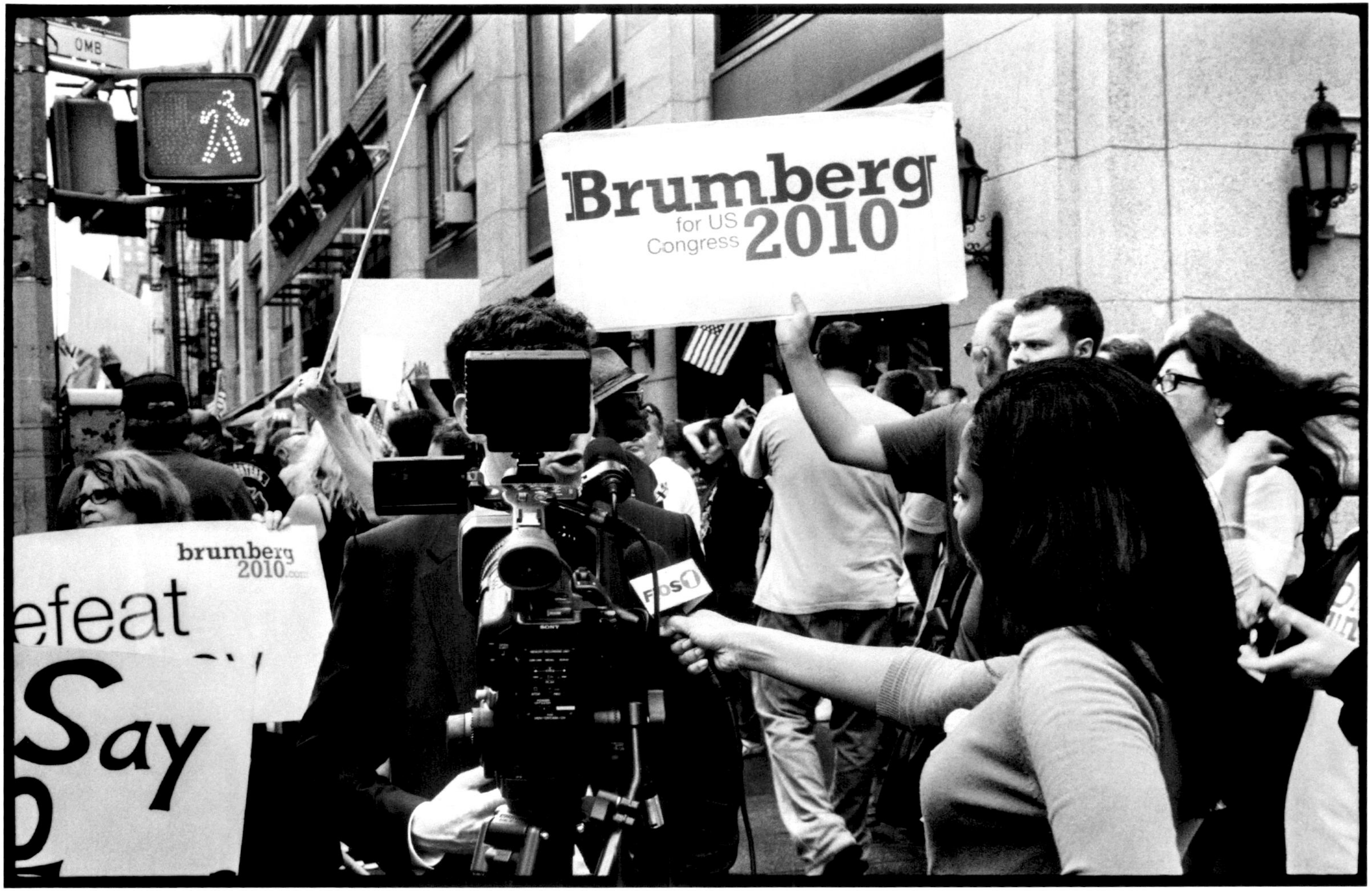
OMB
Brumberg
for US
Congress
2010
brumberg
2010.com
efeat
Say
FOS1
SONY

Neighborhood paper staff, Bayside, Queens, January 22, 2002

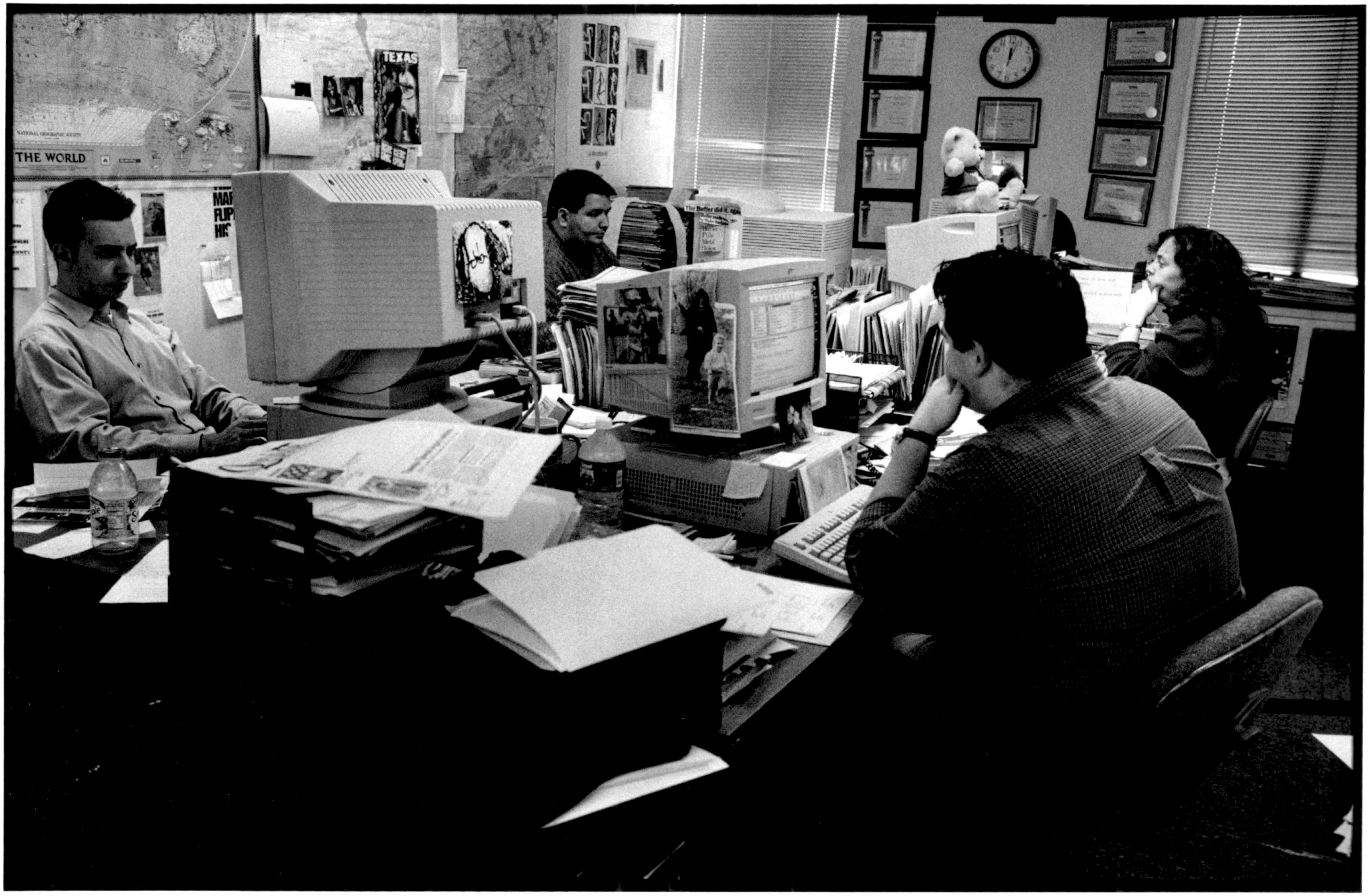
THE WORLD
TEXAS

Protesting *The New York Times*, Midtown, October 17, 2010

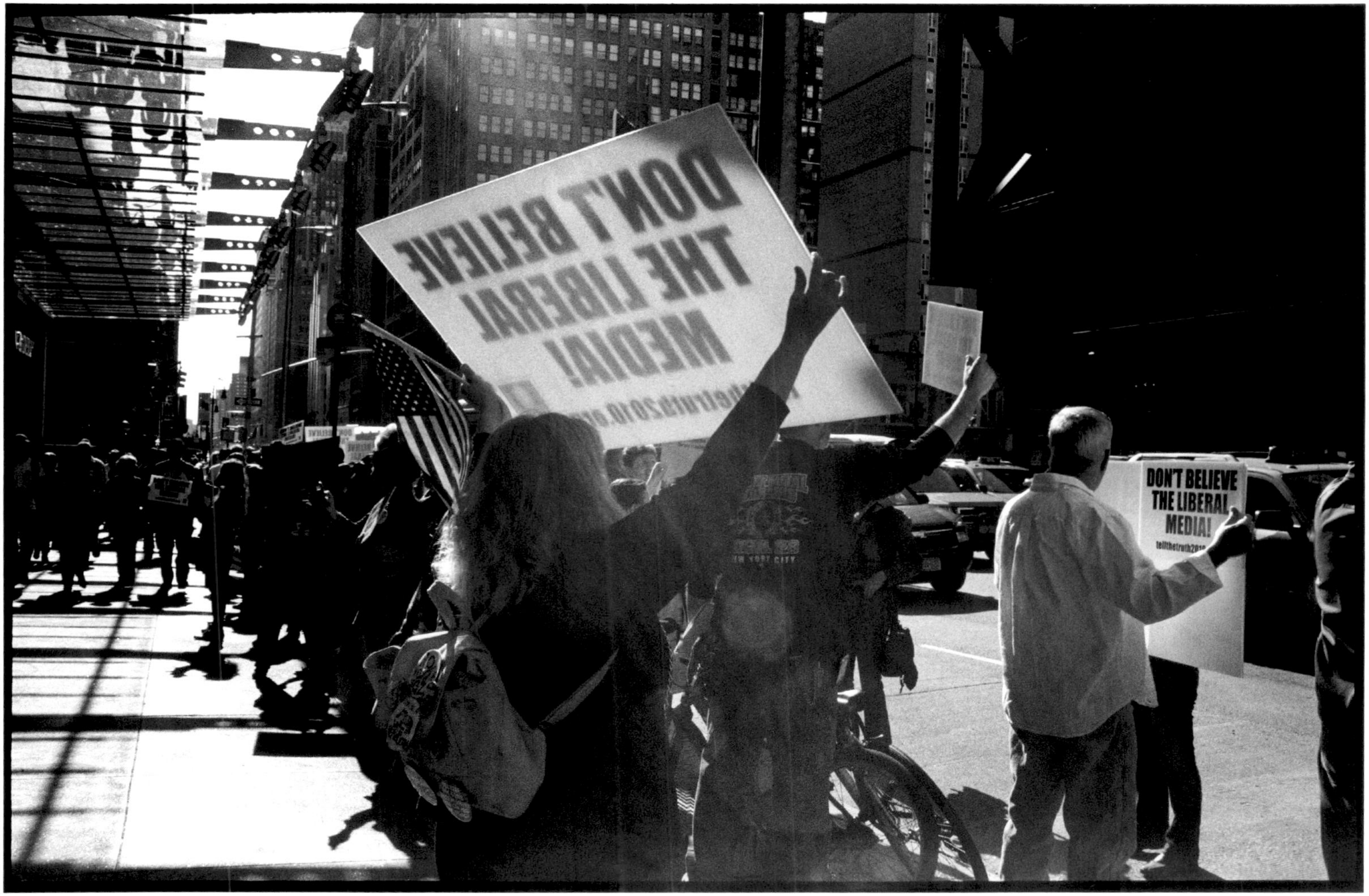
DON'T BELIEVE
THE LIBERAL
MEDIA!

Newsstand, Broadway, Upper West Side, May 21, 2009

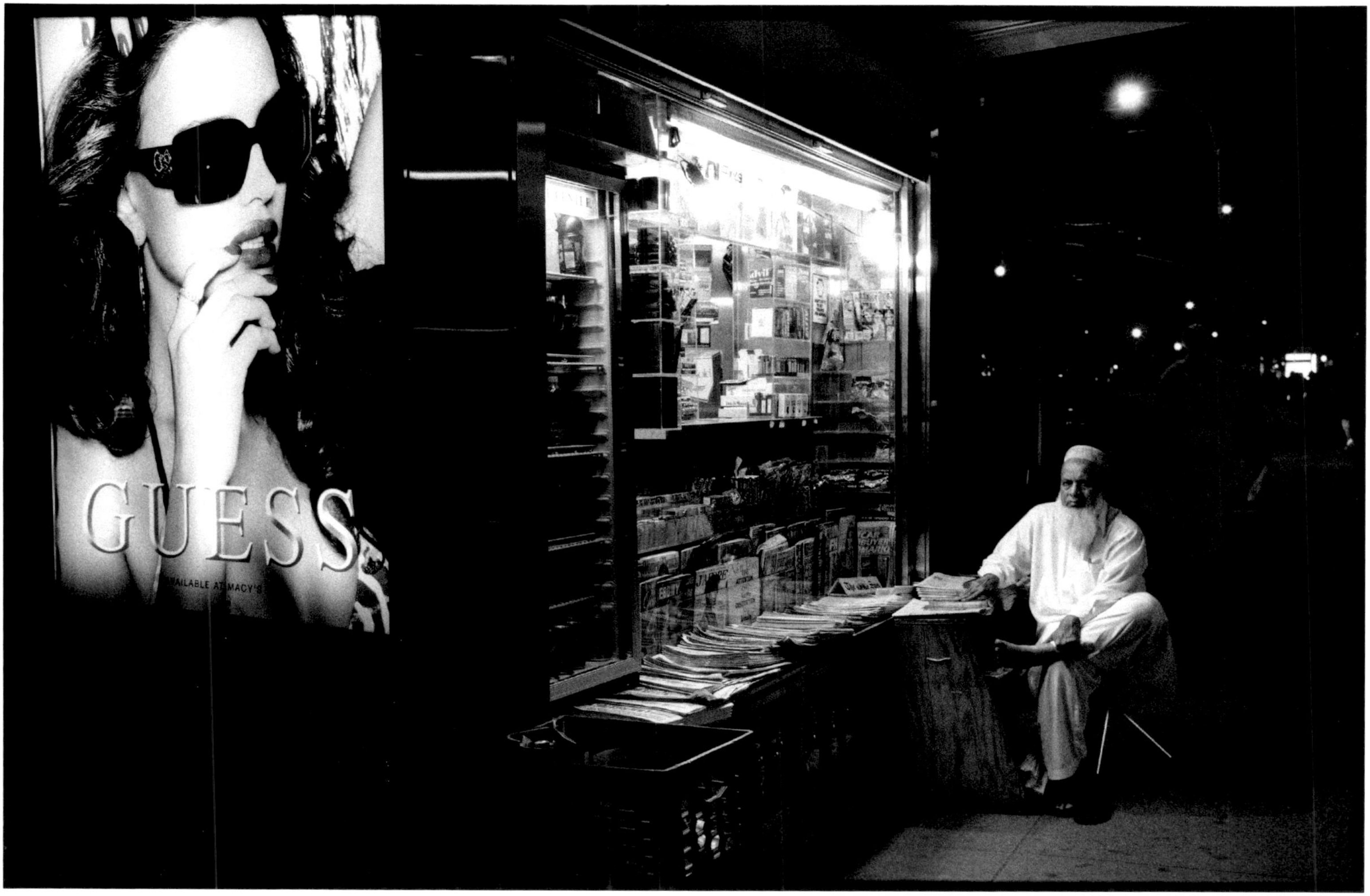
GUESS

Ángel Franco, *New York Times* photojournalist, at a Michel Faulkner campaign rally, Harlem, October 26, 2010

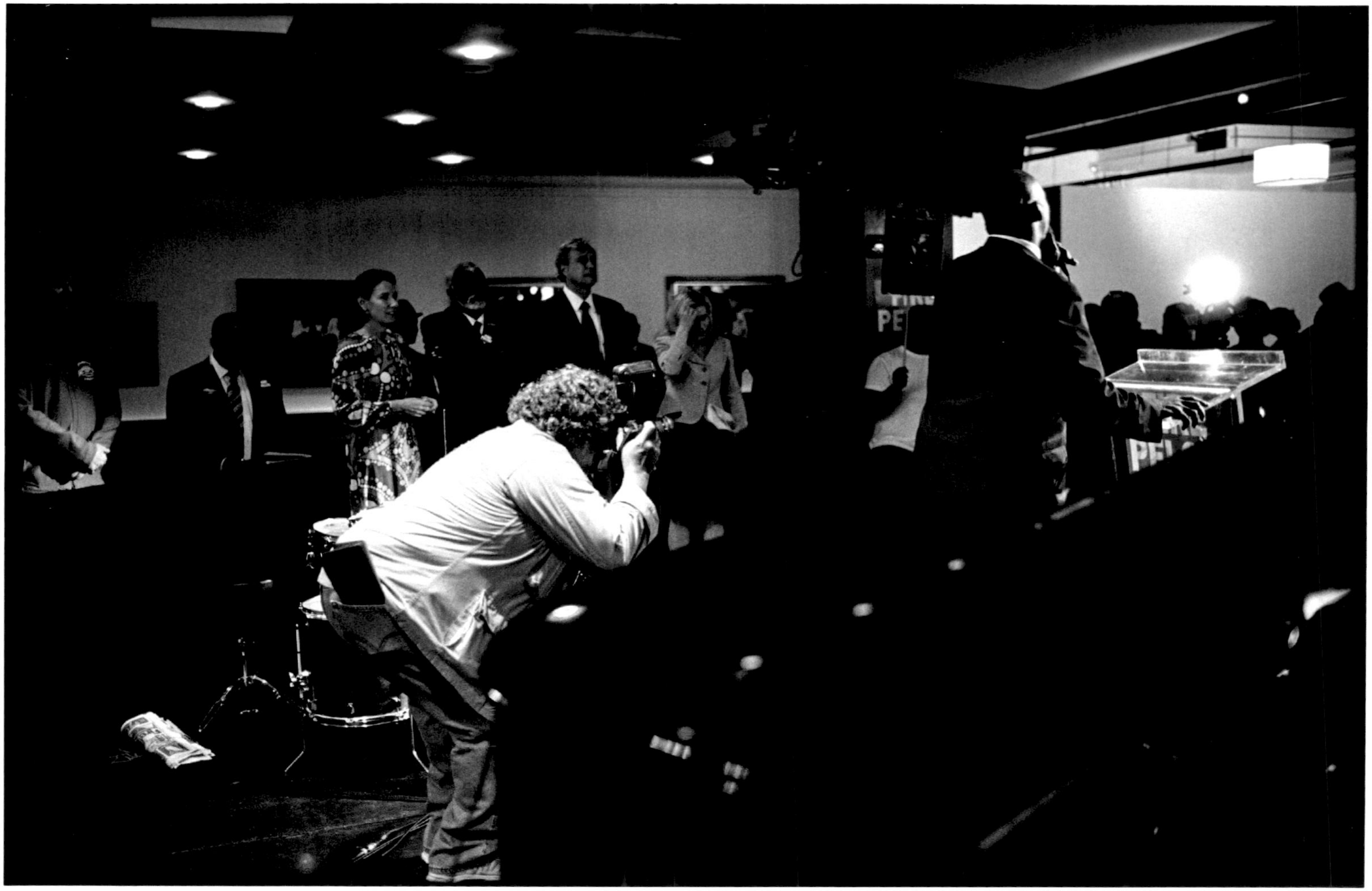

Reporter at the site of a terrorist bombing, Fifth Avenue and 23rd Street, Flatiron District, September 18, 2016

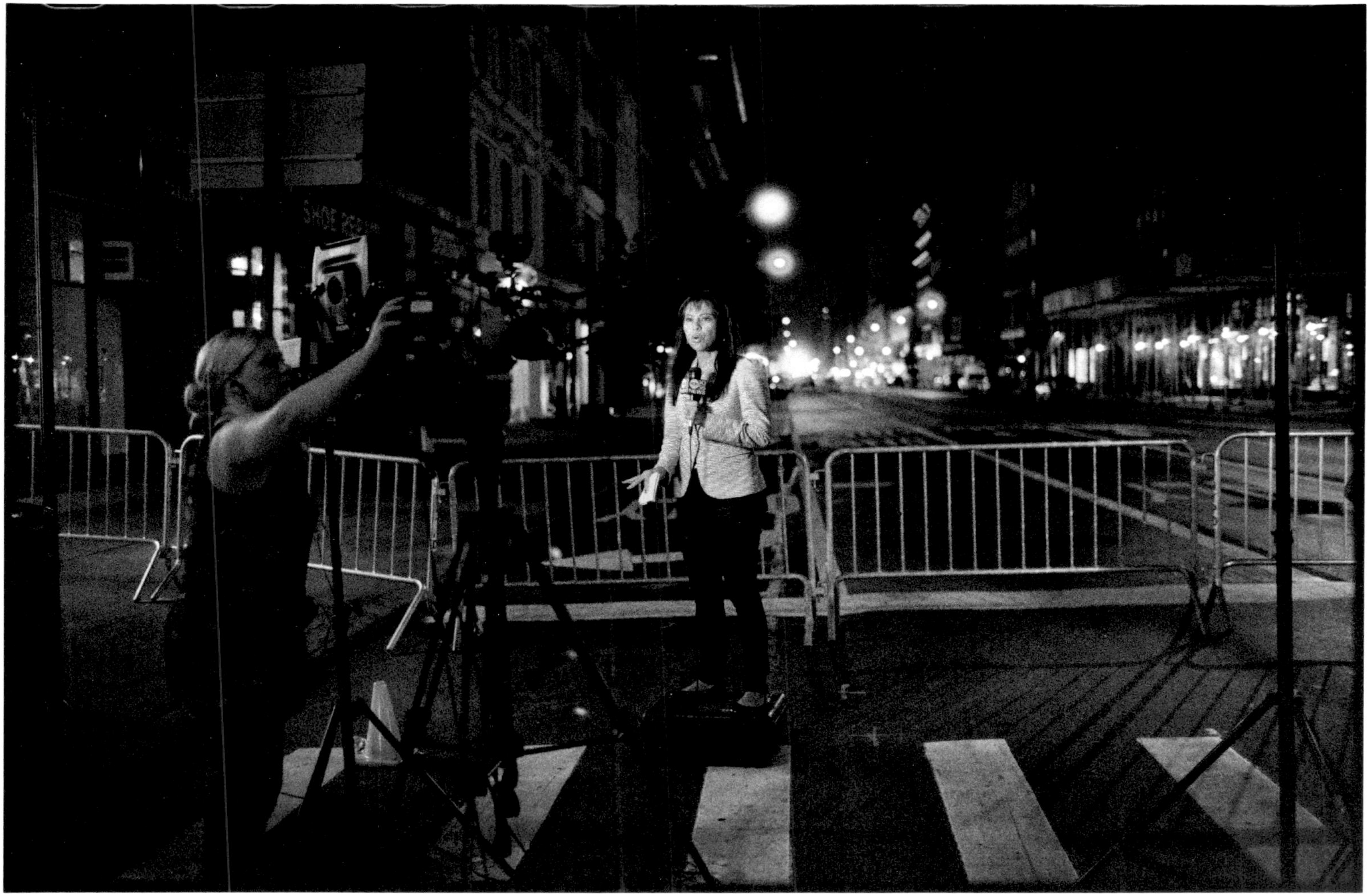

Stephen Witt, editor and publisher of *Kings County Politics*, Kensington, Brooklyn, December 16, 2015

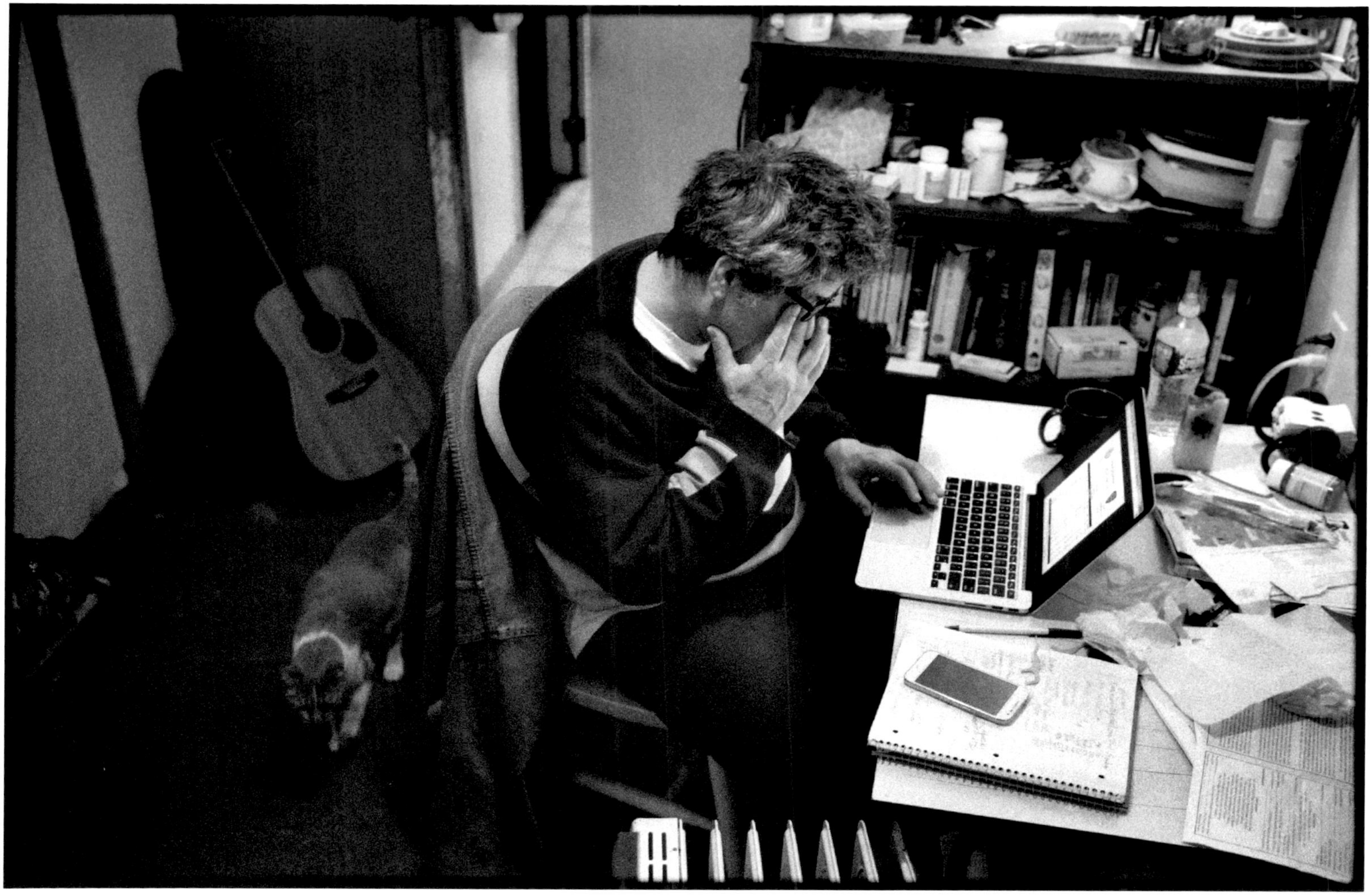

Dedication of David H. Koch Plaza, Metropolitan Museum of Art, Upper East Side, September 9, 2014

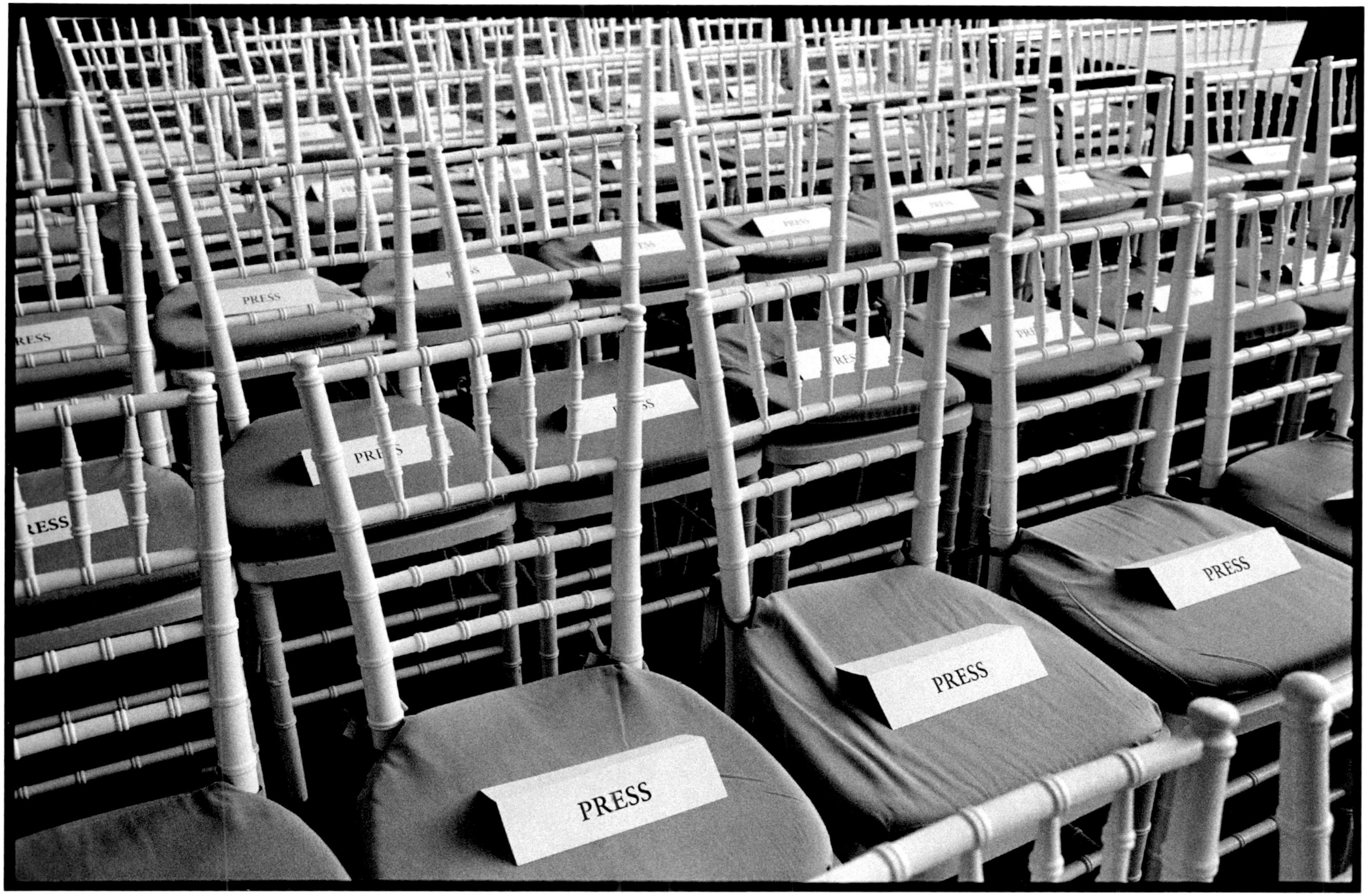
PRESS
PRESS
PRESS
PRESS

Occupy Wall Street event, Park West Presbyterian Church, Upper West Side, February 12, 2012

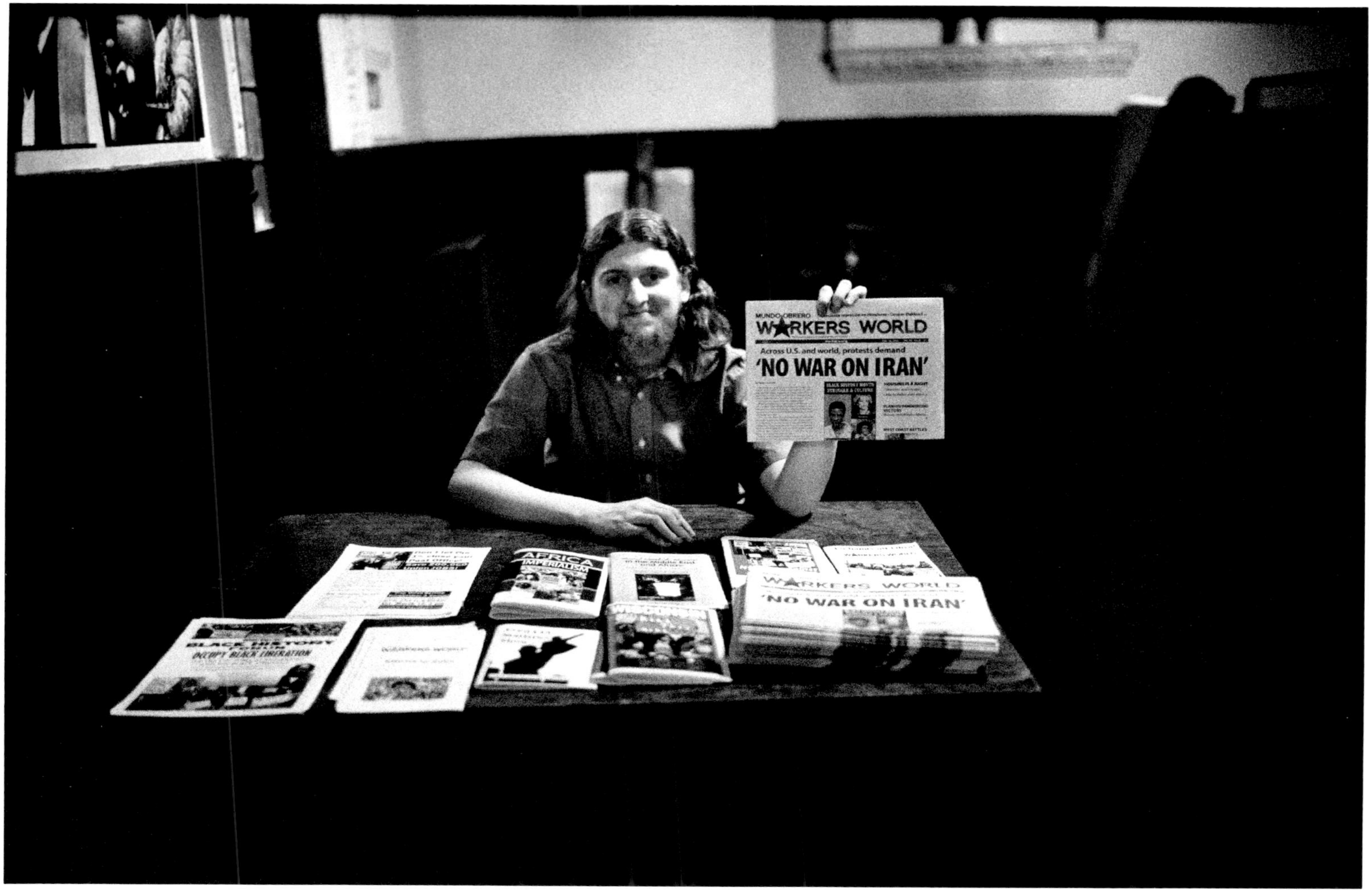
MUNDO OBRERO
WORKERS WORLD
Across U.S. and world, protests demand
'NO WAR ON IRAN'
AFRICA
IMPERIALISM
BLACK HISTORY
OCCUPY BLACK LIBERATION
WORKERS WORLD
'NO WAR ON IRAN'

Reporters wait for Attorney General Eric Schneiderman, West End Avenue, Upper West Side, May 8, 2018

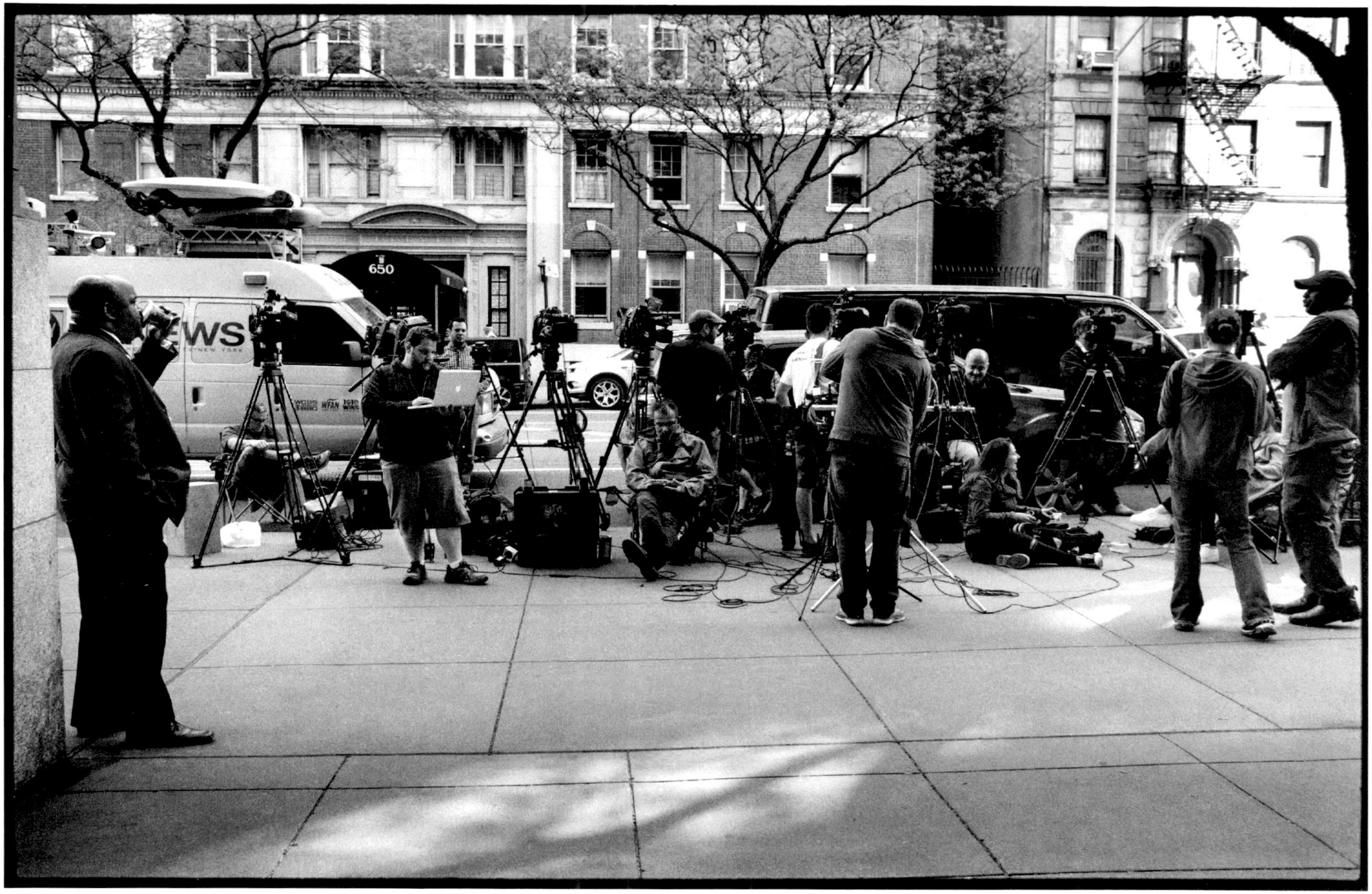
650

TALK

Socializing, exchanging information, arguing

Councilwoman Helen Rosenthal's Second Annual Town Hall Meeting, Redeemer West Side church, Upper West Side, April 27, 2015

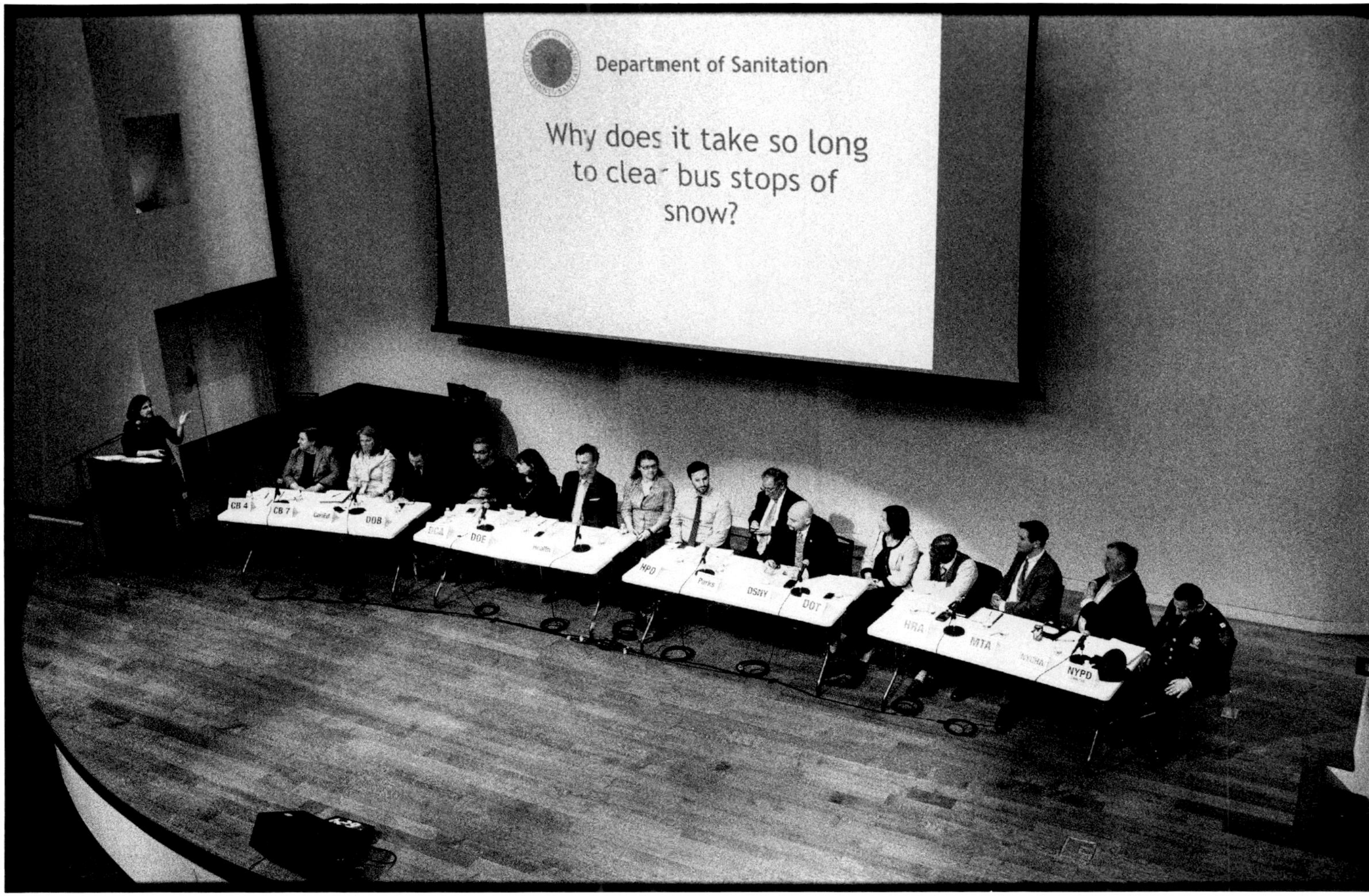
Department of Sanitation
Why does it take so long
to clear bus stops of
snow?
CB 4
CB 7
DOB
DCA
DOE
HPD
Parks
DSNY
DOT
HRA
MTA
NYPD

New Americans Initiative graduation ceremony, 63rd Street YMCA, Upper West Side, June 6, 2018

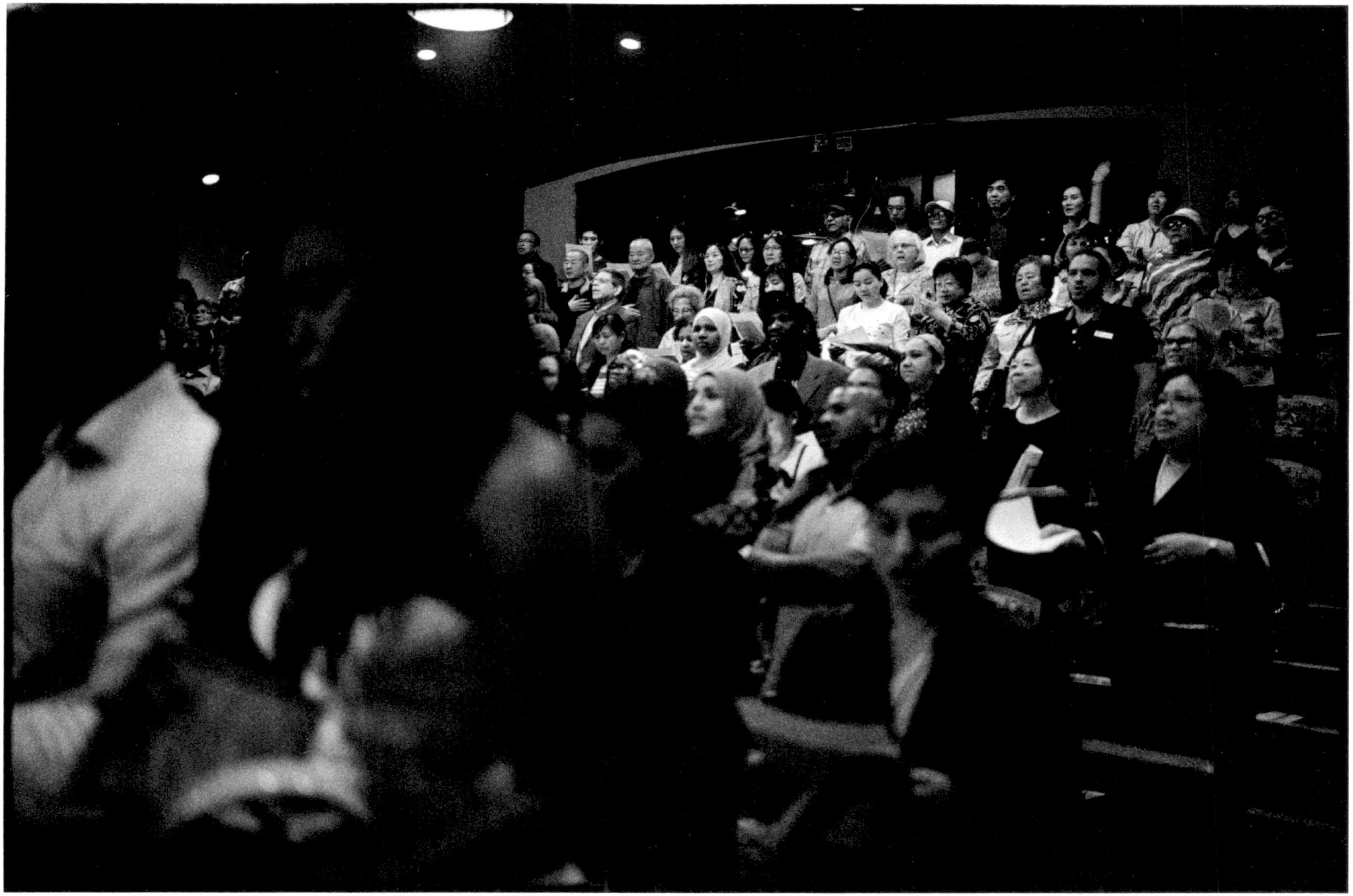

Conversation on Civil Society, Institute for American Values, Columbus Circle, September 22, 2011

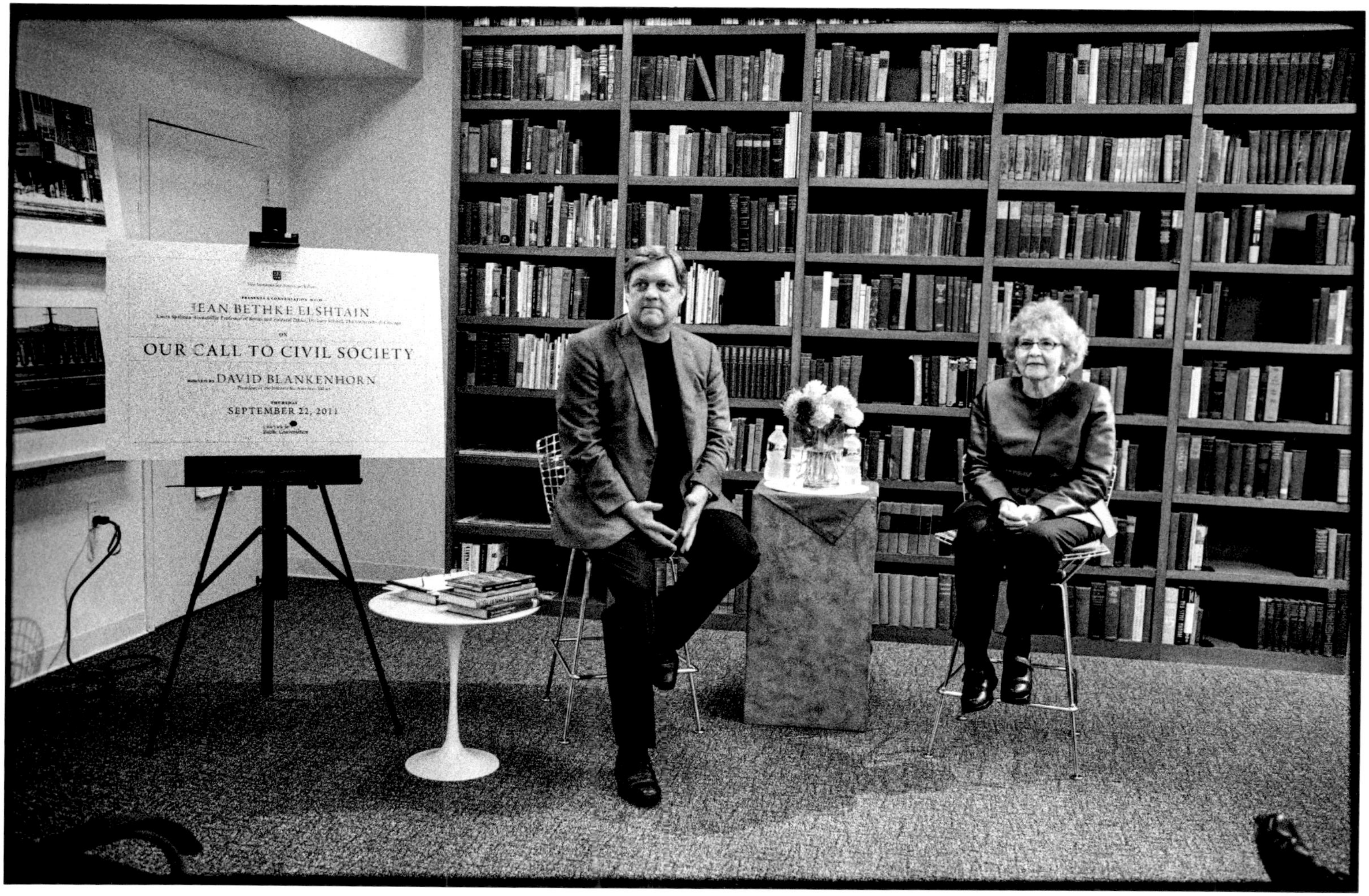
JEAN BETHKE ELSHTAIN
ON
OUR CALL TO CIVIL SOCIETY
DAVID BLANKENHORN
SEPTEMBER 22, 2011

Soldiers' and Sailors' Monument Committee meeting, Midtown, February 24, 2015

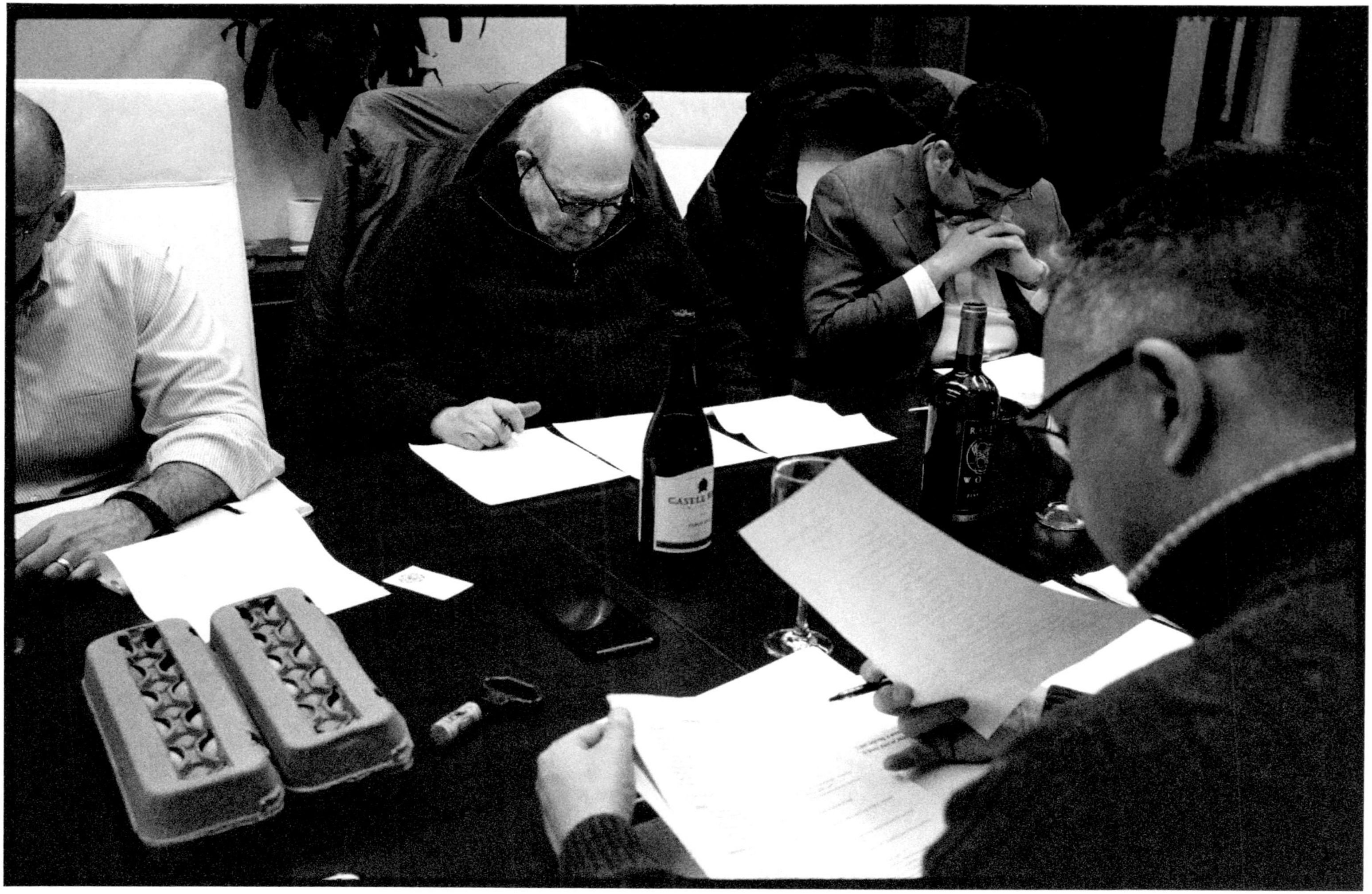

The Importance of Teaching Civics in Schools, Civic Affairs Committee, National Women's Republican Club, Midtown, May 20, 2015

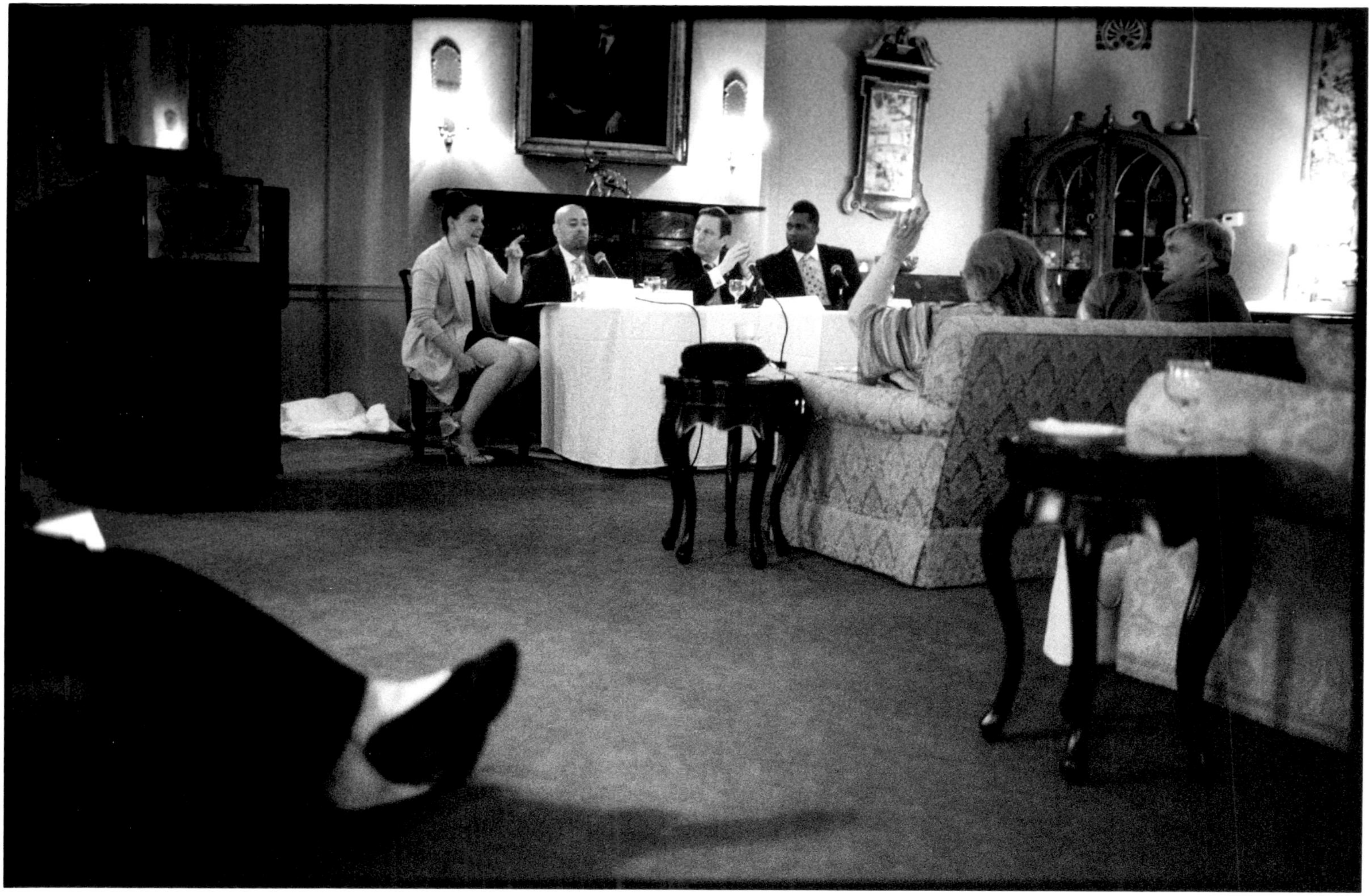

Manhattan Borough President Gale Brewer's Program on Aging in the City, John Jay College, Hell's Kitchen, October 27, 2019

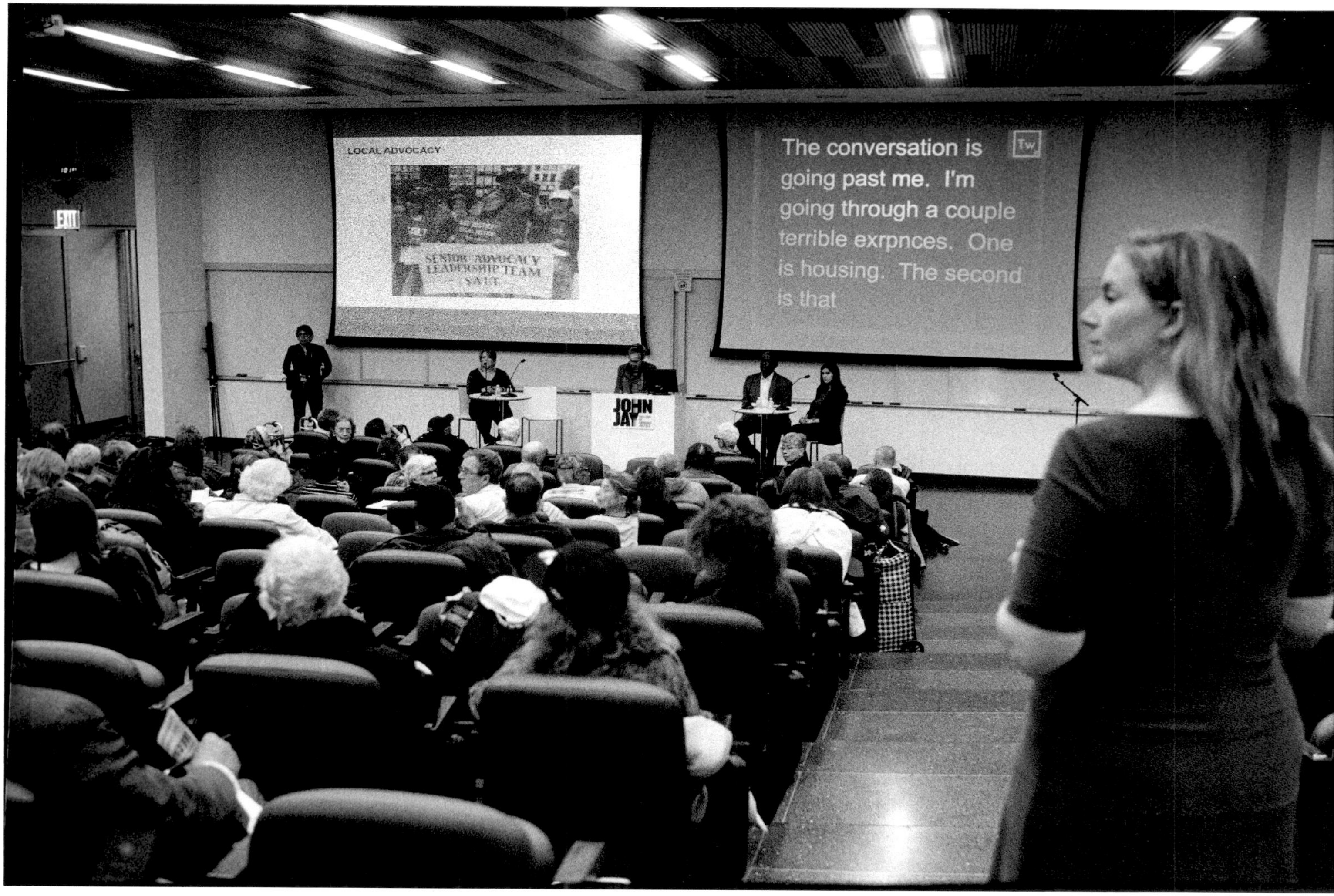
LOCAL ADVOCACY
SENIOR ADVOCACY LEADERSHIP TEAM
The conversation is going past me. I'm going through a couple terrible exrpnces. One is housing. The second is that
EXIT
JOHN JAY

National Association of Scholars, Mighty Maze Conference, Harvard Club, Midtown, March 2, 2013

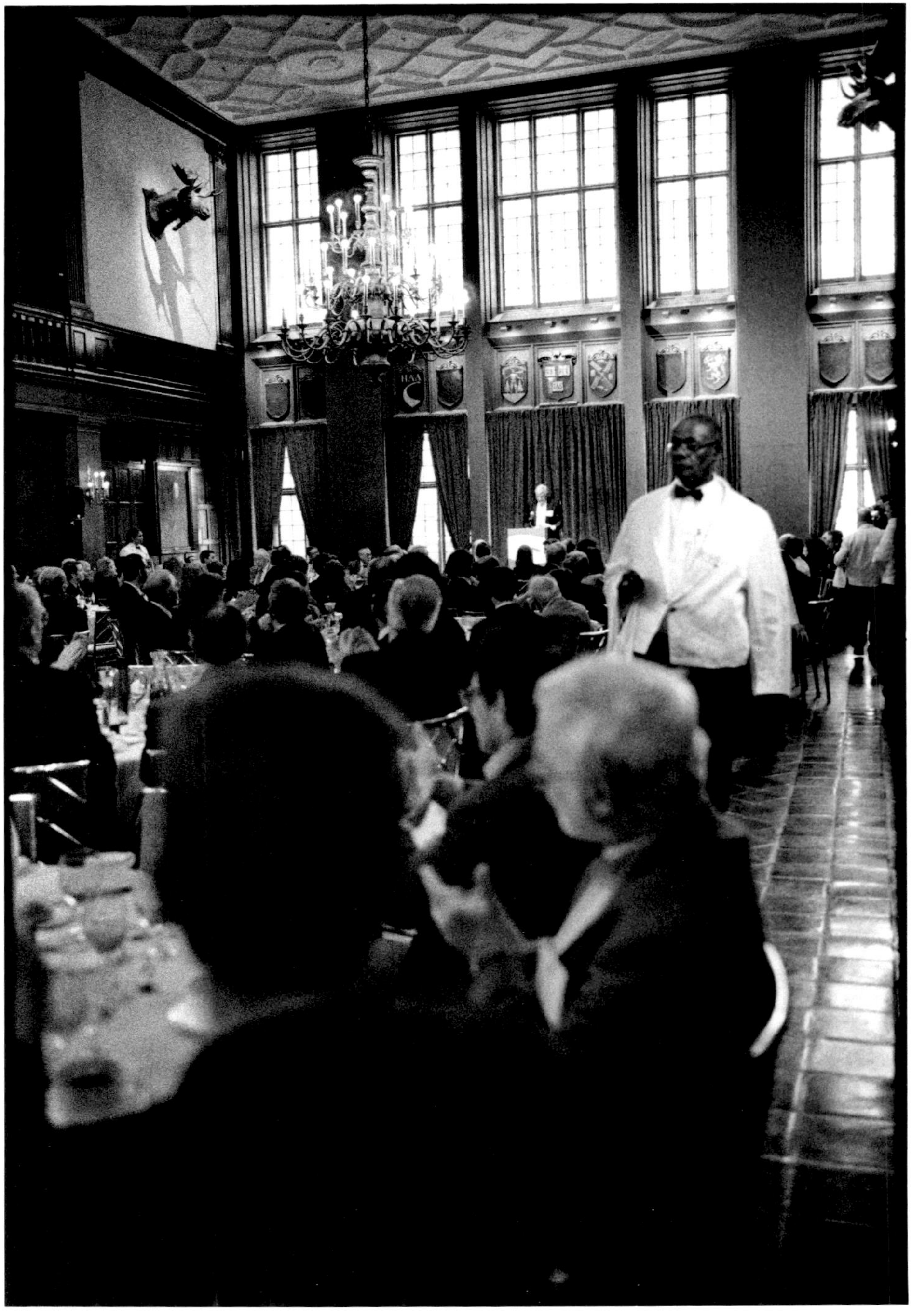

Civic Hall (IT support for progressive organizations), Chelsea, November 25, 2019

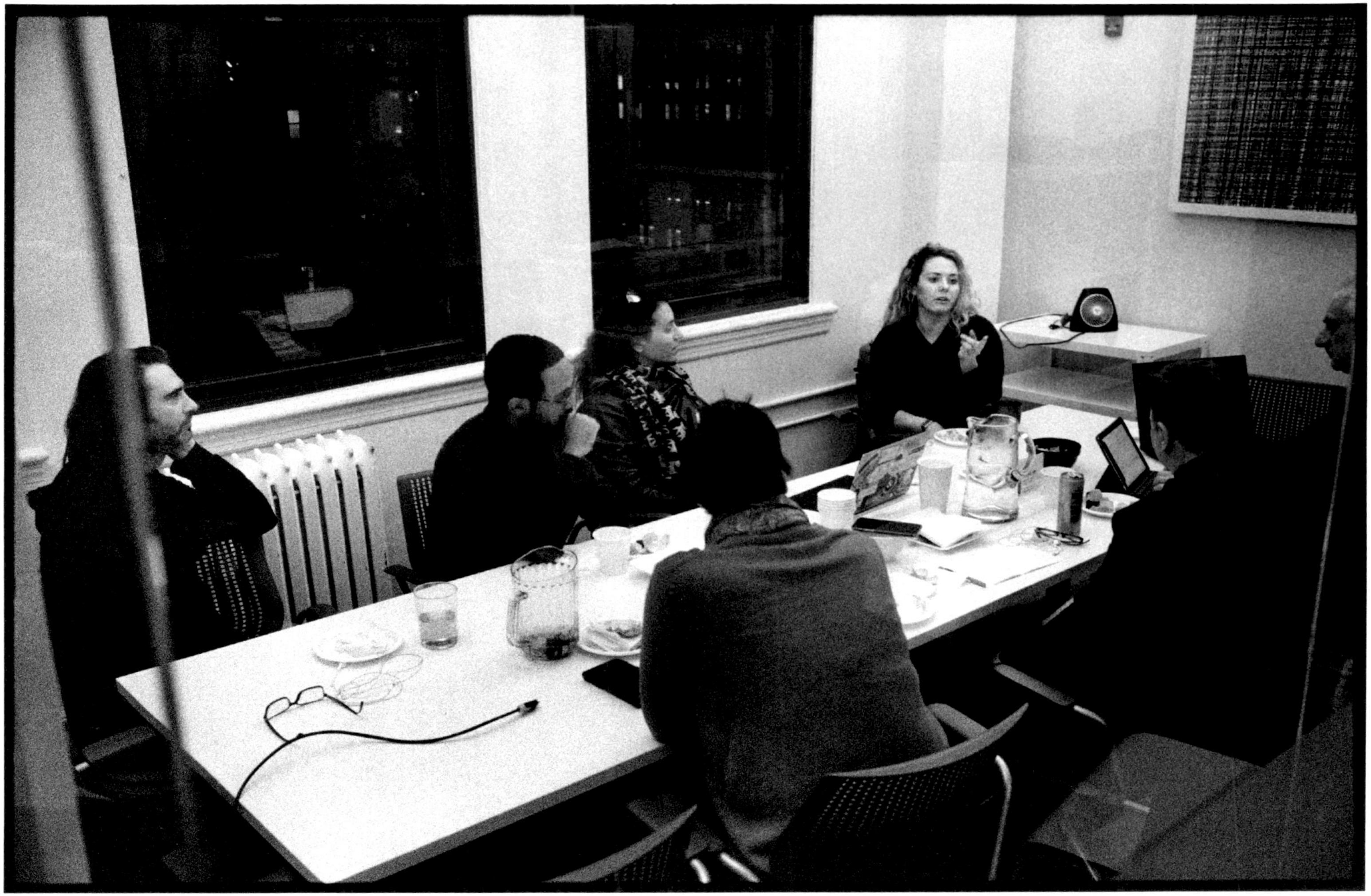

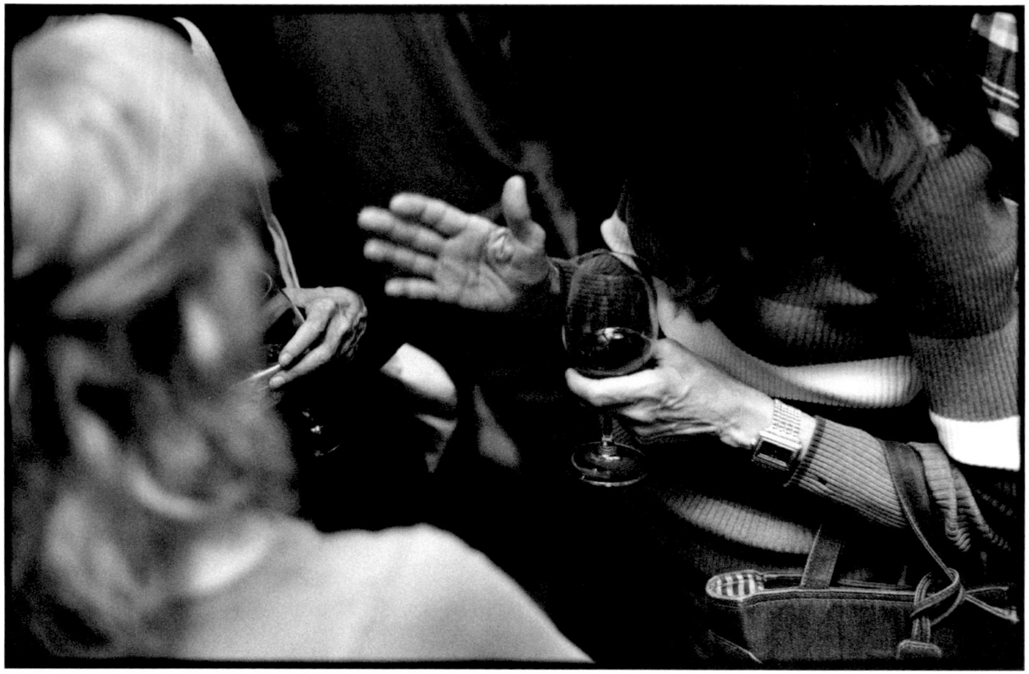

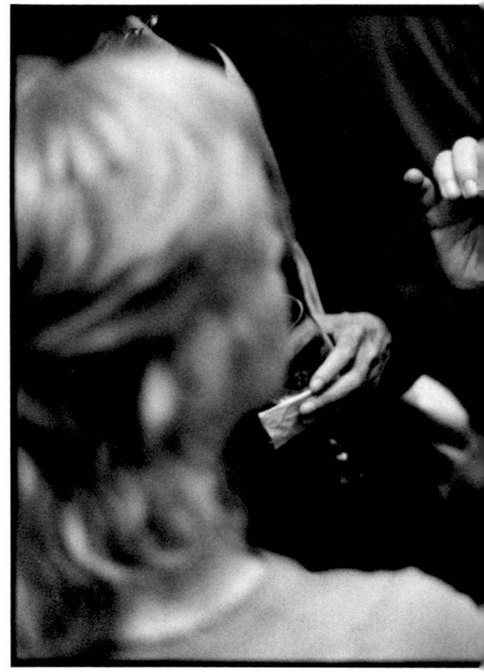

Tea Party 365 social event, Tio Pepe restaurant, West Village, April 27, 2010

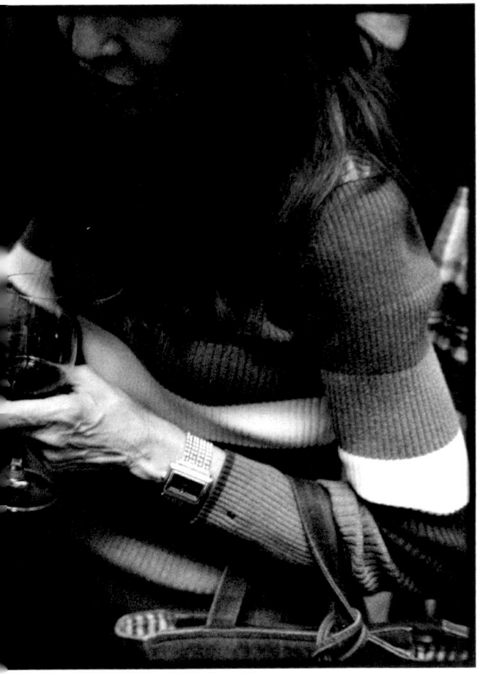

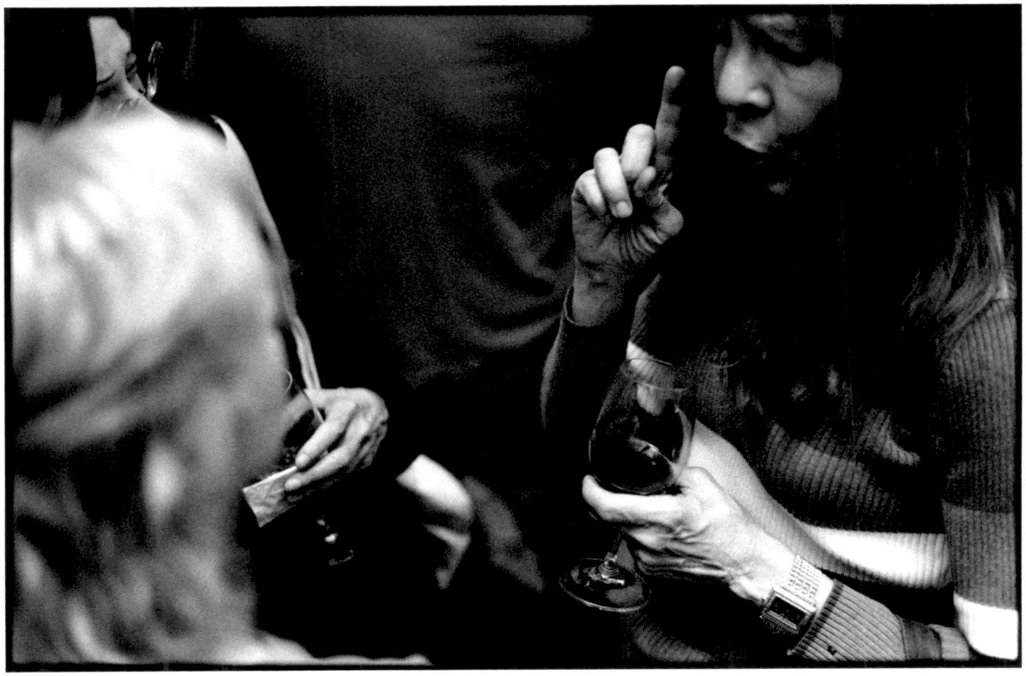

Staff meeting, nonprofit legal services provider for indigent women, Financial District, September 11, 2013

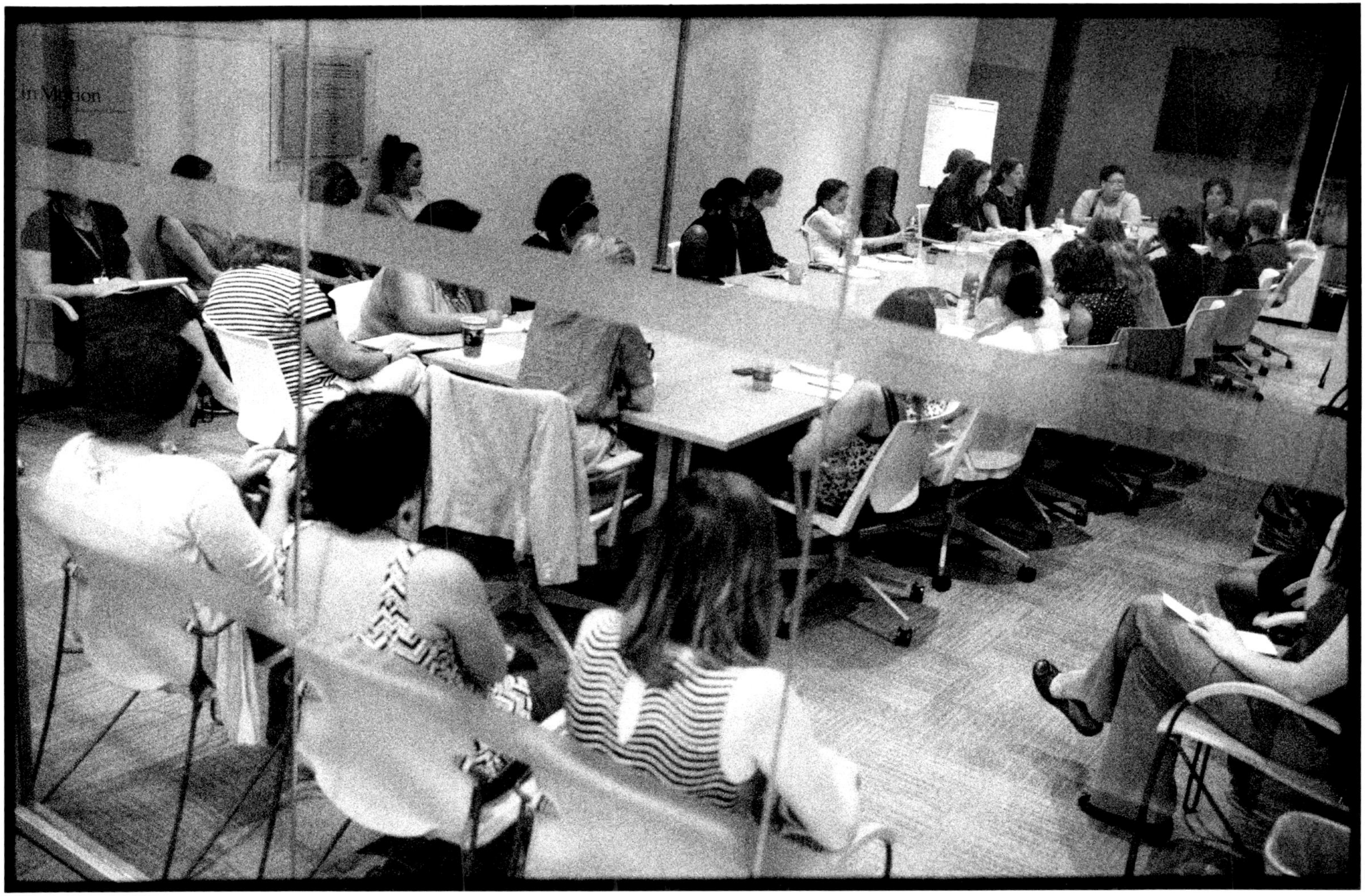

Town Hall meeting about the American Museum of Natural History's planned construction in Theodore Roosevelt Park, Fourth Universalist Society, Upper West Side, October 6, 2015

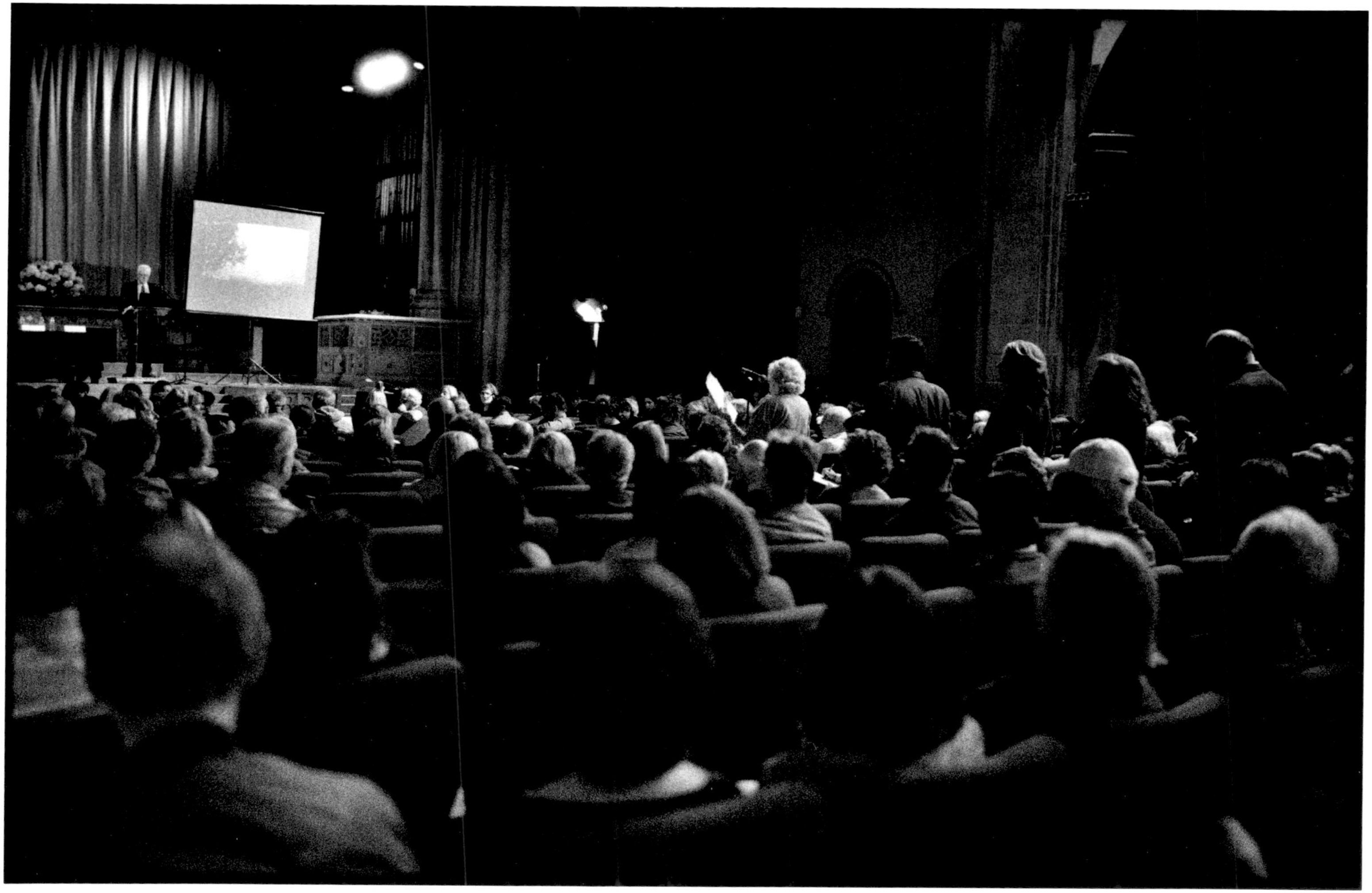

West Side Republican Club, 63rd Street YMCA, Upper West Side, June 6, 2014

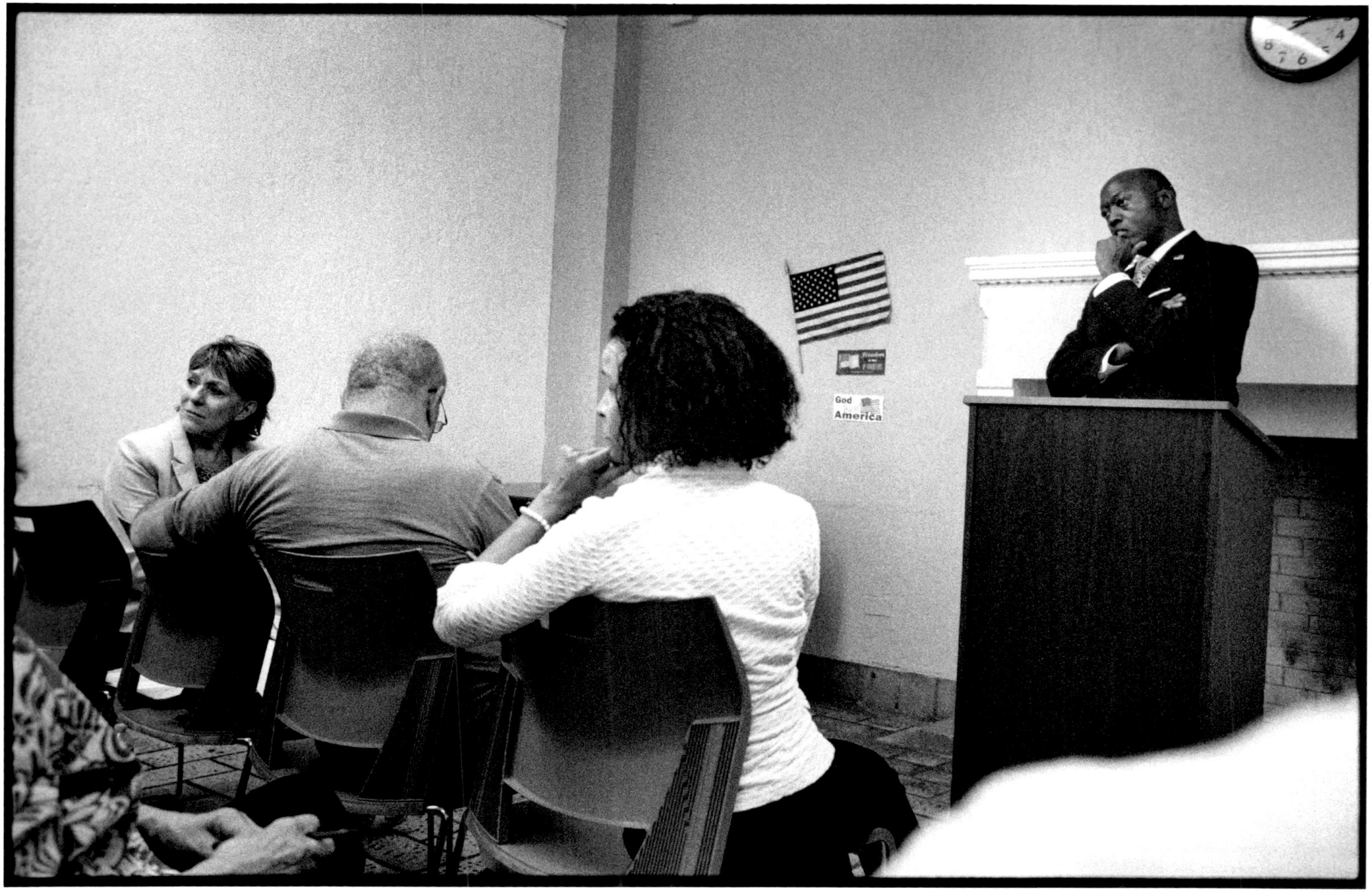
God
America

Build the Block, Neighborhood Policing and Safety Meeting, 20th Precinct, Sector C, 79th Street Rotunda, Riverside Park, August 20, 2020

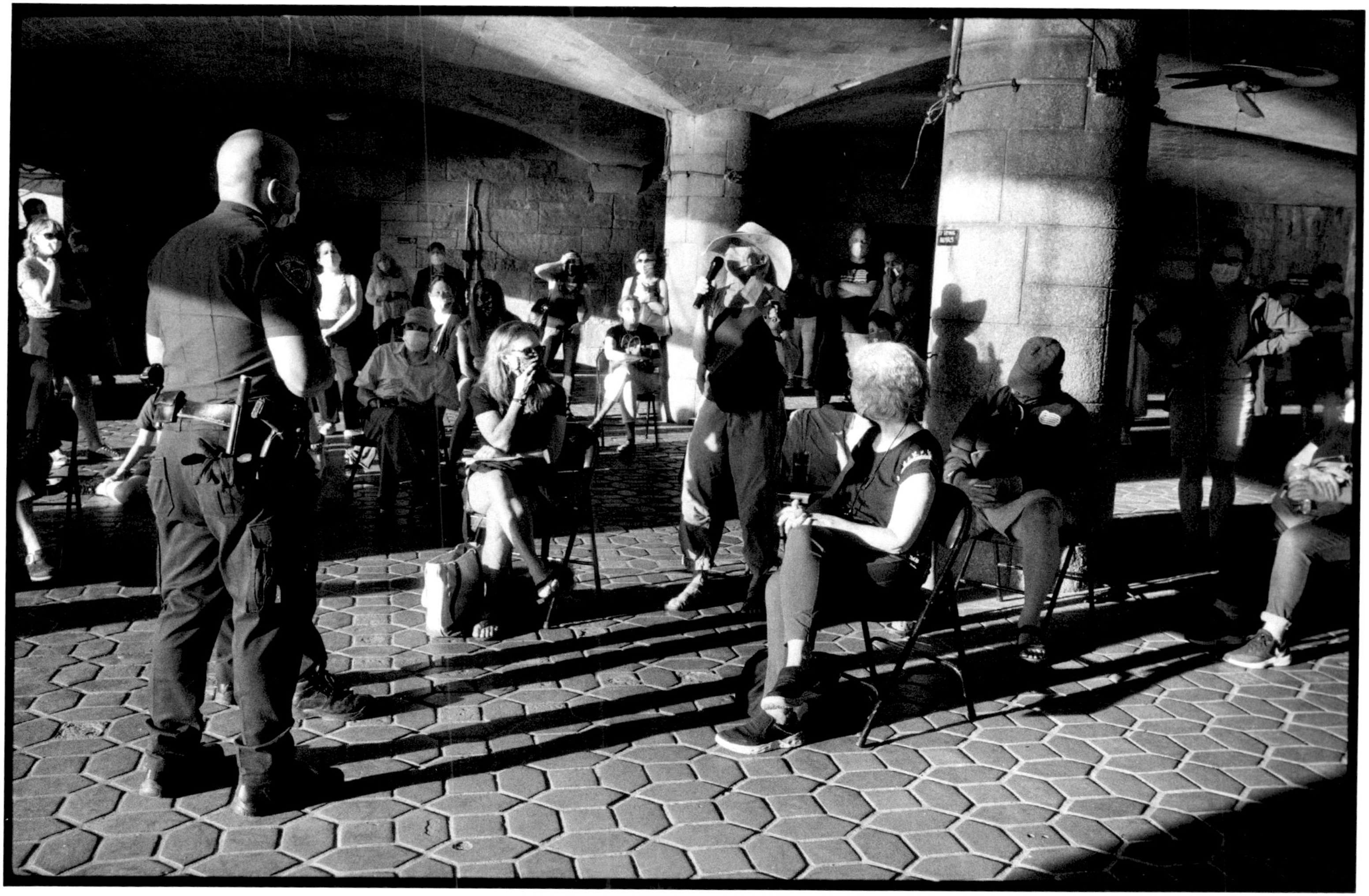

Frank McCourt High School PTA meeting, Brandeis Campus, Upper West Side, April 10, 2013

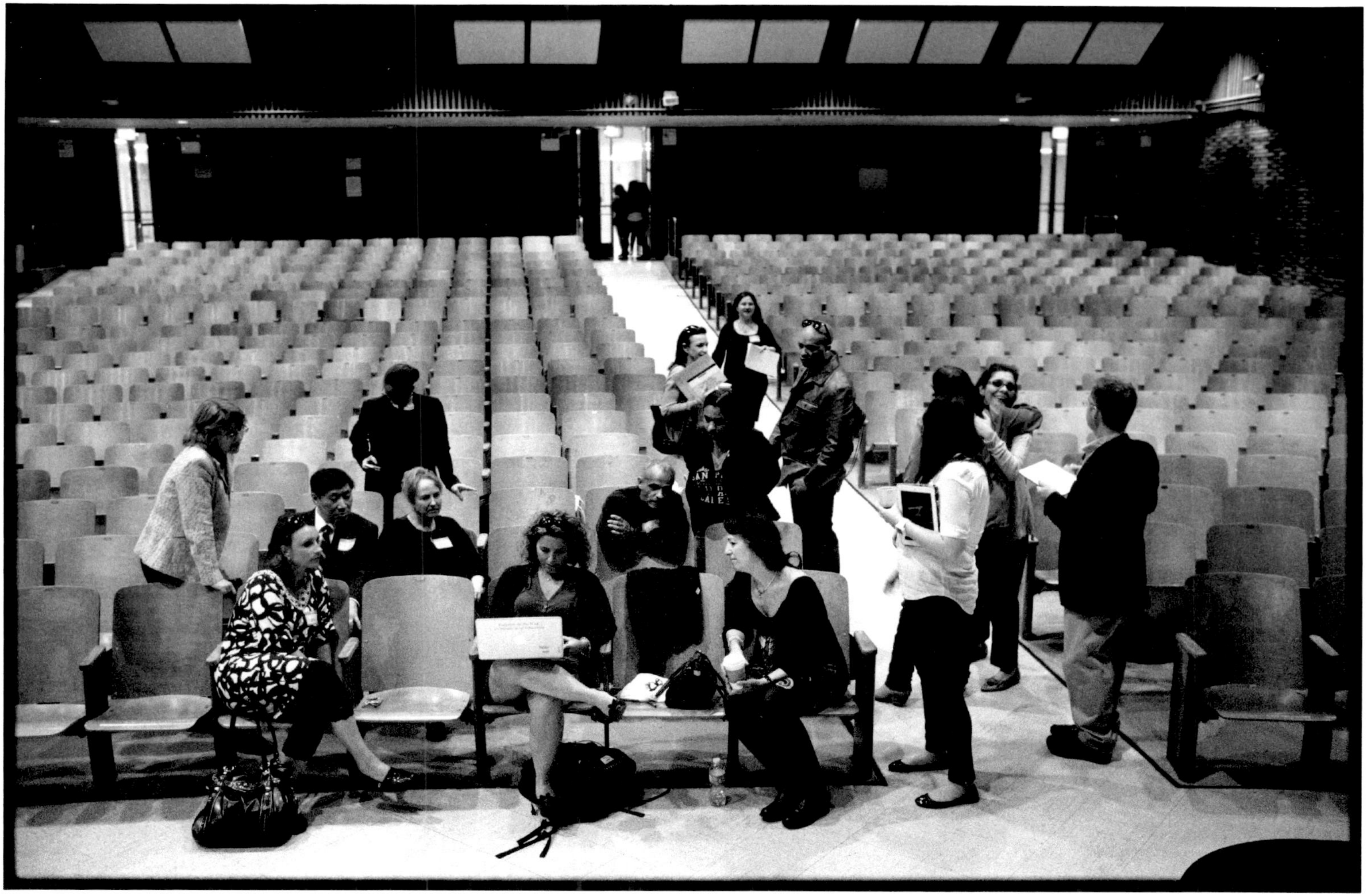

SOCIAL CAPITAL

Volunteers, charities, not-for-profits, communal organizations, and acts by individuals promoting confidence that members of a society care for each other and can be trusted

Aiding an epileptic, Church Avenue subway station, Kensington, Brooklyn, December 16, 2015

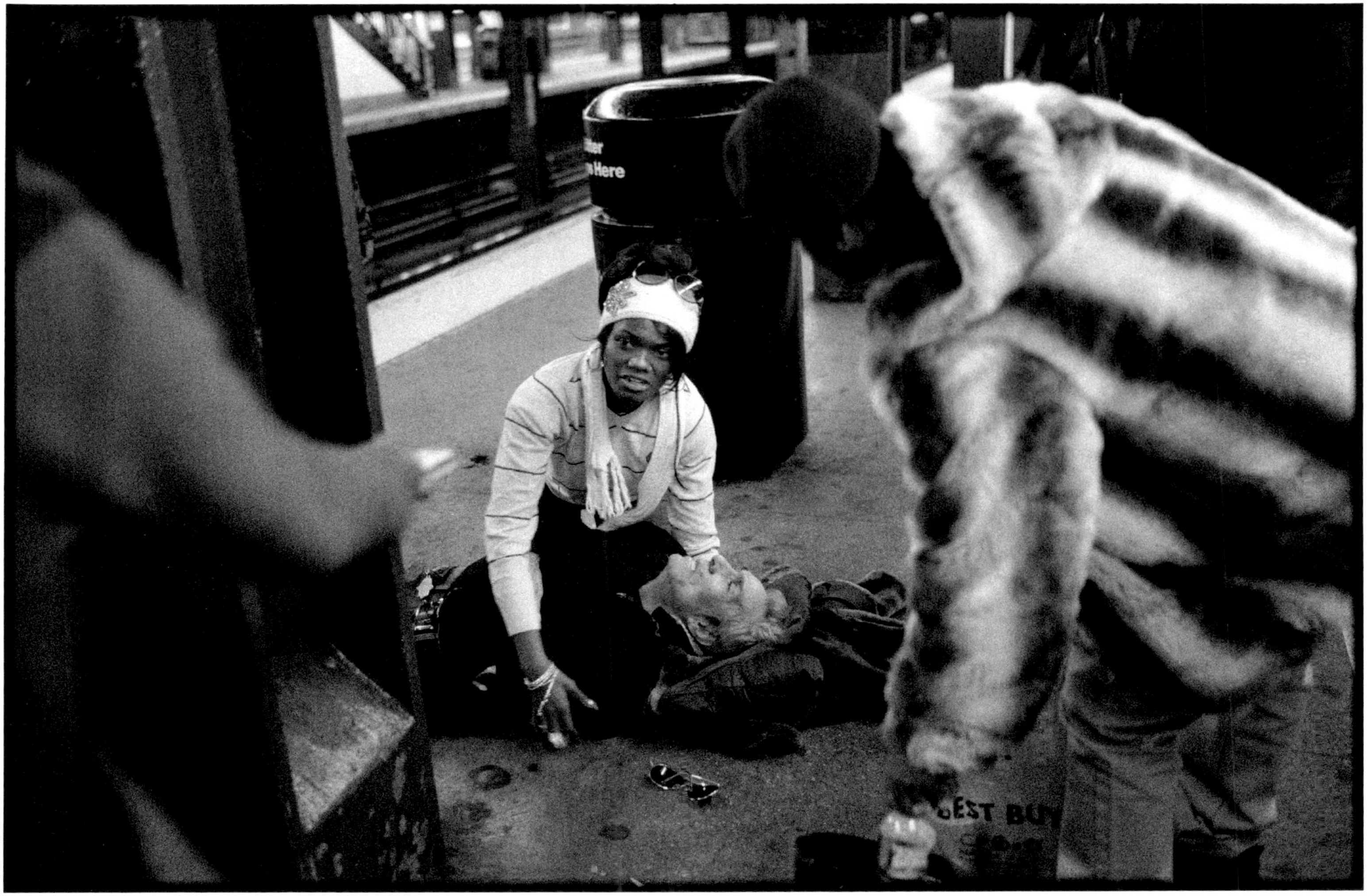

Volunteer maintenance workers, Riverside Park, September 4, 2012

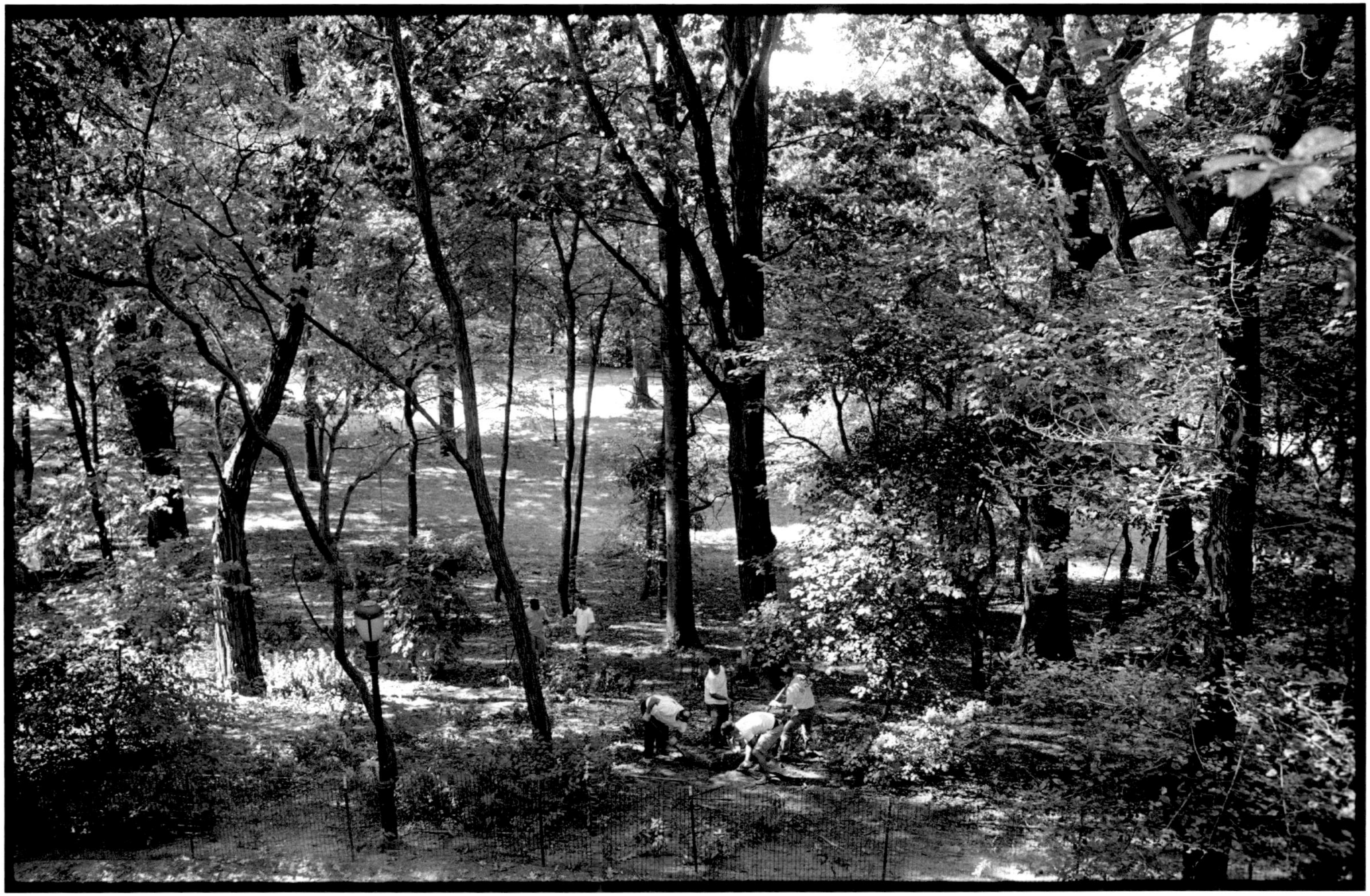

Superstorm Sandy relief workers walked up seventeen floors with supplies, Far Rockaway, Queens, November 11, 2012

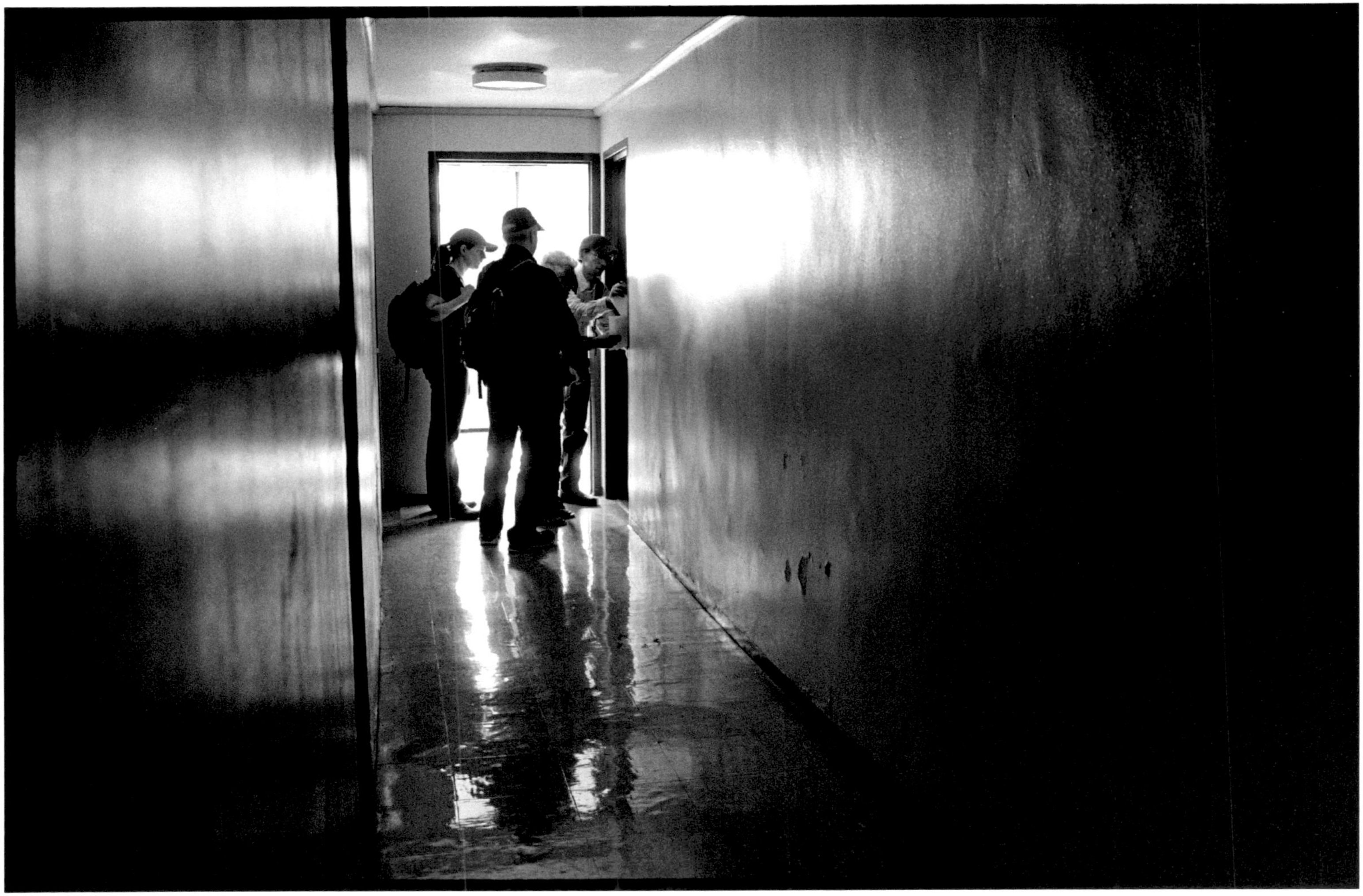

Public Forum: Speak Out on Hydrofracking, Upper West Side, November 2, 2011

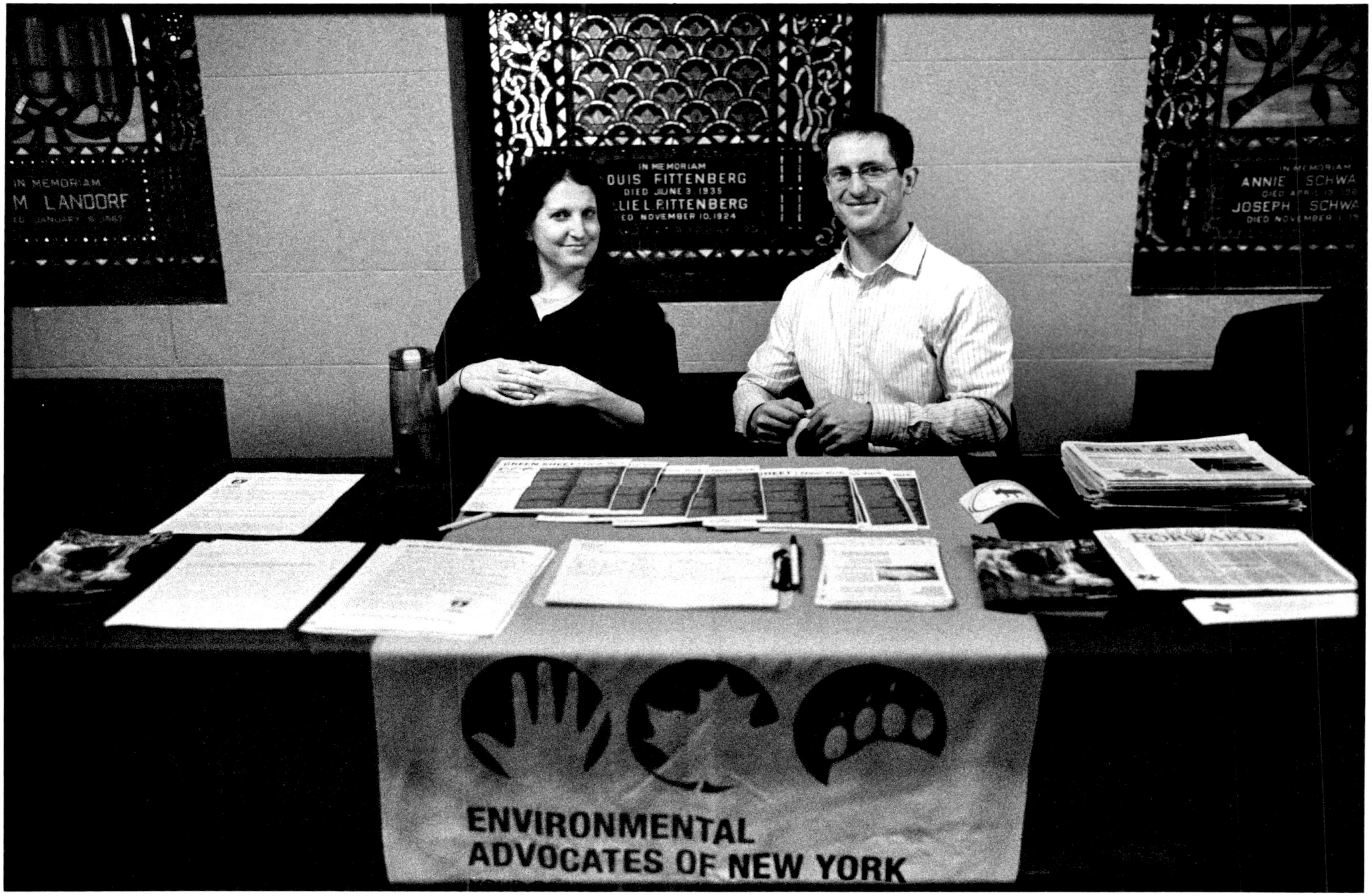
IN MEMORIAM
M LANDORF
IN MEMORIAM
OUIS FITTENBERG
DIED JUNE 3, 1935
LLIE L. FITTENBERG
ED NOVEMBER 10, 1924
IN MEMORIAM
ANNIE SCHWA
JOSEPH SCHWA
ENVIRONMENTAL
ADVOCATES OF NEW YORK

West Side Campaign Against Hunger, Church of St. Paul & St. Andrew, Upper West Side, July 28, 2011

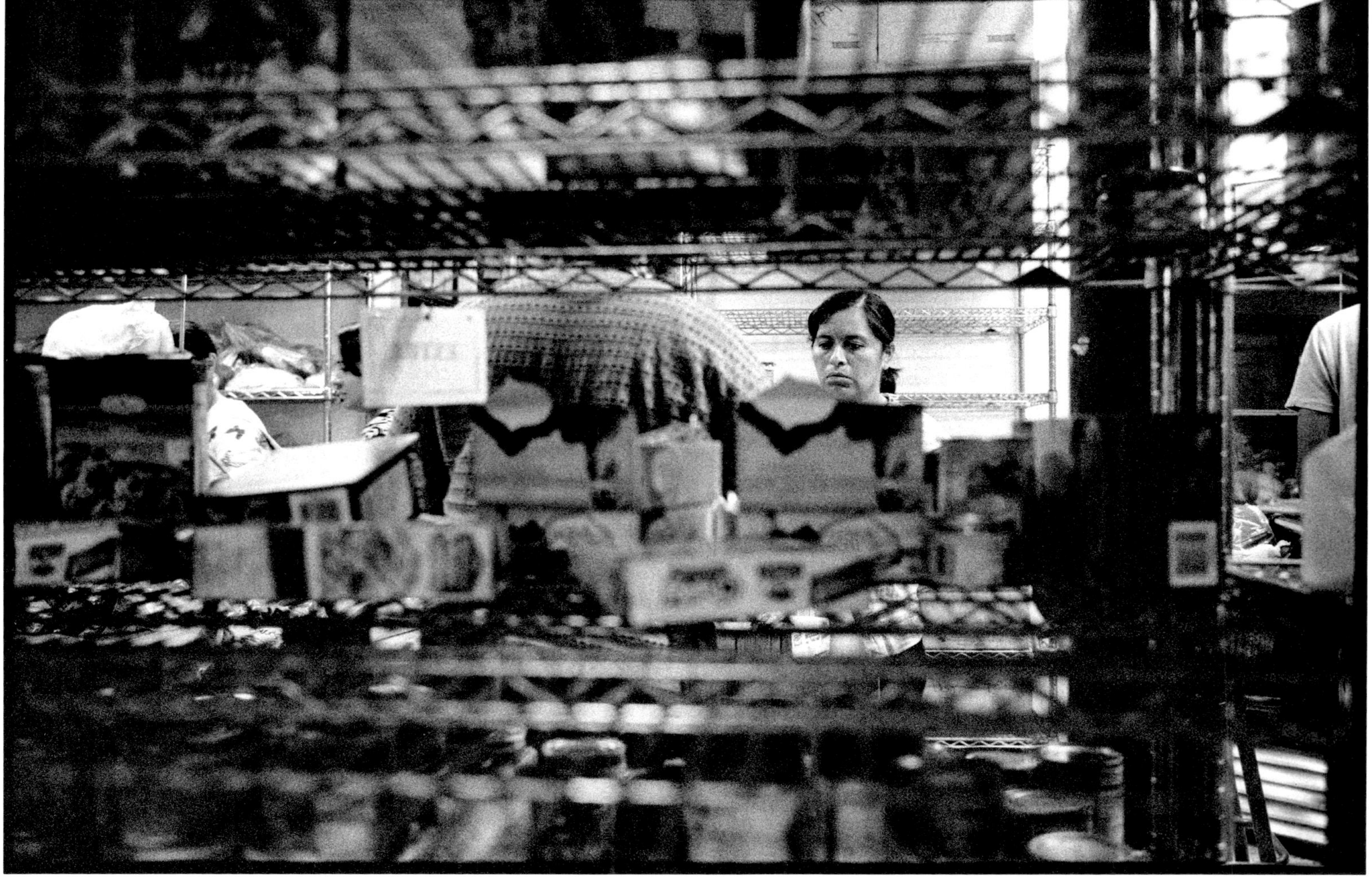

Class parents' hootenanny, Upper West Side, May 4, 2014

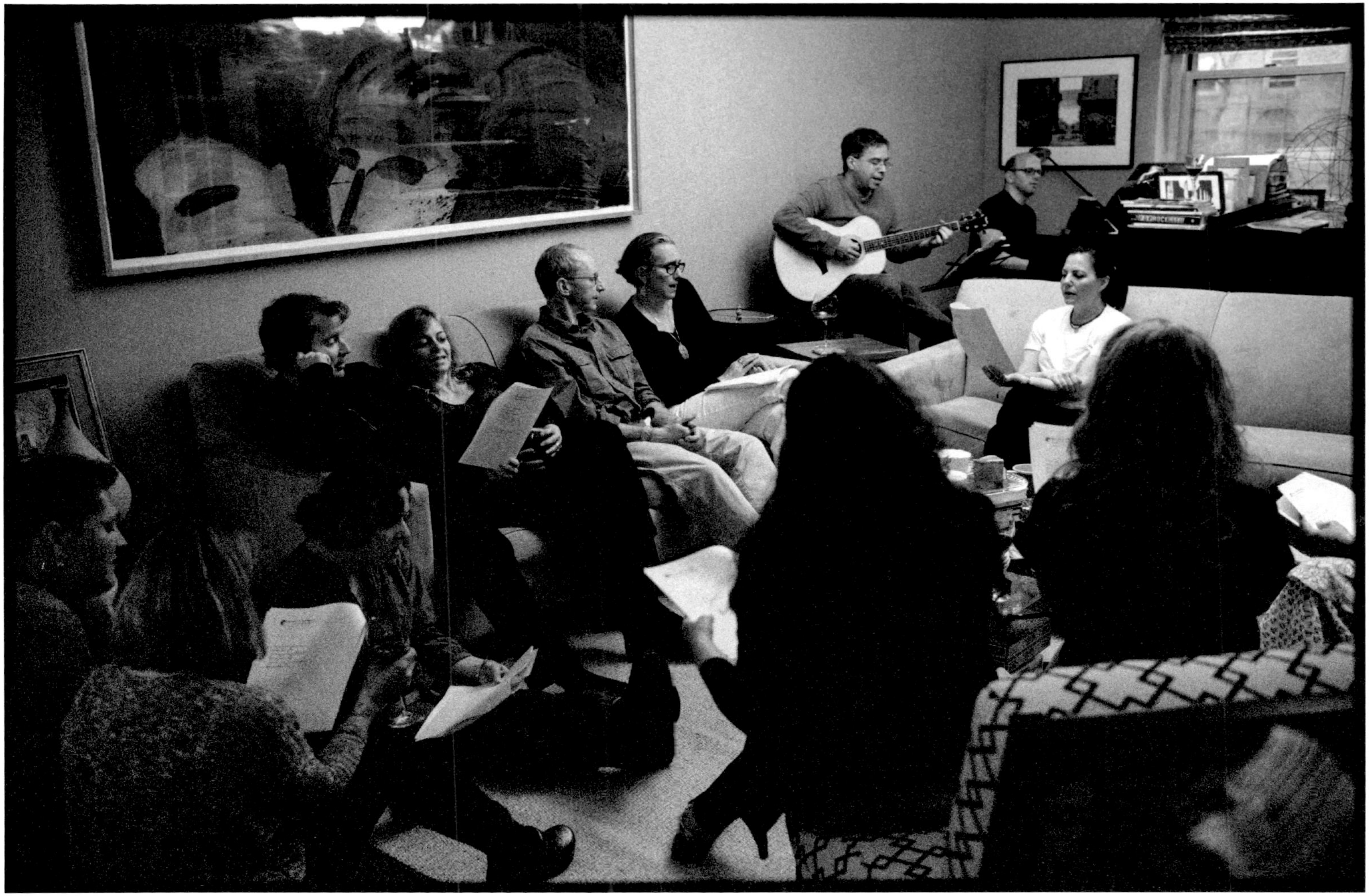

Fundraiser, Joan of Arc Memorial, Riverside Park, May 30, 2017

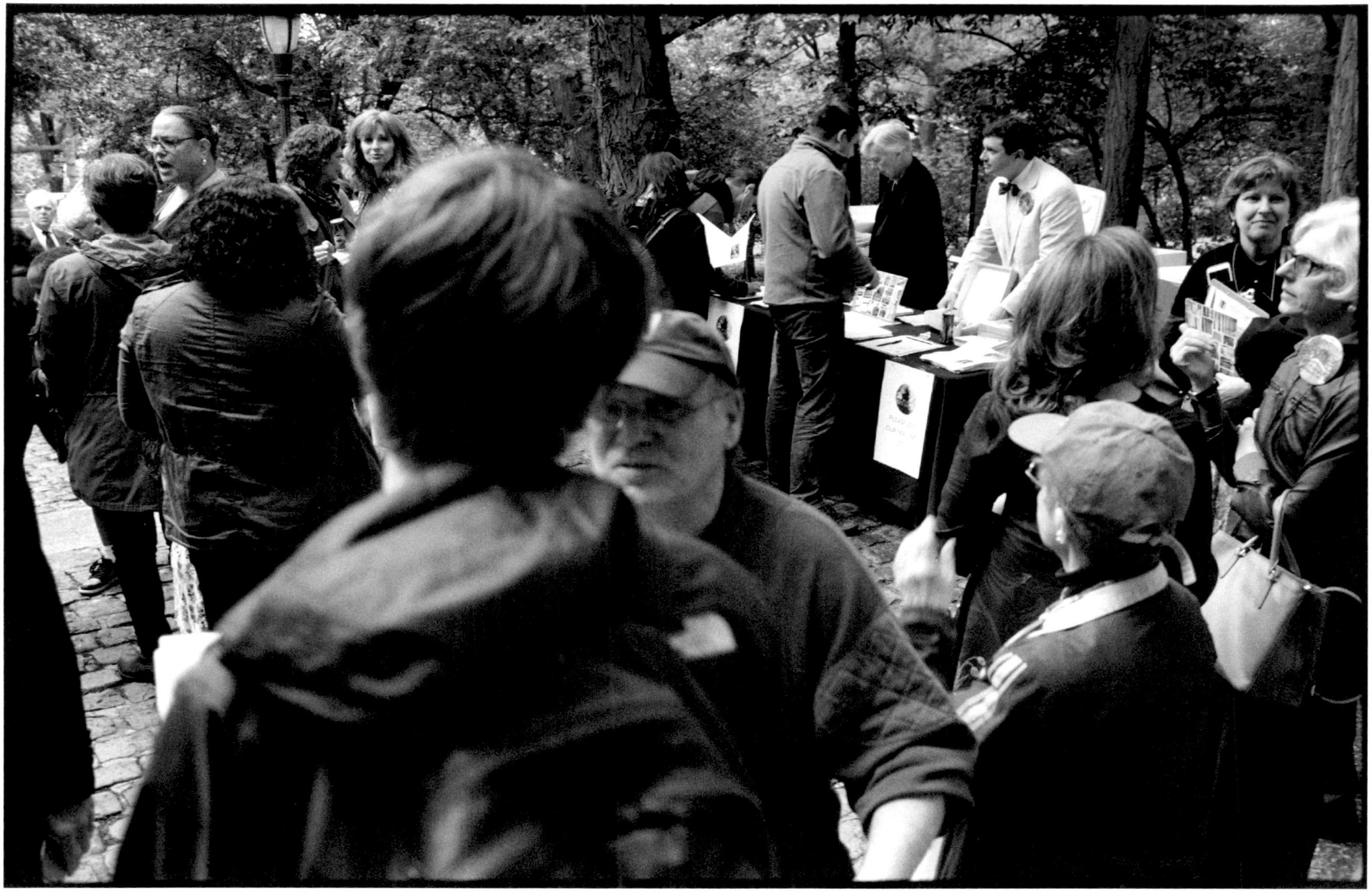

Benefit concert for Superstorm Sandy victims, Jalopy Theatre, Carroll Gardens, Brooklyn, December 16, 2012

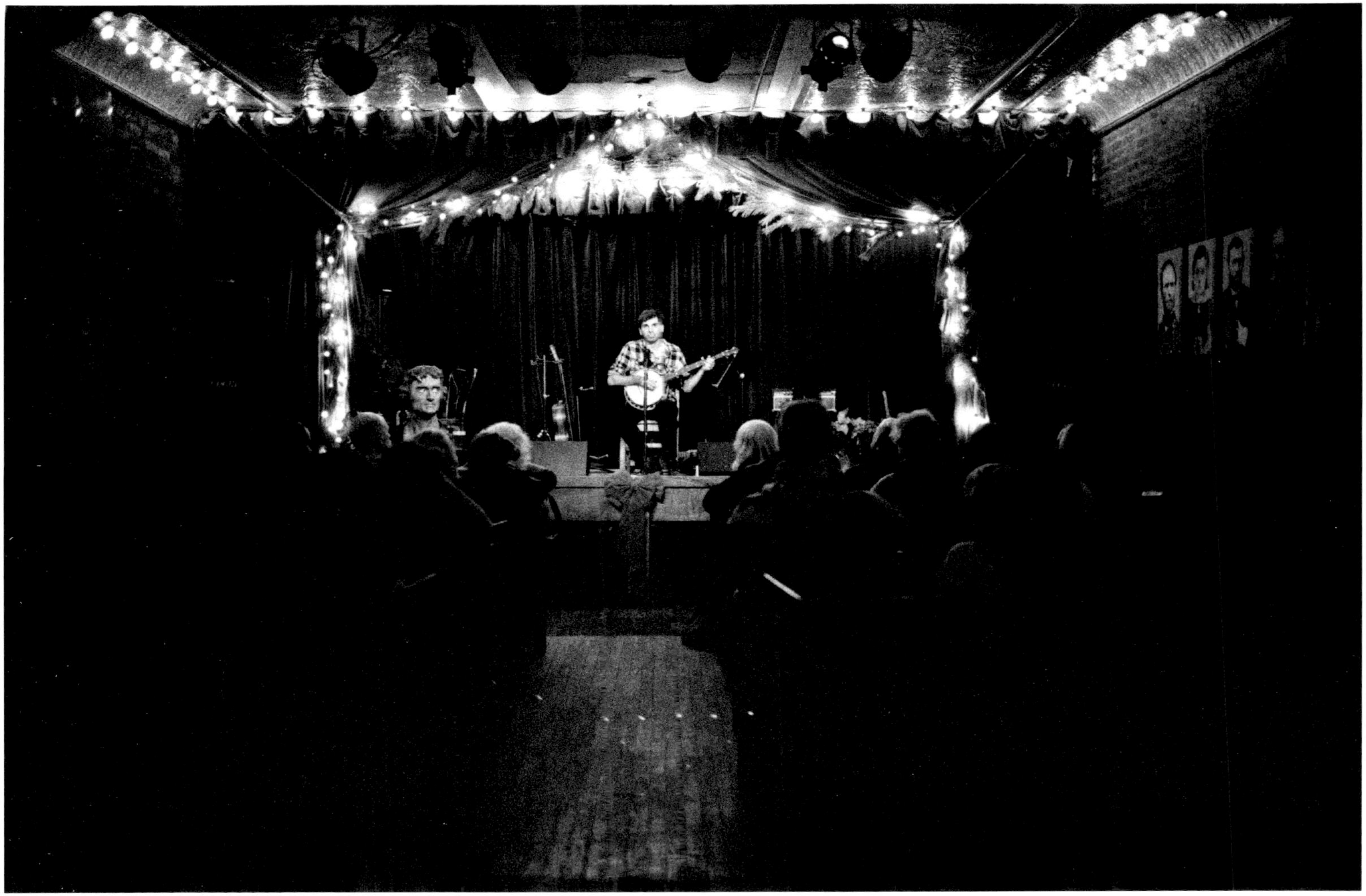

Blood donor, synagogue, Upper West Side, September 20, 2013

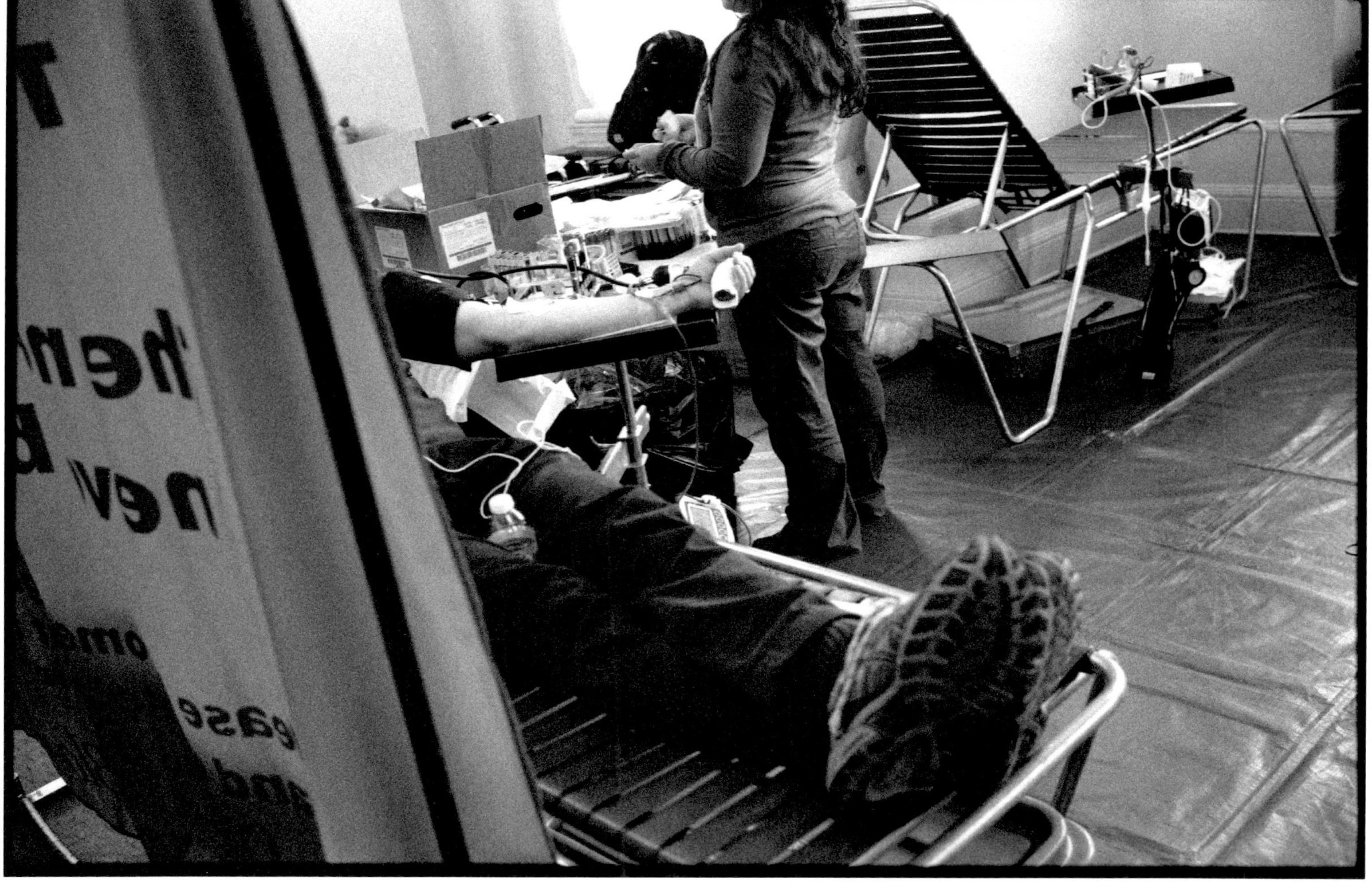

CPR training, synagogue, Upper West Side, March 5, 2014

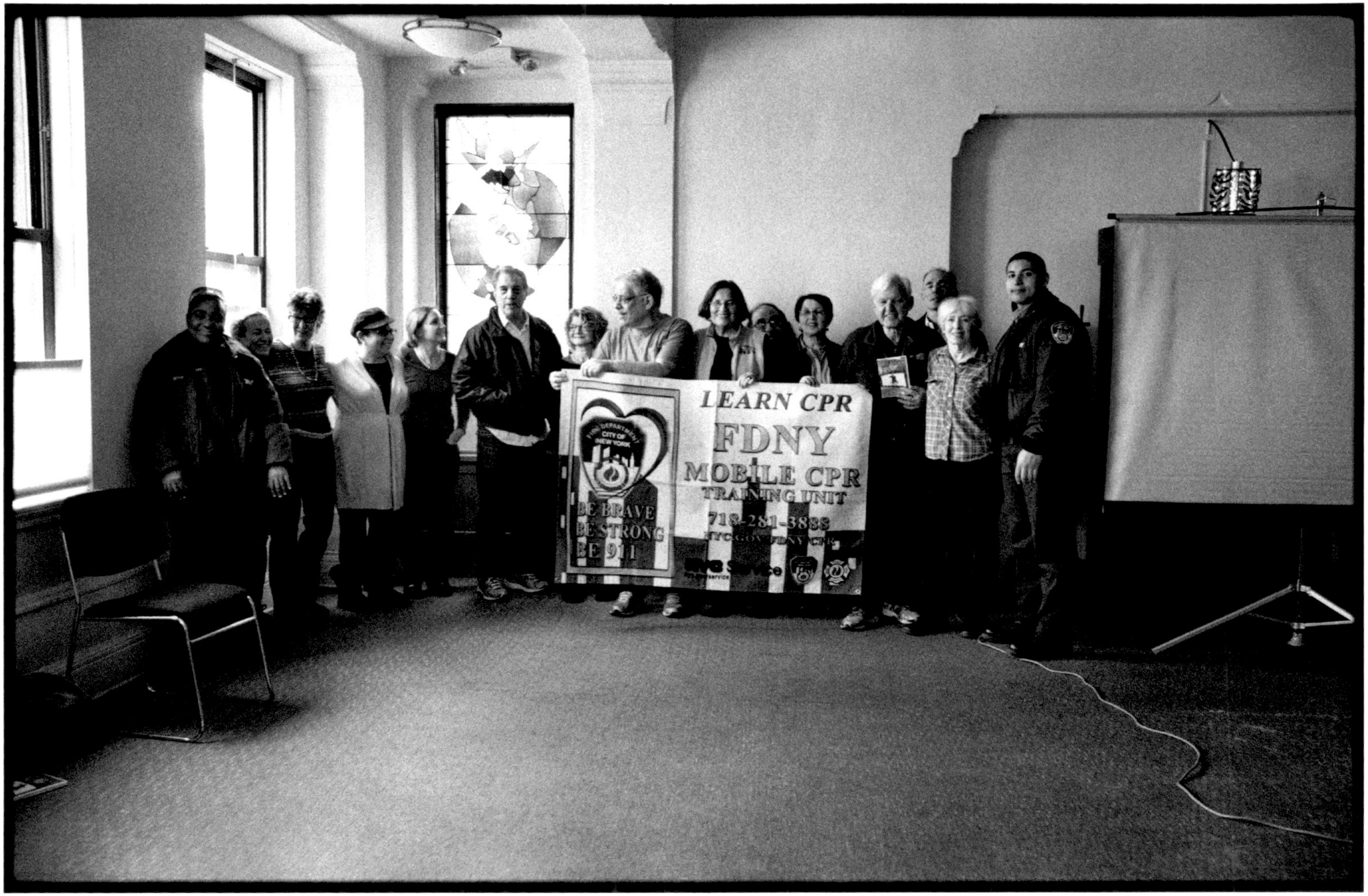
LEARN CPR
FDNY
MOBILE CPR
TRAINING UNIT
718-281-3888
BE BRAVE
BE STRONG
BE 911

Pablo, patriot, West End Avenue, August 6, 2020

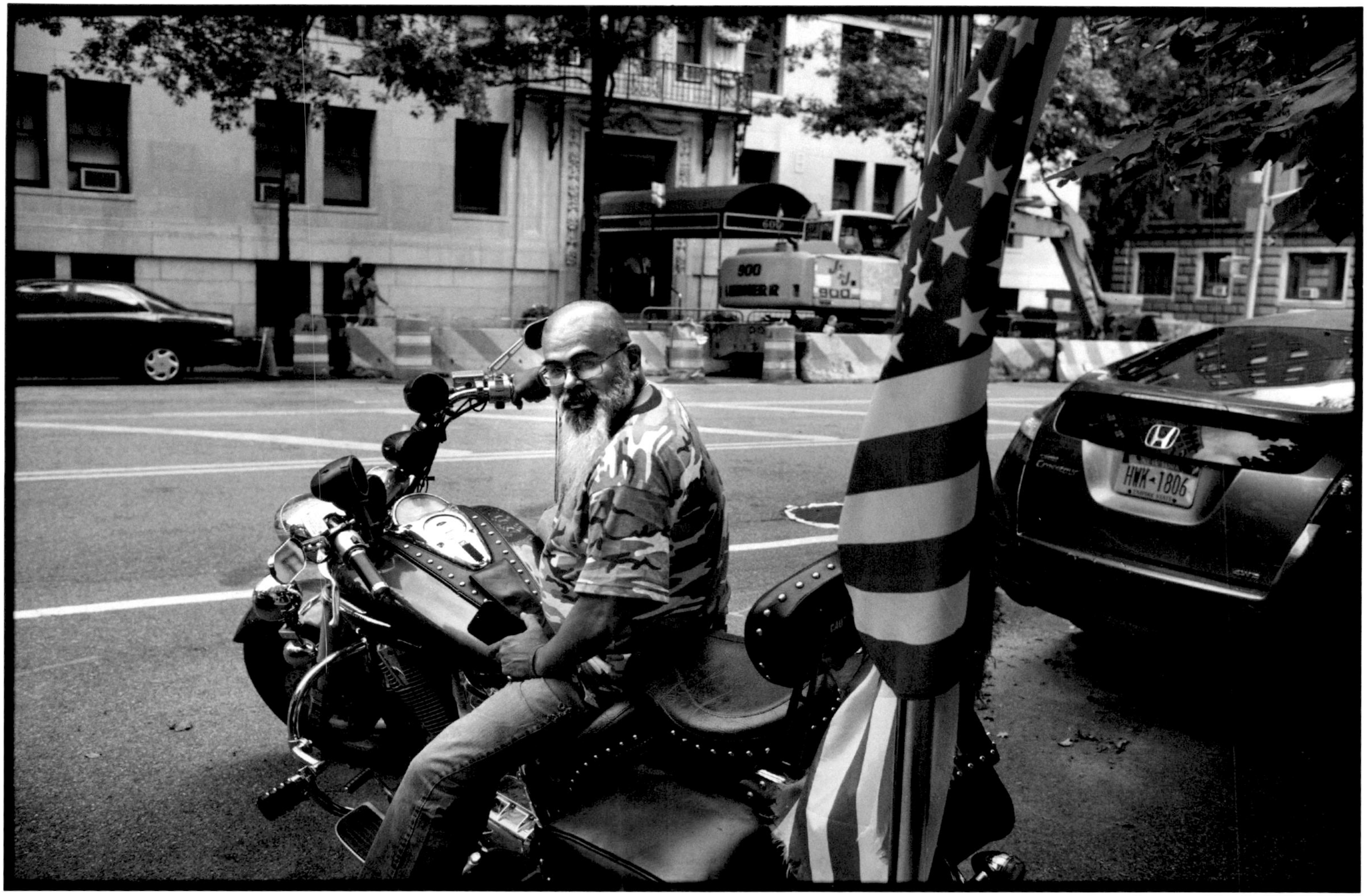
900
HWK 1806

Riverside Park Conservancy, The Interchurch Center, Morningside Heights, October 17, 2018

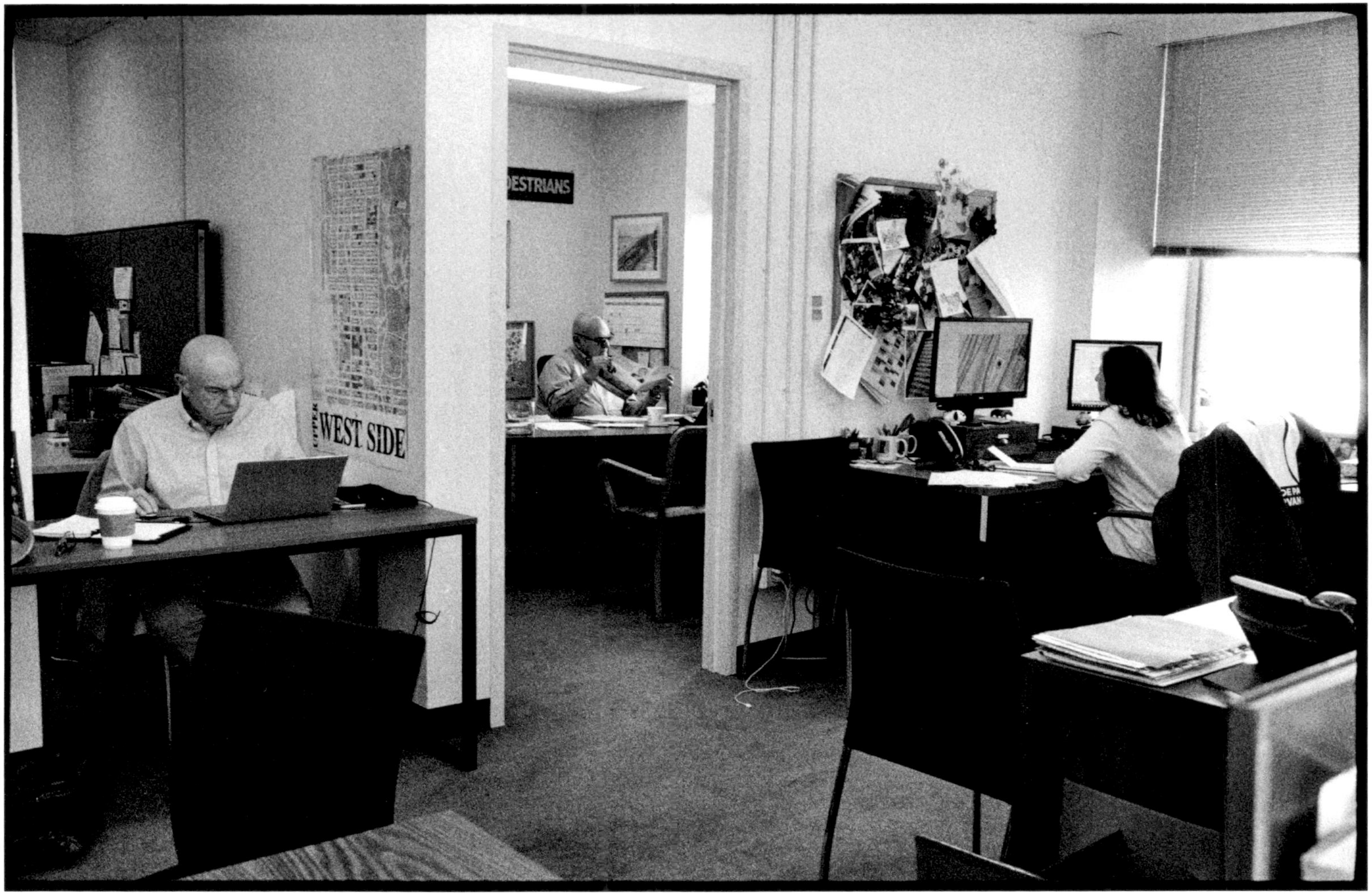
WEST SIDE
DESTRIANS

Homeless men's shelter, synagogue, Upper West Side, October 31, 2009

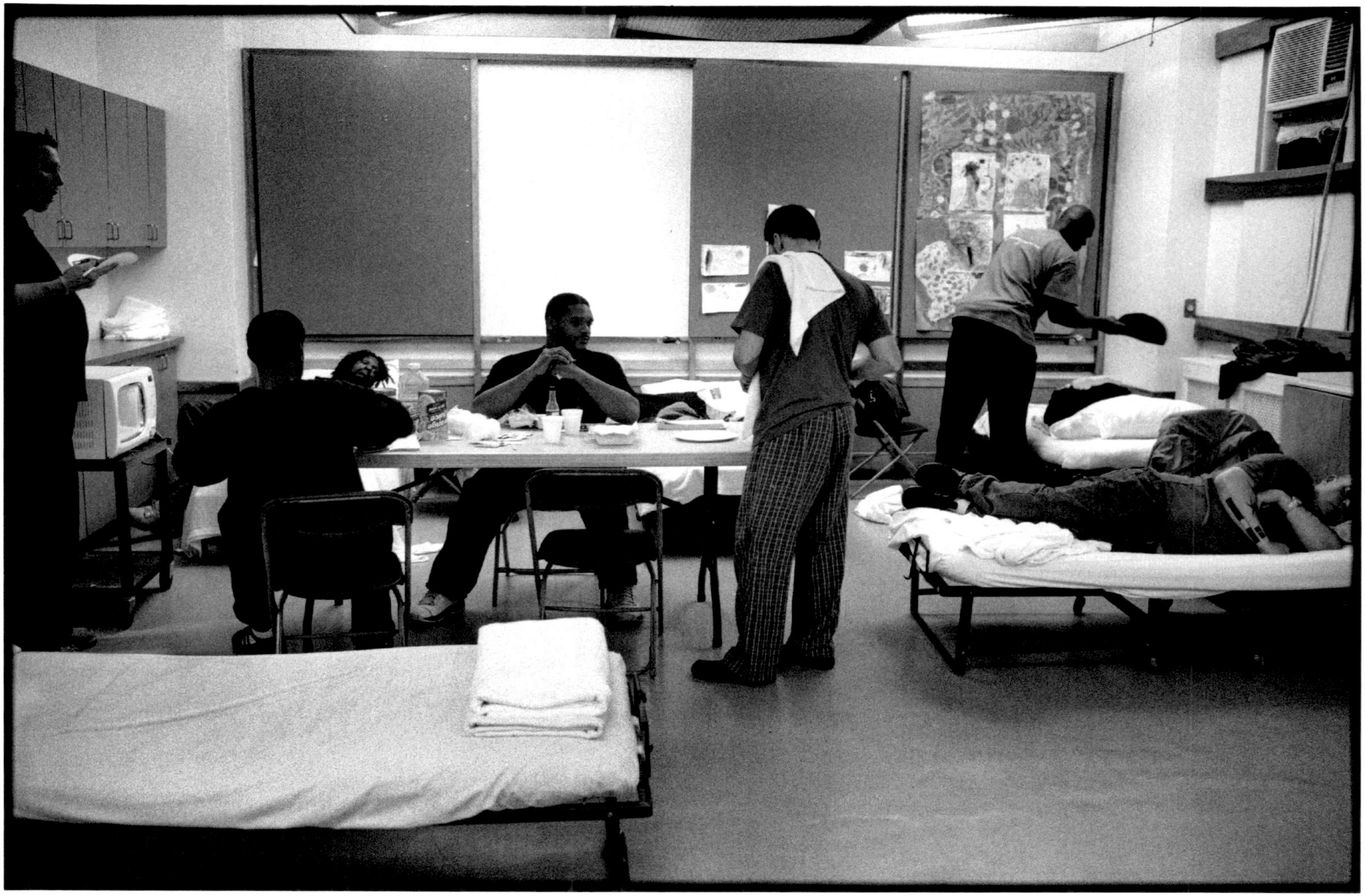

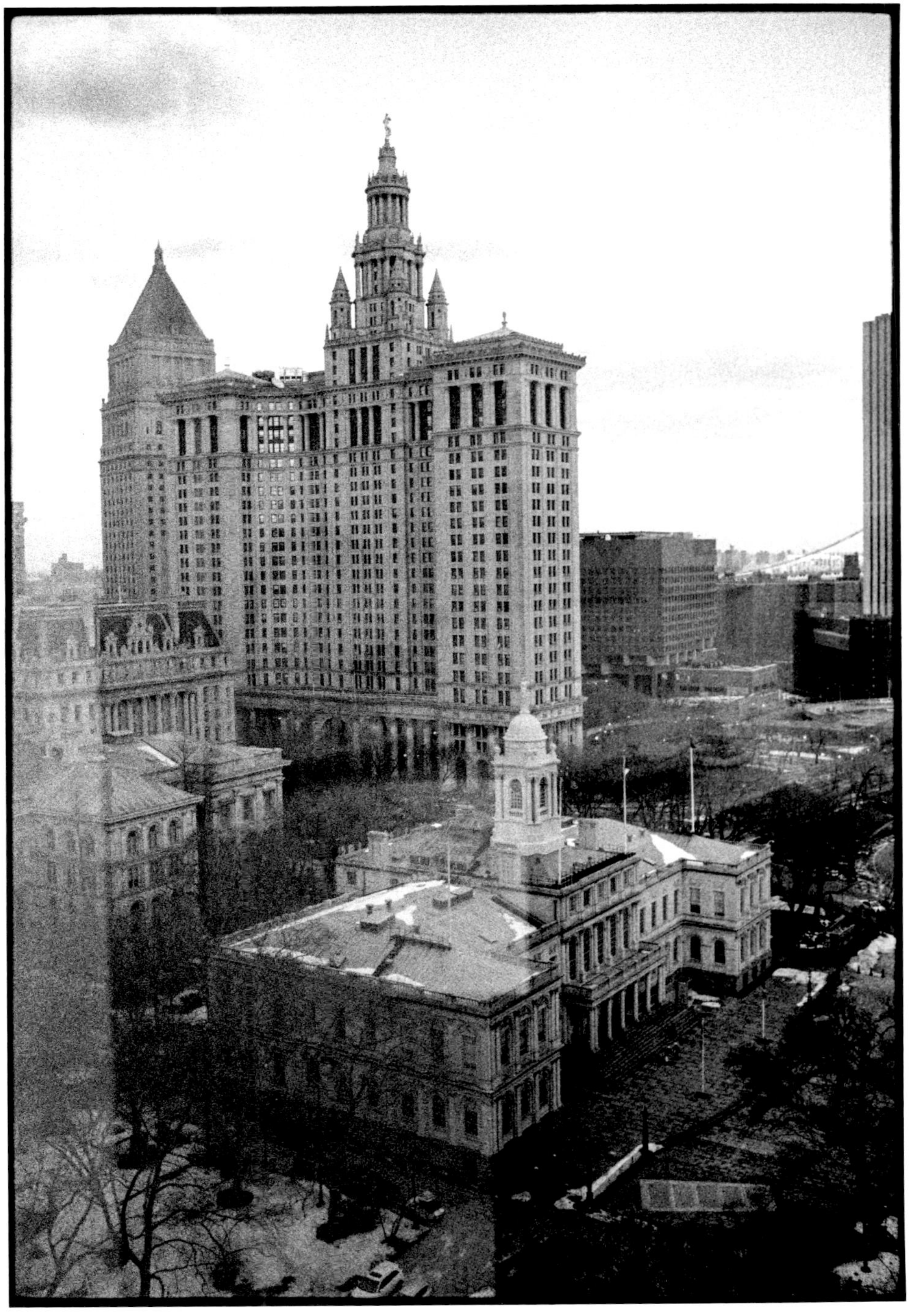

CIVICS

WILLIAM MEYERS

Essay by Nicole Gelinas

APOLLO
PUBLISHERS

Civic life is the life we live in dealing with problems of common concern.

—DAV D TUCKER AND NATHAN TUCKER, "Music and Civic Life in America"

CIVIC MARKERS

Remembering and honoring persons and events of civic importance

Statue of Liberty souvenirs, tourist shop, Times Square, September 15, 2010

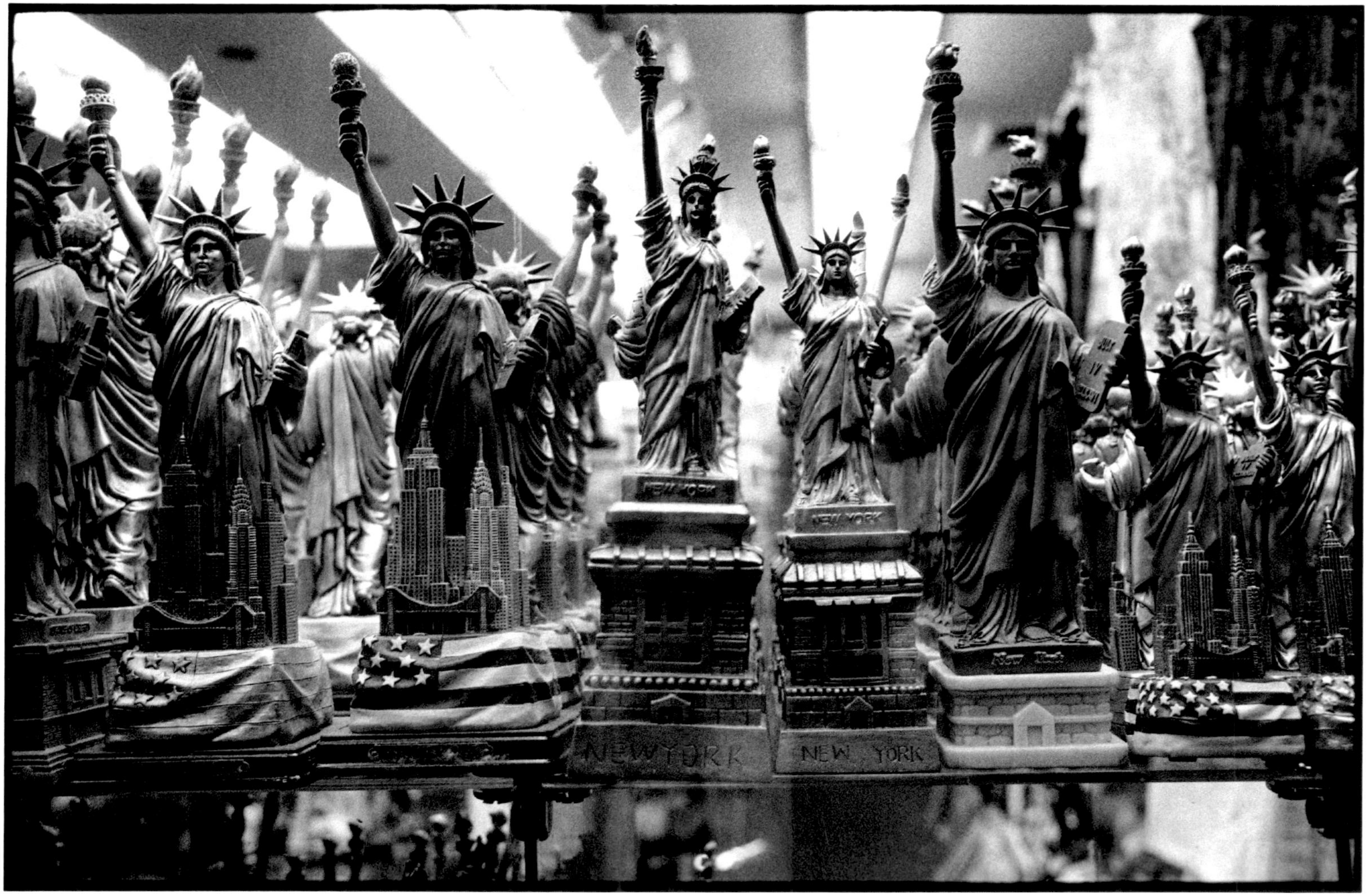
NEWYORK
NEW YORK

World Trade Center site seen from Battery Park City, June 6, 2010

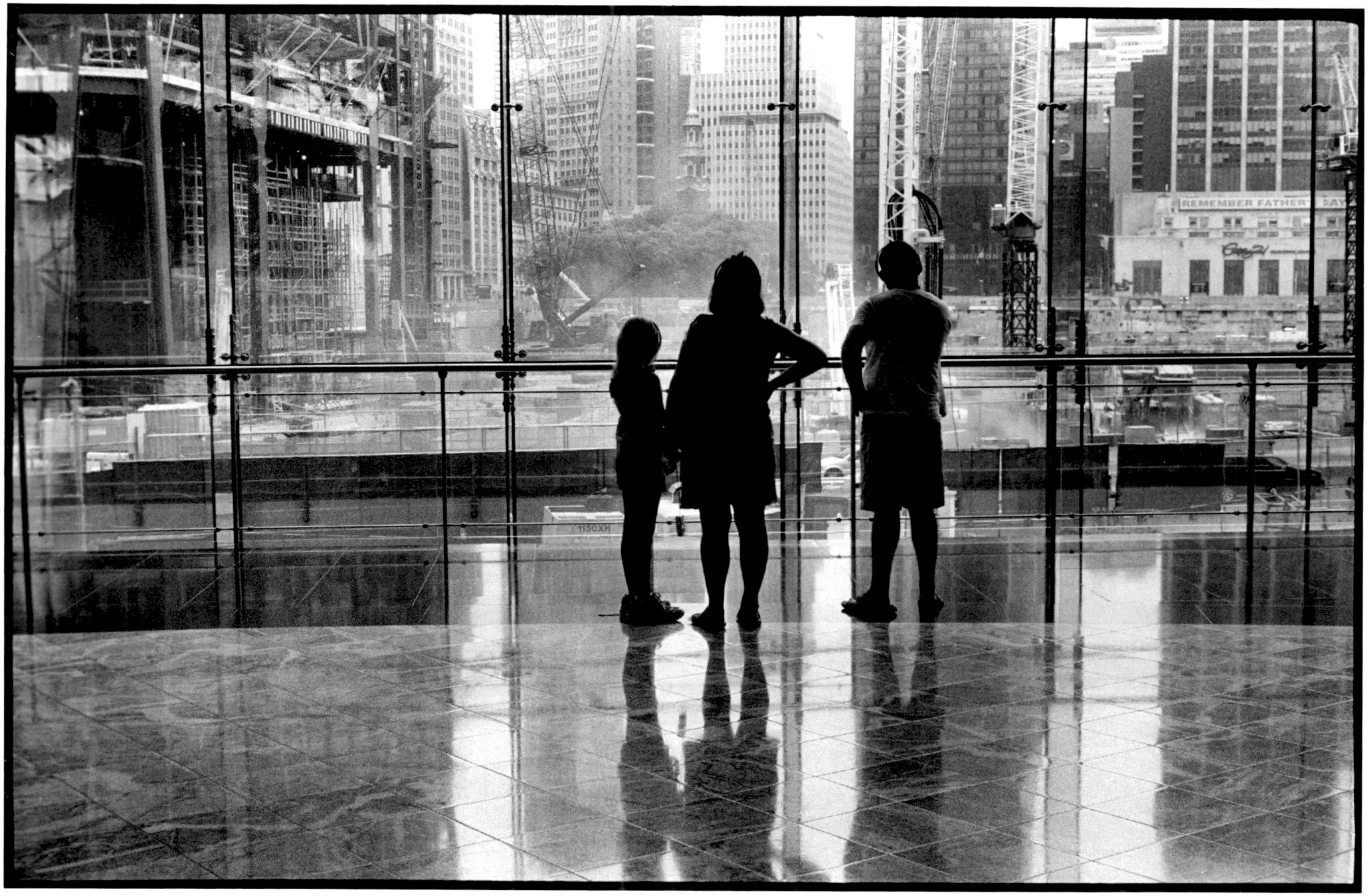
REMEMBER FATHER'S DAY

World War I doughboy, Woodside, Queens, September 29, 1999

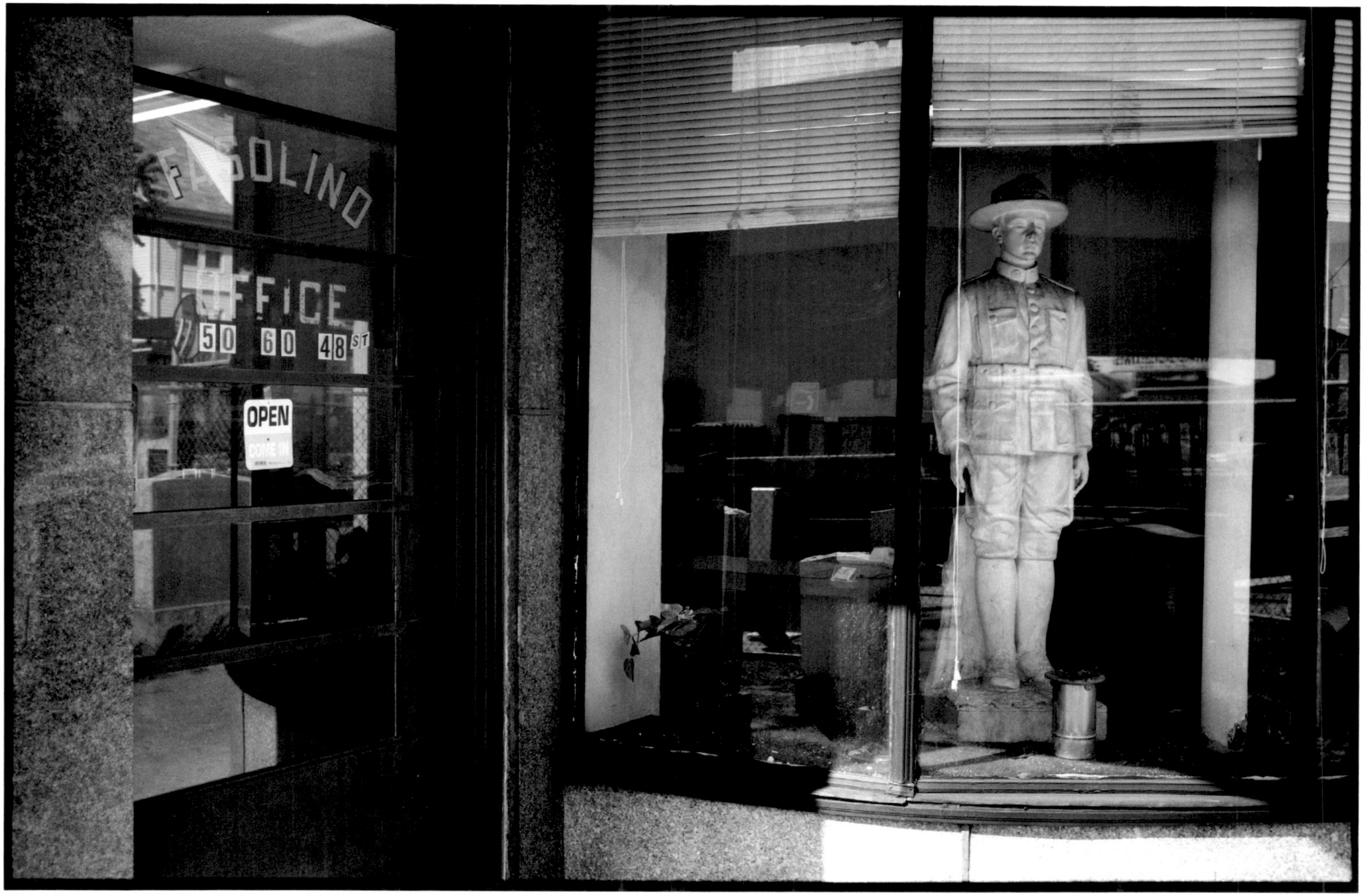
FASOLINO
OFFICE
50 60 48ST
OPEN
COME IN

Daniel Webster monument, Central Park West Drive, February 25, 2009

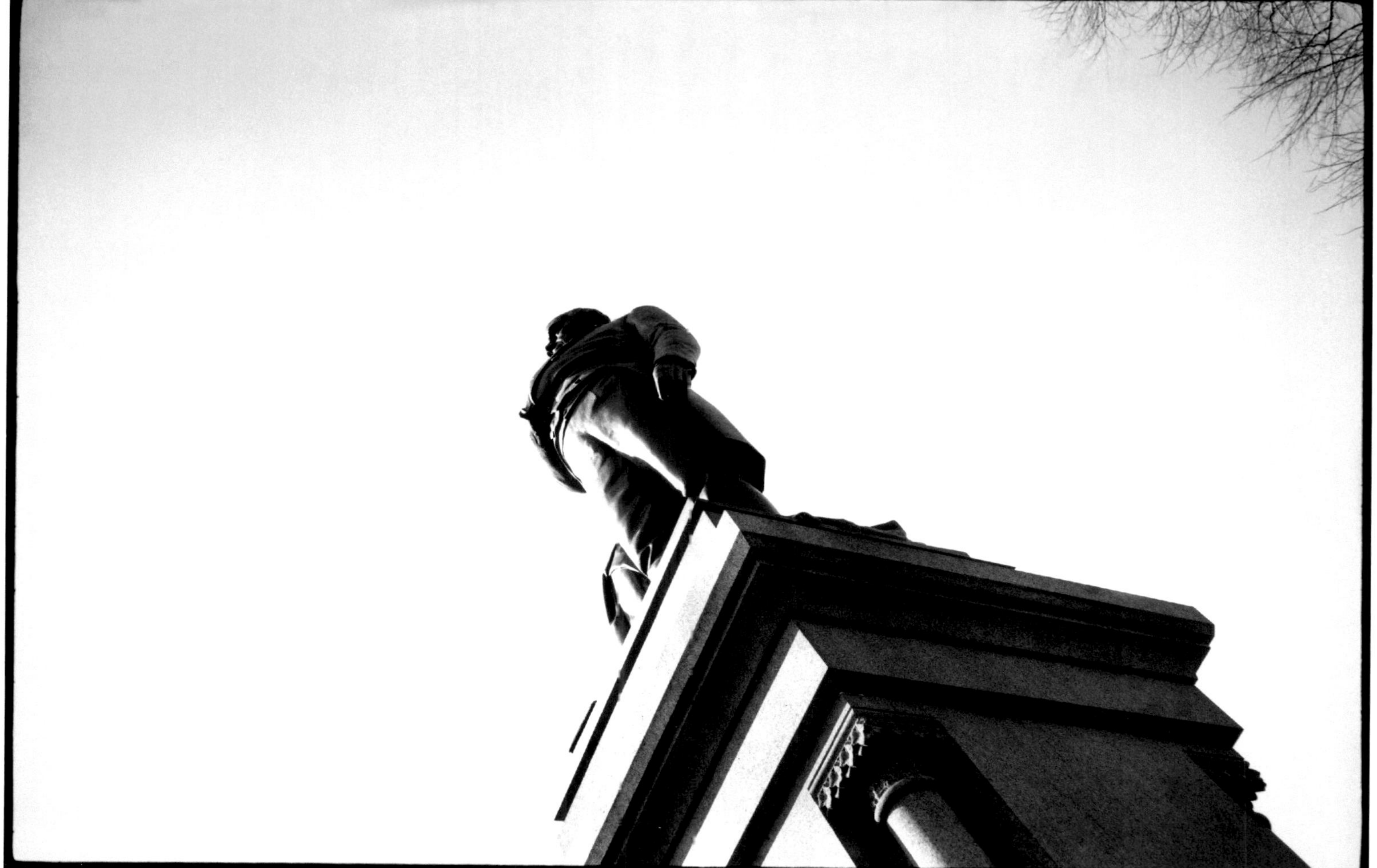

Veterans Day Ceremony, Soldiers' and Sailors' Monument, Riverside Park, November 11, 2020

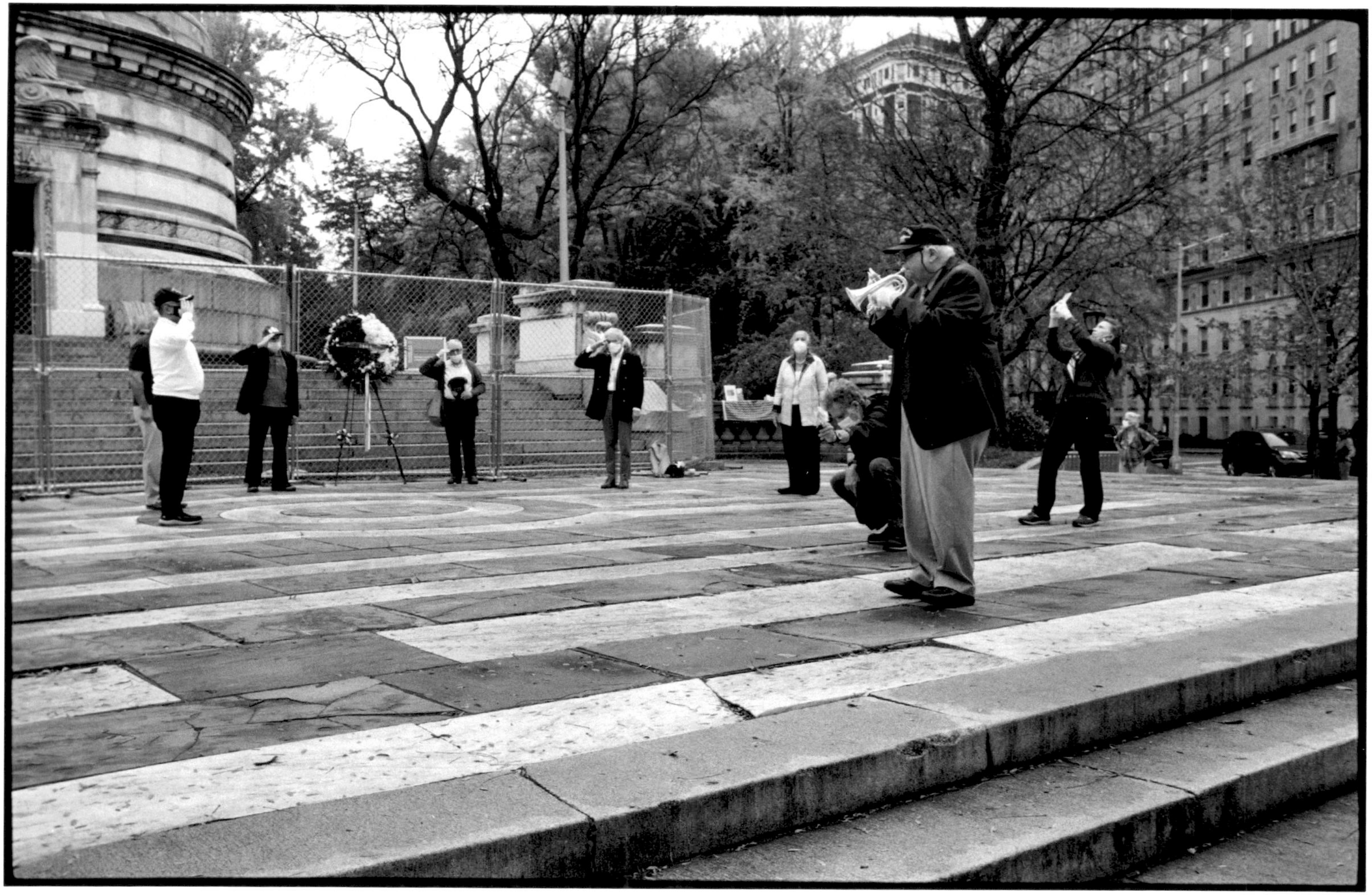

International Women's Day, Apthorp Cleaners window display, Upper West Side, June 30, 2020

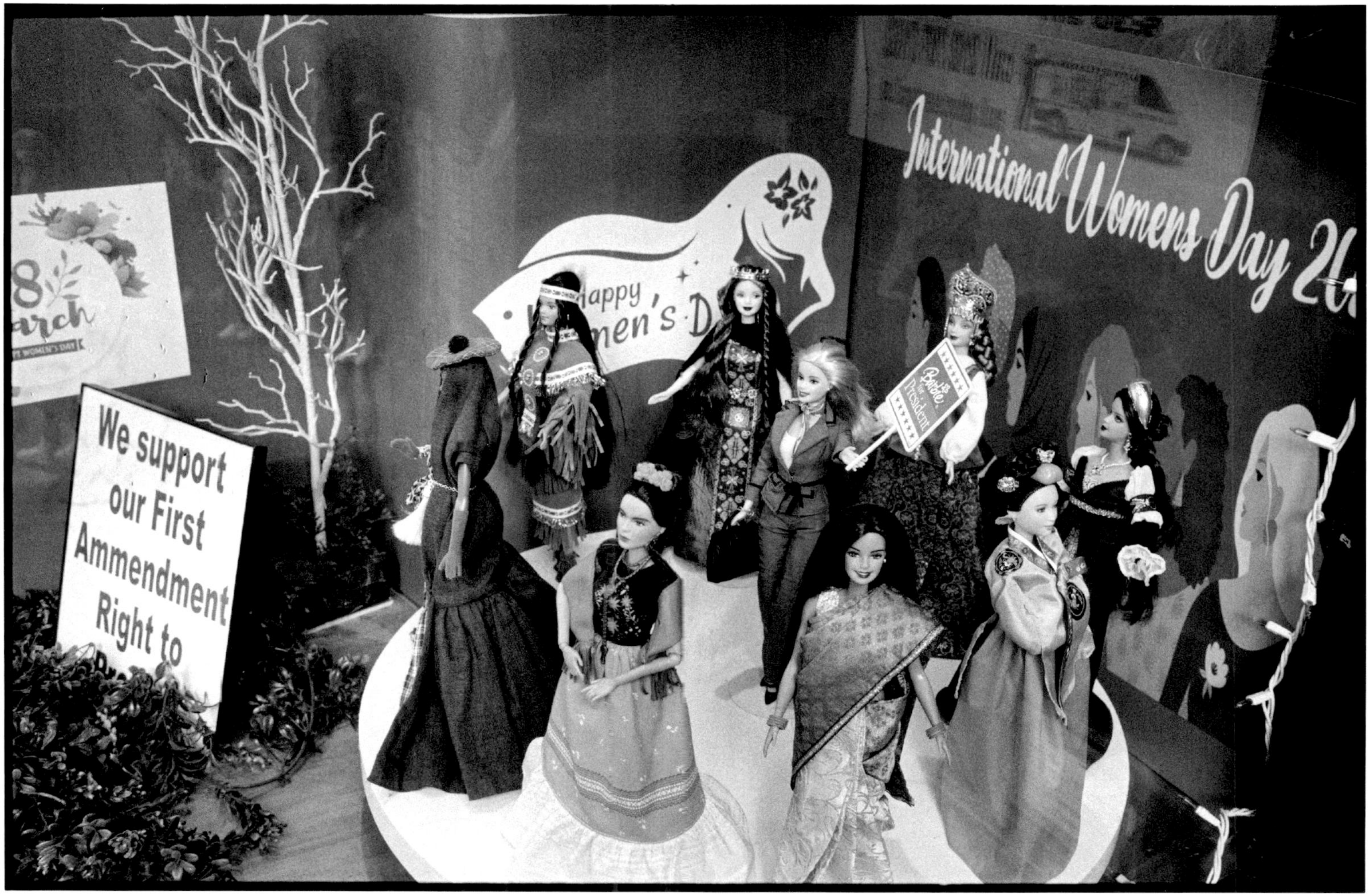
International Womens Day 20
Happy Women's Day
8 March
We support our First Ammendment Right to
Barbie for President

Tribute to firefighter Teddy White, Engine 230, FDNY Memorial Wall, World Trade Center, Financial District, September 12, 2010

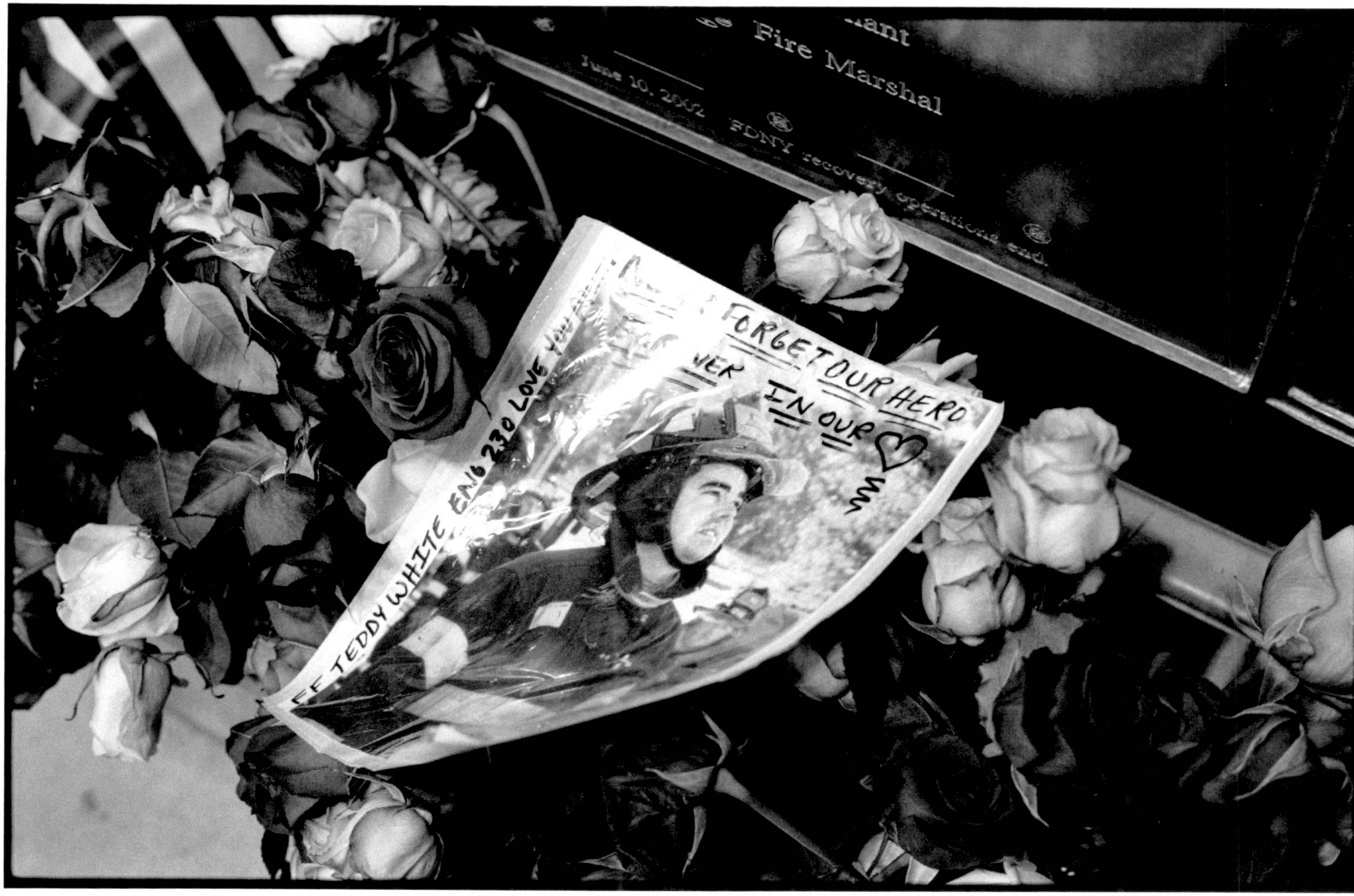
Fire Marshal
June 10, 2002
FDNY recovery operations end.
FORGET OUR HERO
IN OUR
TEDDY WHITE ENG 230 LOVE

Fourth of July celebration, Riverside Park, 2009

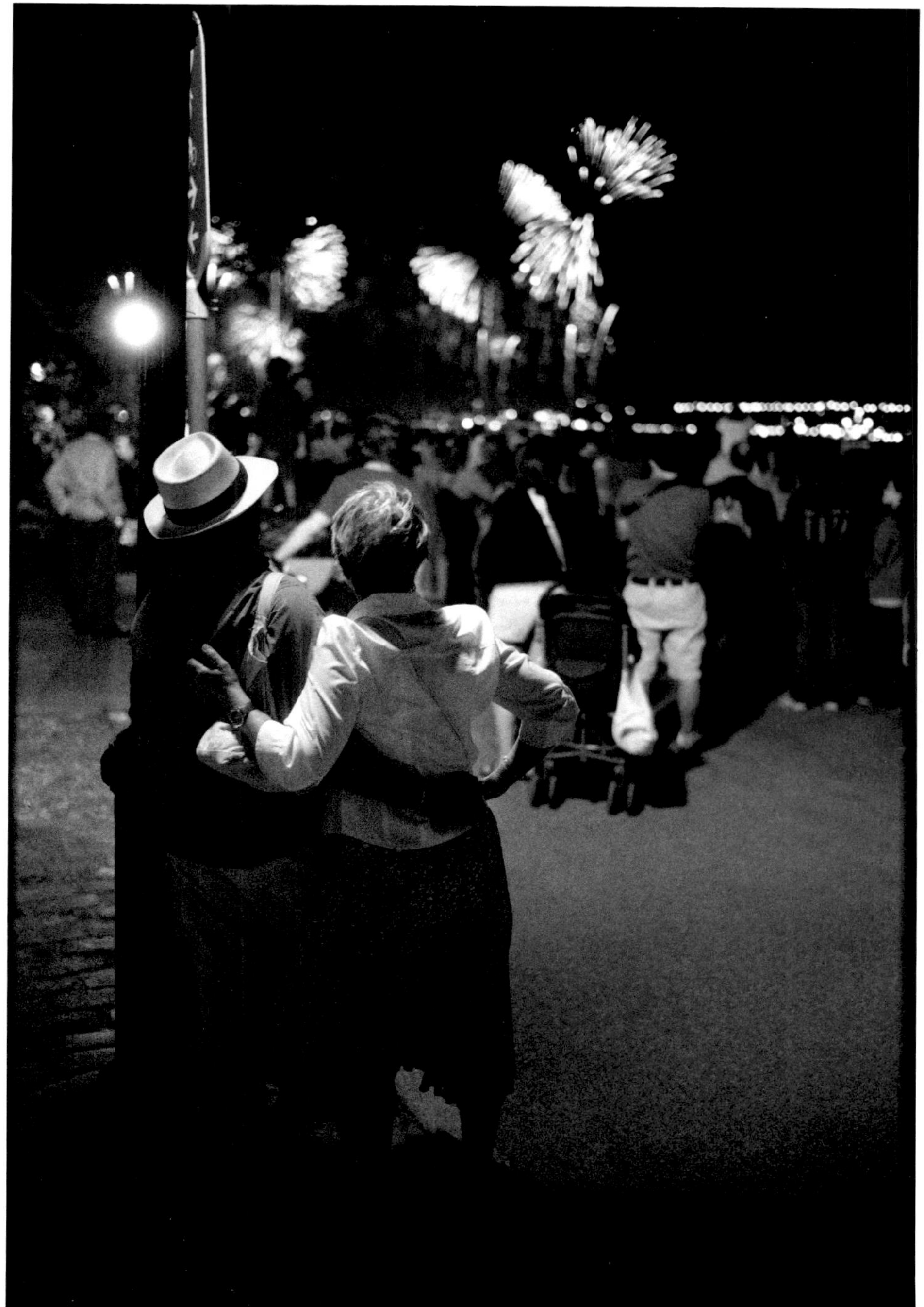

Statue of Frederick Douglass in the rain, Frederick Douglass Circle, Manhattan Valley, March 15, 2015

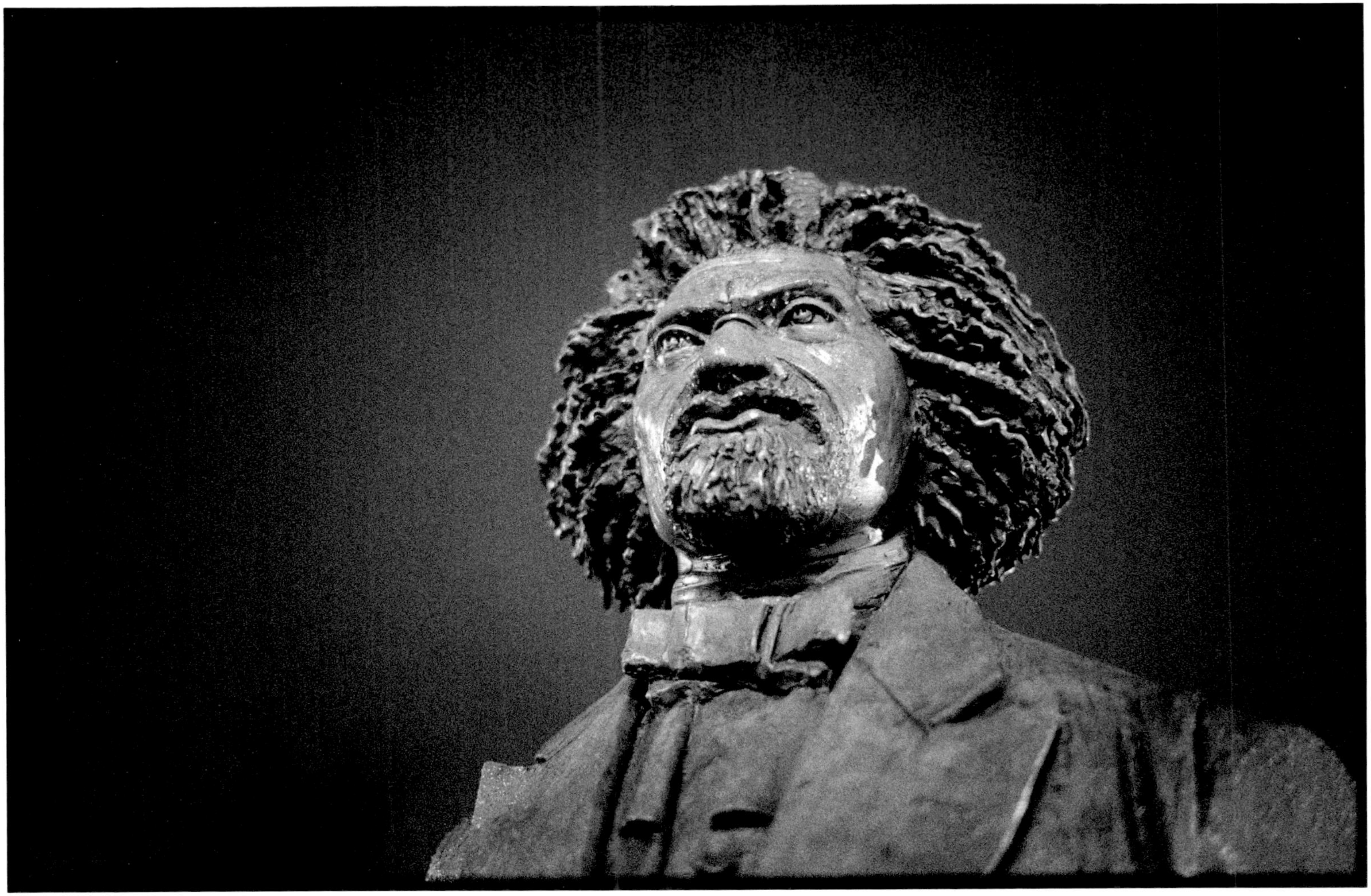

Woman who just became an American citizen, Daniel Patrick Moynihan Courthouse, Civic Center, January 23, 2026

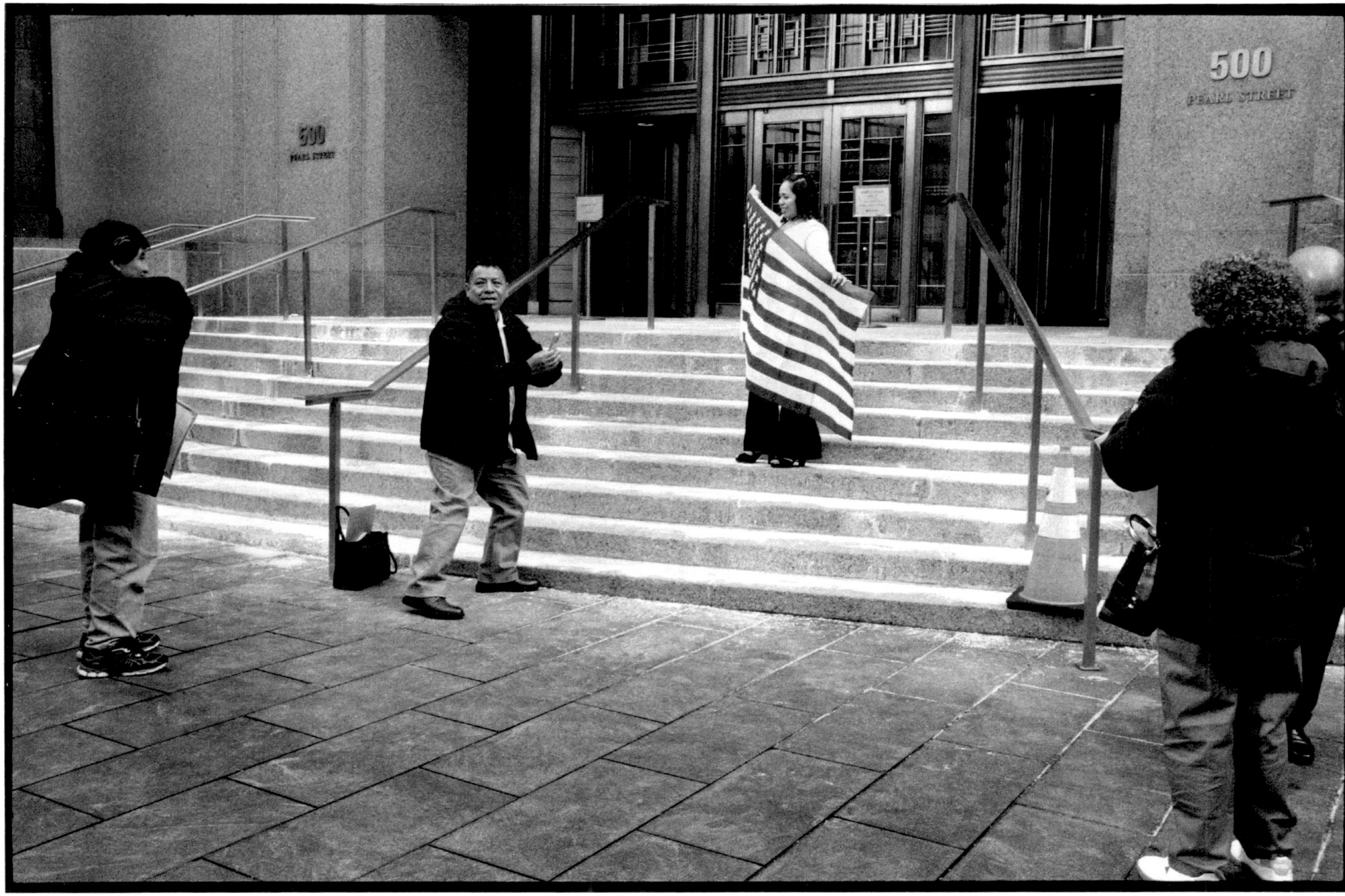
500
PEARL STREET
500
PEARL STREET

Wreaths from Memorial Day after a storm, Soldiers' and Sailors' Monument, Riverside Park, May 26, 2009

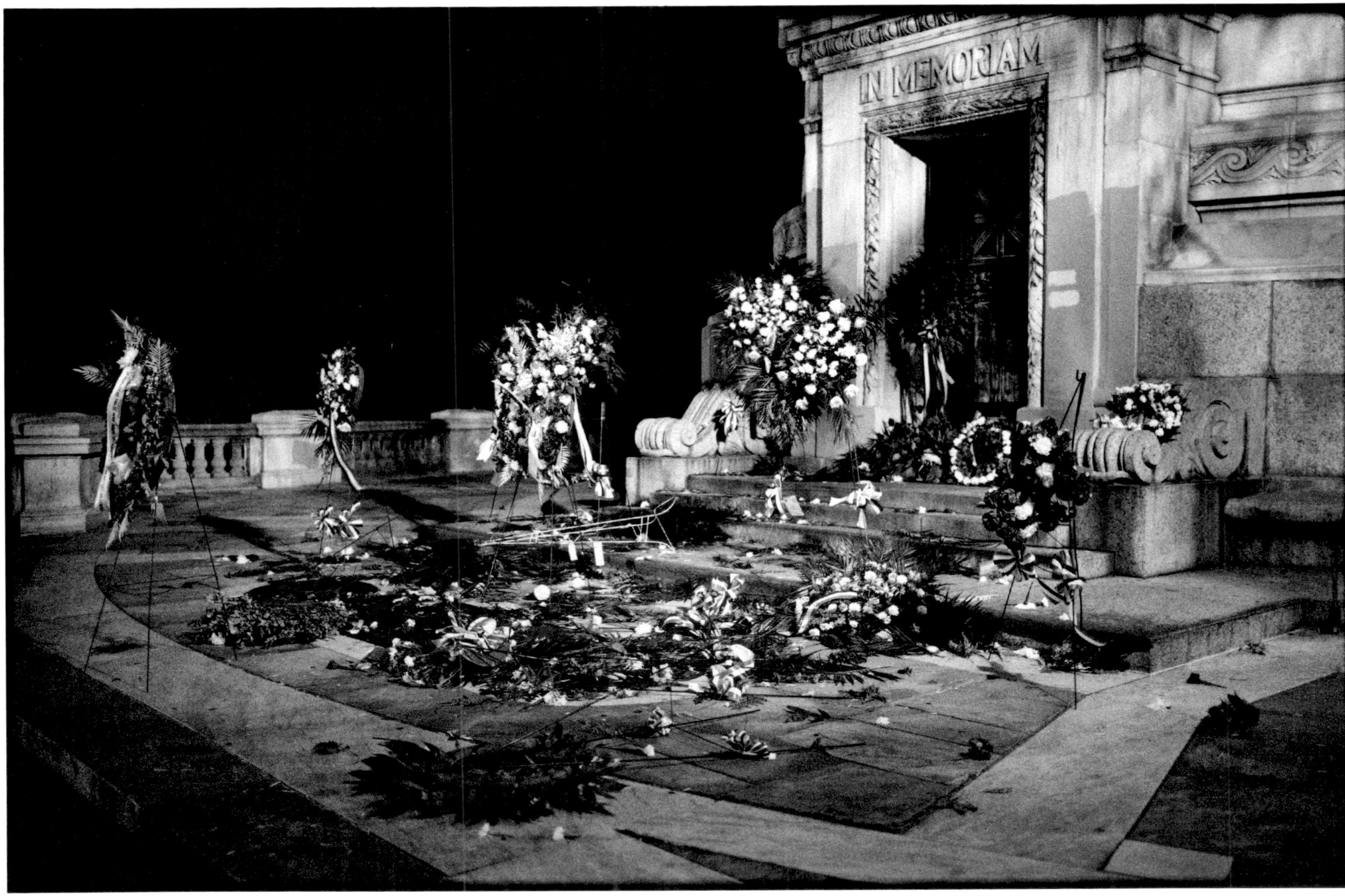
IN MEMORIAM

EVERYDAY PARTICIPATION, SO MODEST AND SO MEANINGFUL

Nicole Gelinas

You never know when you are going to need the people around you. You may set out with your child for a joyful day of sledding in Central Park—and suddenly, after a crash in the snow, need an ambulance. A historic storm may have stilled the elevators in your Queens apartment building—and because you can't walk down stairs, you need someone to bring food to you. You may find yourself under arrest and need passersby to stop and watch, putting pressure on the police to act lawfully.

But who are these people around us? How do they choose their government? How do they govern when chosen? How do they determine their collective priorities, inside and outside of government? How do they communicate their ideas, their wishes, their grievances? What and how do they choose to remember? How do they help, or not help, others? How do they respond when they don't get their way?

The never-ending process of arriving at the ever-changing answers to these questions is called civics. Civics—encompassing the rights and duties of citizens—may seem an obsolete notion in an age when politics looks to be done via stadium rally or X post, and when it is easy, via YouTube, to be instantly outraged about a war halfway around the world and express that anger on TikTok.

We can yell at everyone, everywhere, all at once, so why listen to each other, patiently, painstakingly, one by one?

William Meyers's *Civics* quietly demolishes any notion that the concept of civics belongs to another era. The photos, which were taken in New York City between 1991 and 2026, reveal to us that a functional society depends on people showing up—not just once, but over and over, to figure out, and continue refiguring out, what we think is important, and how will we work together to achieve and maintain a desired result.

As *Civics* reveals, elections aren't just about charismatic presence on the national stage. The most critical elections, because they involve everyday public services, are local and state elections. Running to win a local or state office isn't glamorous. It involves standing alone on the sidewalk by a subway exit, attempting to hand out campaign literature to people who more often than not ignore you. It involves sitting, solitary, in an unadorned office, trying to convince someone on the phone to donate money or time.

It also involves listening to people, all sorts of people with all sorts of ideas, all day and all evening. It involves sitting through meeting after meeting to discuss strategy and tactics with supporters, even though those strategies and tactics, after all that planning, may fail. Finally, it involves being able to lose graciously, smiling as you watch your balloon-festooned victory party turn into a wake.

Governing, too, is as much about meeting small-scale local needs as it is about dealing with big national ideas. The ambulance must arrive when summoned. The water must flow through the pipes. The school buses must show up to pick up the children, and the regular buses must show up to pick up the adults. City council members mostly don't concern themselves with the latest viral video; instead, they hold fifteen-person panel discussions on why it takes so long to clear the snow from the bus stops after a storm, because that's what their constituents want to know.

Quotidian electioneering and governing do happen against a backdrop of grand ideas though. How do people get these thoughts across to the public? They do it by showing up, and then showing up again. Whether the Tea Party in 2010, Occupy Wall Street in 2011, or Black Lives Matter in 2020, protest participants carefully plan what they are going to wear, what their signs are going to say, and how they are going to behave. Then, they hope that the time they have taken will be worth it, that people outside the group will notice and care. Labor union members protesting companies using nonunion labor don't even need to bring a sign. Because they have been persistently consistent in their message for decades, their giant inflatable rat posed on the sidewalk gets their point across, no words necessary.

People holding fringe ideas get an opportunity to communicate their concerns as well. Whether you think the National Security Agency planned 9/11 or that "the Jews killed Jesus," you, too, can peaceably try to convince people of your point of view. A society built on a healthy civic foundation has no fear of such lunacy, because sturdy discourse ensures that the argument will not hold.

How do people get the news they use to form their ideas? They get it from editors sitting at desks, determining which of dozens of possible photos to use to illustrate a story. They get it from reporters from neighborhood newspapers willing to sit through hearings over obscure but important issues such as land use. People can even learn a little about what's going on just by walking by a newsstand—sometimes attended by a vendor with no stake in the news but to earn a living—and reading the headlines on offer on the competing front pages. And when people are unhappy with their news, they can protest in front of the *New York Times* headquarters; the voices from outside of the building are just as protected by the Constitution as those within.

Civics shows that people gather, in groups large and small, not just to push sweeping narratives about broad injustices but also to give immediate aid to alleviate practical problems, sometimes for strangers. A synagogue cannot solve homelessness, but it can shelter a few men on cots. New Yorkers who aren't sure how to help their neighbors after a hurricane can attend a benefit concert in Brooklyn. Causes unknown to the broad public, such as refurbishing a memorial to Joan of Arc are important enough to enough people that they are willing to organize themselves to make progress.

Interacting with the physical emblems of remembrance, too, is a part of civic culture. A child too young to remember the original World Trade Center vanishing into dust watches from a gleaming office building nearby as the new World Trade Center rises. A laminated photo and fading flowers mark the FDNY Memorial Wall. Rain-soaked garlands add organic color to the cold stone around the Soldiers' and Sailors' Monument. These ephemeral offerings show that someone, or some group, still cares. Most statues go unnoticed, unremarked upon, but the people walking by them still unconsciously absorb: here is some history, and I am a part of this history.

Civics also hints at what happens when civic self-understanding dwindles. Veterans must hold one annual ceremony in front of a memorial that is so badly deteriorated, after years of neglect, that it needs a chain-link fence for protection. A store must board up its windows and doors with riot-resistant plywood during a heated national election. A hand rises from a protest crowd, offering only a middle finger, not an argument.

The most indelible images from *Civics* aren't from protests or rallies, nor of the streets or of statues. Rather, they are photos of rooms full of the backs of people's heads. These are the heads of people sitting, unnoticed, often uncomfortably, while awaiting their turn to speak, whether against a museum building's expansion or in favor of a political candidate. They sit in flimsy folding chairs in grand buildings. If they are not there to speak, they are there to listen, each thinking privately about their role in the common endeavor.

William Meyers's photographs have been exhibited in galleries and museums in America and Europe; they are held in public and private collections, including those of the Museum of the City of New York and the New York Public Library. Several of his photographs are on permanent display in institutions including Harvard University and Ansche Chesed. His photo book *Outer Boroughs: New York Beyond Manhattan* was published by Damiani Editore in 2014.

Pictures from *Civics* have been published in *Standpoint* (UK), *The Free Press*, *National Review*, *Parnassus*, and *City Journal*. The New York Historical has thirty-seven prints from *Civics* in its permanent collection and the New York Public Library has one.

Meyers writes on photography for *The Wall Street Journal*. His writing has also been published by the *New York Sun*, the *Weekly Standard* and *Commentary Magazine*. He has lectured about photography in the United States and abroad.

William Meyers was born in 1938 in Providence, Rhode Island. He lives in New York City with his family.

Meyers is represented by Nailya Alexander Gallery.

Visit williammeyersphotography.com for more information.

Visit our website at www.apollopublishers.com.

Published in compliance with California's Proposition 65.

Library of Congress Control Number: 2026905796

ISBN: 978-1-954641-57-0

Printed in the United States of America by Brilliant, Exton, PA.
All separations, image work, and print production by Brilliant.
Photographs printed by Chuck Kelton.

Book design by Dolly Meieran.

Printed on Opus Matte 100# Text.
The typeface is Gotham, designed by
Hoefler & Co. in New York City.

Cover: *Statue of Liberty souvenirs, tourist shop, Times Square, September 15, 2010*

Frontispiece: *City Hall and Municipal Building, Civic Center, January 4, 2011*